PRAISE FOR *Wonder Year*

"For the intrepid family that's keen to raise kids with a broad worldview, the curricular visions and thoughtful considerations outlined in *Wonder Year* will help you get out the door and on the road toward the greatest discoveries of your family's lives. A recipe book for activating the deepest curiosities of young minds."
—CHRIS YAGER, founder of immersive student travel company Where There Be Dragons

"Extended travel—the wanderlust kind—has always felt out of reach for too many because of the expense, the disapproval of others, and seemingly overwhelming logistical challenges. *But you can do it!* This book is literally a 'how-to' guide for a life-affirming family adventure."
—CHARLES WHEELAN, author of *We Came, We Saw, We Left* and *Naked Economics*

"Simply superb! A must-read for anyone considering extended family travel, *Wonder Year* is the new standard by which all other books on this subject will be judged."
—JOHN HIGHAM, author of *360 Degrees Longitude*

"*Wonder Year* opens the imagination to possibilities of extraordinary family learning adventures. A treasure trove of resources and inspiration for parents who desire to be learners alongside their children, transforming and growing on a shared journey."
—COLETTE PLUM, assistant dean, UC Berkeley Study Abroad

WONDER YEAR

A GUIDE TO
LONG-TERM FAMILY TRAVEL &
WORLDSCHOOLING

JULIE FRIEDER • ANGELA HEISTEN • ANNIKA PARADISE

WONDERWELL

Library of Congress Control Number: 2022922985
ISBN 978-1-63756-024-2 (paperback)
ISBN 978-1-63756-025-9 (EPUB)

Editor: Allison Serrell
Cover and interior design: Morgan Krehbiel
Julie Frieder's photo: Charlie Stanzione
Angela Heisten's photo: Darcy Sherman – Sassafras Photography
Annika Paradise's photo: Photography by Jitka
Interior photos taken by the authors

Published by Wonderwell in Los Angeles, CA
www.wonderwell.press

Distributed in the US by Publishers Group West and in Canada by Publishers Group Canada
Printed and bound in China

Contents

A person
susceptible to
"wanderlust" is not
so much addicted
to movement as
committed to
transformation.

—Pico Iyer

Introduction

WELCOME TO YOUR WONDER YEAR. If you've picked up this book, maybe you're dreaming about taking off and traveling with your family. Maybe you have been reading articles about road tripping, listening to podcasts on working remotely, or peeking at family adventure blogs.

Maybe an unexpected layoff served up the gift of time, or stories of families moving overseas to live and learn have you green with desire. Perhaps your experience with virtual work and remote school opened a window, allowing your travel fantasies to pour in with the morning light.

Maybe a friend or neighbor passed this book along to you, and serendipity is amplifying the refrain: *you can do it!* Odds are, something has tempted you, and now you're hooked on possibility. But can you actually hit the road with your family for longer than the usual two-week stint? Can you pull up stakes and embark on an extended adventure that goes well beyond the typical vacation? Of course you can. We call it a *Wonder Year.*

A Wonder Year is a season of discovery. It is an experience of being in motion with your family and adopting a mindset of growth and curiosity.

The educational component of a Wonder Year is called *worldschooling,* which is learning through direct interaction with the world. Our belief is simply this—the world is a very good teacher, and the more interaction our children have with it, the more their hearts and intellect will open and grow.

Wonder Year = long-term family travel + worldschooling

Before you start thinking, *Maybe I've bitten off more than I can chew with this book,* know this: we three coauthors have each taken our own Wonder Year, and thousands of other families have as well. Consider this book your warm welcome to a supportive community of folks who set out on journeys near and far, grand and humble, to learn, discover, and connect.

Wonder Year: A Guide to Long-Term Family Travel and Worldschooling is your handy, creative resource to help you and your family get out there.

Purpose of This Book

Part inspiration and part how-to, *Wonder Year* addresses the most important and challenging questions about planning and executing extended family travel. While you'll find many family travel memoirs and destination guidebooks, this is the first soup-to-nuts companion to demystify the seemingly outrageous prospect of long-term family travel and worldschooling. Packed with practical information and enriched by first-person travelogues, it is the book we each wish we'd had for our respective adventures.

Wonder Year is intended for families at any stage of their journeys. You may be daydreaming about an extended trip, actively planning one, or deep into your travels. We don't recommend an optimal duration, direction, or distance. Please take what you like from these pages to shape your own adventure—be it three months traveling in your home country, three seasons on one or two continents, or three years circumnavigating the globe.

Wonder Year makes it easy and keeps it real. We talk about the psychological and emotional hurdles of making the leap, the lift and release of undertaking the journey, and the social and spiritual impact of the experience. We want to show you that long-term family travel is more attractive and attainable than ever before, and that remote living and remote learning are not actually remote at all.

How to Use This Book

We've structured the chapters of *Wonder Year* to help answer the big questions and allay common concerns about money, planning, safety, and personal care on the road. We also dive deeply into education and offer guidance and tools to help you harness the educational offerings of the world. We paint a picture of life on the road and walk you home when it's time to reenter. You'll also find checklists and a curated list of resources at the back of the book.

This book is written as a complete guide, but not every section will be relevant to every reader or type of traveler. You might skip the discussion of car seats if you're traveling with a teen or not bother with notes on altitude sickness if you are traveling by boat.

Recognizing that some parents crave more structure while others want to wing it, *Wonder Year* is written as a kind of origami, folded seam by seam, ready to be opened, strung together, inflated, or offered as a gift to someone you meet along the way.

Woven throughout the book are short travelogues and personal accounts about the experience of family travel. We share these stories, some from us and some from others, to give you a glimpse of what a Wonder Year can look like. Spoiler alert: it's not all pretty—we do not airbrush the reality of family travel. Our aim is to be your trusted friends all along the journey.

You've Got a Friend!

Before we go any further, allow us to introduce ourselves. Here's a little bit about each of us and our respective adventures.

MEET ANNIKA

My trip was a twelve-month around-the-world adventure with my husband, Will; our daughters, Lorna and Lucy; and our son, Kai. Our trip was anchored around China, Nepal, and Thailand for personal reasons; and then Greece, Rome, and Spanish-speaking Central America for academic purposes.

As a San Francisco Bay Area native, I traveled to Vermont for college and left for the Peace Corps in Thailand just six weeks after graduation. In Krabi, Thailand, I taught English to middle and high school students and facilitated teacher trainings. I also developed microlending projects to help build markets and sustainable products with women's cooperatives in remote areas of the Thai Andaman Islands.

When I returned home to San Francisco, I worked in refugee resettlement, then earned my master's in education from Stanford and taught public middle and high school in the US. I spent my summers working with a very cool organization, Where There Be Dragons, to bring teenage students to Thailand and Laos for immersive language, culture, and service-learning trips. I had the honor of watching teens learn by experience in the world. Our conversations were deep, complex, and the stuff of life itself. I vowed then and there that if I had kids, we would have these kinds of experiences together. I would give them a Wonder Year, even if I didn't have a name for it yet.

When I met my husband, he held travel in the same regard. He had traveled through Pakistan by bus and spent years mountaineering in Nepal. If anything, between the two of us, we needed to dial down the adventure knob to include our kids. Our daughter Lorna was twelve when we left on our "big trip," and she was challenged to leave her friends. But she gained time with oceans—a passion she hopes to study in college—and a deep call to work for a sustainable future. Lucy, our younger daughter, was nine, sad to leave her youth orchestra and her pets, but happy to spend time together as a family. Lucy had spent her first three years in a Chinese orphanage, so time in China was a must on our itinerary. Kai, our son, was eight and easygoing, loved sports, and just twelve months younger than Lucy; the two were natural playmates. As owners of a local record shop, my husband and I made sure that our manager was ready to hold down the fort for a year, and built in contingency plans and regular check-ins.

Living in Boulder, Colorado—known for snow and mountains—we wanted to give our kids a taste of something different, so for a year, we avoided winter altogether and watched the sun set over oceans.

MEET ANGELA

My trip was a two-year odyssey across six continents with my husband, Mark, and our sons, Ronan and Asher. We backpacked through Europe, Australia, New Zealand, Southeast Asia, Japan, South America, and southern Africa, with return trips to an Airstream RV we called home while exploring the US and Canada.

An army brat, I've always had itchy feet. I grew up in the Midwest, road tripping to Carolina beaches and camping in muggy, mosquito-laden destinations with my parents and younger sister. Some of my strongest childhood memories are of fossil hunting, mudslides at nature camp, trekking through the rolling hills of Ohio, and playing "wilderness" in the trees that edged my suburban backyard. I thrive in big-city energy, but I'm at my best when I'm in the woods by a river, makeup-free and a little rough around the edges. My only addiction is to novelty, and travel feeds the beast.

Mark and I met in college and took our first trip together—from Missouri to the backroads of New Mexico—after two months of dating. We bonded

over shared values of exploration and education and are both driven by insatiable curiosity. We like to head to the very, very end of the road together. We've moved over twenty times in thirty years—not easy when the one thing we collect is books—and I'm always thinking about what's next. I like to go anywhere I've never been, but if forced to choose, I'll head to the outer latitudes. When I planted my boots in Patagonia, it felt like coming home. Scotland felt the same.

After earning my engineering degree in the Midwest, I moved with Mark to Chicago and later to the West Coast, where I completed an MBA at Cal-Berkeley. My professional credits include strategic planning, communications, and operations management roles in healthcare and biotechnology. I'm also trained as an executive coach. Since leaving biotech, I've been remodeling residential real estate, always saying I've done my last project right about the time I take on another.

After nearly twenty years in the Bay Area, I turned my planning skills to laying the groundwork for a dreamed-about family adventure to see the world. Deciding the time was right, Mark and I took a hiatus from work, sold our house and belongings, and hit the road with our boys. Ronan was twelve when we started our trip, leaving middle school, baseball, and martial arts behind to go worldschooling. Asher was nine; nicknamed "the mayor," he's always been comfortable everywhere and with everyone. His up-for-anything spirit gets us all out the door.

We arranged our trip in three-month segments, alternating between RVing in North America and parking the rig to backpack to thirty-plus countries. Our sweet mutt, Timber, came along for the camping and shacked up with friends and family when we left the country. We focused on learning about history and art in big cities and sought extreme nature and animal sightings in remote backcountry. Many families chase summer—we like cool temperatures and sometimes gloomy days, so we chased fall. The original plan was to travel for one year, but it was going so well that we made it two. We checked out potential new hometowns as we traveled and ultimately relocated to Boulder, Colorado, after our journey, landing in a spot that led me to my two coauthors and the conversations that catalyzed this book.

MEET JULIE

My trip was a thirteen-month adventure, mostly in the US with Charlie, my hubby; Johnny, our only child who was eight at the start of the trip; and Max, our very large and handsome dog. We traveled in a twenty-four-foot class B motor home. It was the best year of my life.

When I was in college in upstate New York, I half-jokingly changed my name to juliafreedom. I thought it had a nice ring and reflected my free-spirit and adventurous sides. Plus, I was named for my father's mother, Julia Frieder, who traveled the world at the age of twenty-two.

I went to grad school in Indiana, studying public policy and environmental science, and I've worked in a range of positions seeking to drive positive change through policy, finance, education, and individual action. I had the wonderful opportunity to spend a year in New Zealand as a visiting research fellow to examine sustainability Kiwi-style. I returned to the US and adopted Colorado as home.

In Colorado I met Charlie, a modest, gray-haired hydrogeologist with a bike and a camera. We fell in love, got married, and had Johnny boy right away. Charlie and I shared a love of the mountains and of travel, and we would hike, talk, and dream of taking a year off. There was no single event or windfall of time or money. We just worked hard to figure it out. We saved, made a budget, rented out our house, sold a car, and used some savings. I quit my job, and Charlie got a sabbatical for one year.

We loaded an RV with four bikes, three kayaks, a 72-watt thin-film solar panel, three bowls, three sporks (part spoon, part fork), and a pogo stick. We left some space for discovery and set out on our thirteen-month "Going with the Flow" tour. Along the way we volunteered as family ambassadors for a nonprofit water protection organization and did community service projects across the country. We met with sustainability champions from Alaska to Florida, and River Heroes working to protect local watersheds.[1] Charlie and I created a worldschooling curriculum that used water and sustainability as a framework for experiential education. Fortunately, for all three of us, Johnny was at a time in his life when he was eager to try

anything, liked hanging out with his scrappy parents, and wanted to do real work like chopping wood and fixing bike flats. He was then and is now a super adventurous, curious, and kind kid.

A Word on Collaborative Writing

As you can see, we three coauthors had very different journeys. Upon our decision to collaborate, we found great delight and connection in talking about our experiences. Emerging from our conversations were themes, wisdom, and realizations that added up to more than the sum of our respective trips. Good ideas come from collaboration, and we found that coauthorship filled out our stories. In addition, we interviewed many domestic and international travelers, as well as families with diverse perspectives and different styles, and have included these voices in our book. We hope you'll feel welcome to pull up a chair, grab a cuppa, and join us in this wondrous conversation!

Cloudy with a Chance of Curveballs (and Pandemics)

A word on uncertainty: Yes. It will. It may. Definitely. Or maybe not. Or never. Or possibly. In the summer, or in the winter. As sure as we are traveling through space on a "pale blue dot" in a galactic festival of chance and randomness, *it* could happen, and *it* could be *anything.* You could meet your life partner deep in the Tatshenshini River gorge, cut your hair short and finally go fuchsia in Romania, lose your rig in a tsunami—or even find that a novel coronavirus spreads ridiculously quickly around the world.

When COVID-19 hit, we three coauthors pondered a pivot and considered a rewrite of this book. We paused and mourned the loss of lives, of livelihood. We quarantined and stopped hugging friends. Sheltered at home, we asked ourselves whether families would still need a worldschooling guidebook. Our gut, our research, and our inclination said *absolutely yes.* Moving through the experience of COVID changed perspectives, altered priorities, and created new opportunities with remote school, virtual work, and family togetherness. This is a silver lining and a new reality.

After all, we are wired to wander. The world awaits. You've got this, friend. *Now let's go!*

Tapestry
Main Street
Hotel Reception
Restaurants.
Churchill Boutique
Place de Quebec
Tourist INFO

CHAPTER 1

The Case for a Wonder Year

When setting out on a journey, do not seek advice from those who have never left home.

— Rumi

LET'S FACE IT, modern society did not invent the family road trip. Humans have been traveling for millennia, and for many reasons—sustenance, survival, soul-searching, security. In this chapter, we look at what has motivated people to travel over time, why we each decided to take a Wonder Year, and whether it may be a good choice for you and your family.

The Case for Travel

Travel bug. Travel itch. Wanderlust. Bucket list. So many of us yearn to be on the road, soaking in adventure and experiencing other cultures and faraway places. Whether escaping the rat race, emerging from a pandemic, or cashing in on a sabbatical to pursue the dream of family travel, more and more families are moving around.

You could say we evolved for long-distance travel: to hunt and gather, secure resources and water, avoid predators, and quench a thirst for exploration. After all, our forebears were really good at foraging, at traveling; they did it for hundreds of thousands of years. But let's look at what stokes modern-day travelers to get up and go.

WANDERLUST

We often talk about a love of travel as *wanderlust*. The word is derived from the German *wandern*, "to wander," and *lust*, "to desire." In the fullest sense, wanderlust is that overwhelming desire to explore your world and deepen your connection to people and history while walking toward the unknown. Psychologists have posited the existence of a "wanderlust" gene in some people; correlated with extroversion, exploration, curiosity, and a migratory lifestyle. Certain people seem to love change more than others and just want to wander and try something new.[2]

Guðrún Jóhannsdóttir grew up horseback riding and tent camping with her family in the highlands of Iceland. As a young girl spending time in the countryside, she remembers watching the few cars pass by and always wondering where they were going. She just wanted to get in a car and go, too, wherever it could take her. Many years later, Guðrún is doing just that—leaving Iceland for many months each year to explore Europe and Africa with her large adventurous family.

FOR ADVENTURE

Classical explorers were some of the earliest adventure travelers. From the 1400s through the 1600s, they navigated oceans, mapped the skies, bagged mountains, and established new routes. We do not glorify their trade; we know theirs was not just saffron and gold.

Today, many travelers heed the call to adventure and set out to find their physical or social limits. They do it for mystery, for challenge, and for meaning and transformation.

AS PILGRIMAGE

The practice or path of awakening is evident across cultures and time periods. Many religions have a pilgrimage, a journey to a physical holy site or a metaphorical or spiritual period of contemplation, transformation, and ascension to the sacred. In the Middle Ages, the Santiago de Compostela was a popular pilgrimage ending at the site believed to be the burial grounds of Saint James. It's now a UNESCO World Heritage Site and a European Cultural Route;[3] and today, pilgrims and other travelers follow the paths on foot, by bike, in silence, or with a friend. Some feel that these modern treks, expeditions of the soul, bring them closer to history, to themselves, to their physical limits, and ultimately closer to their spiritual ideal.

FOR PURPOSE

Just as early travelers were seekers, when we trace their historic routes around the world, we become modern seekers on our own journeys, looking for change, love, truth, or enlightenment.

TO PURSUE SIMPLICITY

The ideal of simple living is a motivator for some travelers. There's great liberation in being able to carry on your back everything you need to survive. It wakes up your senses and brings your intention back to the basics, unencumbered by material possessions and focused instead on daily nourishment, shelter, water, and clothing. Living simply is practical, too. It's usually easier and cheaper to occupy a 285-square-foot motor home than to pay down a thirty-year mortgage and maintain a 2,000-square-foot house.

Laura, a mother of two who spent a year in Costa Rica, was excited to get out of her busy suburban world, pursue a simpler lifestyle, and give her kids a new perspective on self-sufficiency. Her Wonder Year helped her strip away the excesses of modern parenthood and come to enjoy hanging clothes on the line. Laura and her family found deep satisfaction in living without a car, slowing down, and walking to the store. She enjoyed seeing her kids release themselves from the grip of video games because there was lousy Wi-Fi. The whole family adapted to their simple lifestyle and filled up on time together.

TO RECONNECT AS A FAMILY

Some of us feel so crazy busy that there's rarely a night we can sit down together as a family for dinner—let alone connect with and enjoy our quickly-growing-up kids. Maybe you are concerned that technology and social media are disrupting family life. Travel can bring families together and dial down the noise, and for many, it can feel like a great reset to an overbooked and overscheduled life.

TO UNDERSTAND FAMILY HISTORY

Some people travel to connect with and imagine the experiences of their ancestors. Annika and her family traveled to China to fall in love with their adopted daughter's homeland and to meet the caregivers at the orphanage where Lucy spent the first three years of life. John and Eydie traveled to West Africa to show their son, Brook, the village in Benin where John, as a young man, spent two years in the Peace Corps.

BECAUSE WE CAN: DIGITAL NOMADISM

A new technological and social reality has opened many doors for the professionally adventurous. Infrastructure for digital nomadism is steadily growing, and this presents more opportunities to pursue the travel dream. We have new marketplaces, new ways of transacting, and new models of community that support mobile lifestyles. Industry experts predict that by 2035 there will be one billion digital nomads working remotely around the globe.[4]

Whatever the reasons or context, traveling as a family sets us into motion together on a winding and textured road that may be at once restorative, cathartic, familial, purely pleasurable, or outside of our comfort zone. It is here, in these momentous, magical, unfamiliar spaces, that we become more deeply connected to history, to fellow travelers, and to ourselves.

Why We Chose a Wonder Year

ANGELA

"Breaker breaker 1-9, what's your handle?" Mine was Blue Eyes, given to me by my Grandpa Ed. While I rode shotgun in his RV, he'd let me talk to semi-truck drivers on the CB radio, and we'd count punch buggies. These are the first trips I remember—tagging along on his fishing excursions to lakes in nearby Indiana and Kentucky, where he'd bait my hook and spit tobacco on the minnow to attract bigger fish. I loved how cozy and contained the RV was, especially where I slept, in the narrow bunk above the cockpit.

I have always loved to travel. I'm lucky that my house was a happy place to grow up in, but if I scan over the course of my life, almost all my favorite memories were made away from home. The *unknown* has always held sway.

My husband and I took many trips together in our early years as a couple, and in hindsight, I realize we made our most important life decisions on the road. We were camping in Montana when we committed to marry. Nestled inside a cabin sheltering us from a Wisconsin blizzard, we resolved it was time to move west. Sitting next to the Luxembourg Gardens fountain in Paris, watching preschoolers play with their sailboats, we decided to try for our first child.

We had that child, a boy, a year later. And then quickly, life piled up. So did stuff and responsibilities. A decade after moving to the Bay Area, we found ourselves with two sons, two very busy jobs, and a house we were working to fill. We were doing what was expected of us, but it no longer felt like *us*. Somewhere along the way we had lost sight of what we loved most—simplicity, time together, and adventure: learning and trying new things, delighting in each other's delight. The idea for a Wonder Year was born from a desire to find those things again, to break some rules and invite the unexpected. We also hoped our kids would gain perspective and experience ways of life other than the one they'd known. Soon we realized there was no way we could *not* go—and while it was going to be complicated to uproot our lives, it wasn't impossible. Four months later and forty years after my first overnight in an RV, I found myself in one again, this time calling it home.

ANNIKA

My love of the road trip probably began the summer I turned ten and our family drove from our home in the San Francisco Bay Area to Jackson Hole, Wyoming, in our VW van with just three cassette tapes. I sat in front with a stack of AAA maps, which I read with the intensity of a novel, looking out into the high desert of Nevada with awe, imagining the lives of the ranchers on the adjacent frontage roads, kicking up dust swirls. The high desert offered perspective. My mom had passed away less than two years earlier, and we were left a family of three reeling and reacting from events outside our control. Travel became healing.

Two years later, my father taught a two-week course at the Polytechnic University of Milan in Italy. My sister and I stayed with the family of a faculty member in the suburbs while he worked. We watched kids our age playing soccer on ancient cobblestone roads, ate strawberry risotto, and saw a whole new way of life.

That Italian summer, my father came to life again and we officially found our footing. We traveled around Italy, Greece, and Switzerland for four weeks after he was finished with teaching. My frugal father, enamored with a bullet train, told the cashier, "Hang the cost . . . I want to ride that train!" Words that were unimaginable weeks before. Those joyful adventures through new places with my dad and sister shaped the form of my life; it was my first Wonder Year.

As I mentioned before, Will and I had planned and saved for our own Wonder Year for ten years before we left. But as the time for our journey approached, I realized it was coming at *the* perfect time. Parenting, stressful jobs, and busy lives had been pushing us off our center for years, and knowing that the time was set for "The Big Trip" was the sweet reward waiting on the horizon.

JULIE

When I was thirteen, my father married my stepmother, Joan, aka Noanie, and they took the new stepfamily on an extended road trip through the American West. We rented an RV in Denver and trucked our way through mountains and mesas, salt flats, and parks.

We camped under the stars, made chili in our outdoor kitchen, took a raft trip on the Snake River, and ground corn in Puebloan fashion at Mesa Verde, crisscrossing our way through the expansive West. I was a curious teen from Cincinnati, Ohio, coming of age in tube socks and pigtails.

Twenty-seven years later, my son, John David, was born, named for his beloved grandfathers and bound to generations through memories and love. Soon after his birth, my father and stepmom passed away—Dad from cancer and Noanie from a broken heart. Life is short. You never know. *Get out there now* is the reason I always wanted to travel.

We have dear friends John and Eydie who, several years ago, traveled around the world with their twelve-year-old son, Brook. They started on bikes in Ghana, trekked in Nepal, studied Spanish in Mexico, and found themselves in the Peruvian Andes.

At the time, our Johnny boy was in elementary school manufacturing letters and numbers in what seemed to me to be a two-dimensional curriculum. I was increasingly frustrated by this and was actually looking at options for changing schools. When John, Eydie, and Brook came to visit upon their return, they shared stories of educational adventures. It struck me and opened my eyes to possibility. We played pin the flag on the country and marveled at their stories. We were amazed at Brook's cultural literacy, global awareness, conscientiousness, and grounded sense of preteen self. We figured if they could do it, so could we. John, Eydie, and Brook got the gears spinning and helped us commit to our trip. It all made sense, felt natural, and we are forever grateful.

The Benefits of Travel

In the course of researching this book and talking with current and past travelers, we heard many stories about how extended travel helped people's sense of well-being.

Travel offers many benefits. In our experience, it can:

HELP US NAVIGATE STRESS

While traveling, we remove many of the stress triggers of home and work. We have more time for exercise and activity, reading and listening to music, taking long walks, connecting with family and friends, being in nature, experiencing the change in seasons more deeply, and feeling free. We dare you to notice a rising tide, watch a moonrise, or photograph a sunset with your kids and not feel more relaxed! Now, do that for months in a row and imagine the effect.

Ship Creek Beach, New Zealand

We pull the RV off the highway, on New Zealand's southeastern shores, for no better reasons than the kids are starting to bicker and I need to use the restroom. The temperature reflects layers of sharp, intermittent breezes bursting from Antarctica, and a bright, hot summer sun. Sand spills into the parking lot; weathered driftwood lines the walkways.

As we read the informational placards about brackish water, a kind woman interrupts to tell us there's a pod of Hector's dolphins over the dunes, swimming just offshore. *Come quick.* So, we scratch our informal worldschooling plan and race toward the beach. Past the break, we can focus on rare, diminutive dolphins jumping, surfing, and surfacing in tandem. We watch them in wonder. A crowd of travelers takes video by hand and selfie stick.

"Let's go in," my thirteen-year-old daughter, Lorna, says to me, in her puffy jacket.

"Gosh, we should," I reply, standing beside her in my fleece and leggings, as if *someone* should, but not the forty-seven-year-old mother that I have become. Not the woman who sees every potential hazard around her. Not the woman who has a plan to get to the town of Haast by lunchtime.

"We might never get this chance again," she says.

And in me is this cavalcade of why-nots: Sweet Jesus, that would be cold. Doesn't this current come directly from an ice cap? I would ruin the videos and photos of the tourists, maybe become a subject of their videos. What if the surf is too strong? What if I can't swim out past that surf break? But when I look at her, I know what I should do. The voice inside that says *Don't do it* is the voice that urges me to play it small. It's time to reclaim my outside voice.

I don't see any offending offshore rocks or signs of a riptide; and secure in the knowledge that my daughter is a competitive swimmer, I take off my fleece, T-shirt, and shoes and stand next to her in my sports bra and leggings. "Come on."

A man in a down parka tells us that we should make clicking noises to attract the dolphins once we're in. Duly noted. I stand for a few waves to ice my feet and realize a slow entry is a bad idea. Instead, we watch for a break in the waves and dive into the frigid turquoise waters of the Tasman Sea to swim toward a pod of wild dolphins.

Seconds before a beachcomber alerted us to a pod of wild dolphins swimming in the Tasman Sea.

We time our entry in between wave sets and easily swim past the break. The cold takes my breath away; I inhale in gulps. Once I can finally breathe with some success, about fifty feet offshore, I start making a frantic clicking noise and look back to my husband on the beach who directs us toward the dolphins. Lorna and I swim side by side for more than ten minutes next to these gorgeous creatures squealing with shared delight. We can feel and hear them swirling underneath us, their *click click* sounds at our feet. Suddenly five feet away from us,

a dolphin breaches, pauses to give us the side-eye, and dives below.

My husband meets us at the shore with our dry clothes. I don't even feel the cold. I just feel alive. I'm finding the will to get uncomfortable, to even spend hours reheating myself for the chance to greet a dolphin in the Antarctic currents, to let go, to share wonder with my daughter, to interact bravely with the world, to look her in the eye, and know that I'm striving to be the kind of adult that I want my daughter to become.

While traveling, you may miss some of your go-to stress reducers that are effective at home, but the good news is that you can develop new practices on the road. There is more discussion on maintaining well-being on the road in chapter 6 (Health and Personal Safety) and chapter 8 (On the Road).

As a bonus for the planners among us, the organizational process itself—putting together itineraries, researching destinations, and solving logistical problems—can be enormously fun and satisfying. The anticipation is an exhilarating prelude to the great adventure.

BOOST CREATIVITY

Engaging in new rituals and experiencing new places can stimulate creativity and prompt fresh ideas. One of the fundamental truths of travel is that it offers many new experiences, thus promoting "cognitive flexibility"—the brain's ability to jump from one set of ideas, activities, or learning approaches to another.[5] Traveling is rich with novel experiences; at every turn, every day, down every trail, there are unexpected sparks and nonstop innovation. We learn to think outside the box because we *are* outside of our box.

MAKE US MORE TOLERANT

Travel exposes our own biases and prejudices. It offers us new perspectives, bringing us face-to-face with fresh ideas and different cultures. Travel expands our cultural awareness and sensitivity, building tolerance, appreciation, and respect.

FEED OUR CURIOSITY

You can't exactly make someone curious overnight. But give a child 365 consecutive days of new experiences and educational adventures while traveling, and curiosity will bloom.

The Case for Worldschooling

You may not know this, but as a parent you have the right to withdraw your child from traditional school and choose an alternative means to educate them. What happens when your concept of education expands beyond the four walls of a classroom? What happens when you notice learning opportunities can be anywhere at any time? The world becomes your school. Worldschooling is the educational foundation of a Wonder Year. Simply put, it is learning through direct interaction with the world.

Worldschooling is an educational *approach*—it is not something you sign up for; there's no one to register with, no dogma or governing institution. There are many resources to help you design what worldschooling looks like for you and your family, and we're going to walk you through several of them in this book.

Over the past couple of decades, the term *worldschooling* gained traction. Several traveling families who considered themselves worldschoolers brought awareness to the concept as they shared their experiences online and in popular media. You might also come across the term *roadschooling*. For clarity, in this book we use the term *worldschooling* to mean it all. We want everyone to feel welcome whether you are traveling in the US or overseas, full time or part time, following a curriculum or going with the flow.

By rolling into worldschooling, you are making a choice to step forward and align yourself with the forefront of innovative educational models. Public and private schools are recognizing the value of travel as part of education. International Baccalaureate (IB) programs promote "intercultural understanding and respect . . . as an essential part of life in the 21st Century."[6] Leading universities encourage study-abroad programs. Some people may tell you worldschooling lacks academic rigor, but the evidence will be clear when your kids return to traditional school from a Wonder Year with grit, confidence, and a global frame of reference. Each of the coauthors' children (six in total spanning third to ninth grades) slid right back into school, advancing to the next grade without missing an academic beat.

What better way to prepare your kids for a future, more interconnected, world than to show them the world? Interacting with the world at a young age plants seeds of inspiration and understanding in our children. We know that young brains are heavily impacted by the experiences they have—so why not share with them the art, architecture, history, food, culture, and texture of societies beside the one in which they were raised? Most of us long for greater connection to both fellow humans and the environment. Ask yourself how our future adults can protect the rainforest when they have not seen the rainforest, or connected with *any* forest, for that matter? We strive to protect what we know and love.

One of the limitations of classroom learning is that we tend to learn *about* others. With worldschooling, we begin to learn *from* others. It's an exchange. Learners begin to create their own opinions based on direct experiences, rather than simply repeating what they hear from others or read in a textbook. You can't fake a personal interaction. Your kids might come to the conclusion, for example, that countries maligned in the mainstream US media are full of good and kind people. Worldschooling is fact-finding; worldschooling is peace building.

It's been said that everything you need to know, you learn in kindergarten. The Blew family took this to heart and traveled for two years with their son, Braedon, when he was between four and six years old. After doing their due diligence, they placed him in kindergartens for one to three months at a time around the world. In Mauritius he was the white minority in his African, French creole–speaking class. He joined kindergartens in Thailand and Vietnam for similar durations. Braedon learned about friendship and practiced being the new kid. His dad says, "Four years later, he's a confident kid who is comfortable with new experiences and can find common ground with anyone. We attribute these qualities to an early life on the road where the structures that can hold us back were blown open."

We believe an early experience of travel is an investment that will deliver a lifetime of social, cultural, emotional, and academic returns. Let your children recognize the cultural lens we all carry. Let them get excited by the real-time lessons that travel presents as they navigate public transportation, breakfasts, schools, and bathrooms. How can biking through Angkor Wat, tapping a maple tree in Vermont, or walking the streets of Madrid *not* be fodder for future passions and out-of-the-box thinking?

Twelve years after her return from a Wonder Year with her husband and three kids, Meredith Davis reflects on the long-term benefits of family travel:

> Worldschooling is something that shapes kids' character, informing decisions they'll make about college and career and their own families. In Ecuador we had a guide who grew up in the rainforest. We learned a heap about flora and fauna, but perhaps more than what we learned was *how* we learned—by touching, tasting, and seeing. [Our kids] have a desire to know geography, they enjoy eating new foods, they like to explore, and they're not afraid of change. They are not afraid to ask questions. Our kids recognize the value of getting firsthand accounts, and they respect other cultures and their stories, history, and knowledge.

A Wonder Year can be a time to focus on emotional intelligence rather than grades. Many Wonder Year families use this period to explore well-being and happiness, as well as cultivating a rich inner life from various angles; indeed, many families embark on a Wonder Year and use worldschooling for the purpose of boosting mental health for the whole family. As parents we can model the search for joy; we can reinvent, repurpose, and remind ourselves that the journey never ends, that education is an exchange, a dialogue of giving and receiving.

A Wonder Year presents opportunities for risk-taking, personal challenge, and problem-solving—all twenty-first-century essential life skills. In taking a Wonder Year, you are standing up and moving in the opposite direction of expectation; heeding the call takes courage. Navigating a medieval village or struggling to make yourself understood in a new language takes perseverance. A wrong turn or a missed bus might uncover the better discovery. The lessons are life changing.

Deadvlei, Namibia

We wake at 3:30 a.m., having committed to a desert safari in Namib-Naukluft National Park that starts at 4:00. Unlike a typical safari into a fauna-rich savanna, our aim today is to explore the massive sand dunes in the oldest desert in the world.

At this hour and without moisture to cloud the stars, we have no trouble seeing the universe spread above our heads. The boys remark on the profound quiet. There are no planes flying over, no road noise bouncing across the barren plains—only the distant sounds of jackals announcing a kill echoing across the vlei.

Ronan is psyched when he sees the safari truck, a repurposed Toyota Hilux with a mounted bed insert to accommodate nine passengers in open-air theater seating. We sit four across. Our guide hands us a worn woolen blanket perfect for one but insufficient to shield us all against the bracing predawn wind. We rearrange and put the boys in the middle so they get the most warmth.

The road is like those we drove on yesterday to reach our outpost: gravel and dirt. Ninety percent of Namibia's roads are unpaved, and although great effort is made to keep them in good condition, sections still make for a rough traverse.

The temperature drops further as we near the entrance to the national park, where a wall of cool fog fills the valley. From the Sesriem entrance gate, our eventual destination is the Deadvlei claypan. Along the way, we see mountain zebra, oryx, and ostrich, and we learn that there are five types of sand dunes. Those in Namib-Naukluft are star dunes, which means they have been formed by winds coming from multiple directions over the past several million years.

At Big Daddy, an over one-thousand-foot-high dune overlooking Deadvlei, we stop and venture out to climb one of those star dune's rays. The dune is massive, and the line of hikers stomping up the ridgeline ahead of us nearly disappears in the haze between sand and sky. Ronan bounds out of the truck and starts the heel-toe-heel-toe trek along the narrow channel laid down by hikers across the years. Mark, Asher, and I fall in behind.

The air is warming quickly, and our elongated shadows stretch down the dune's side. There are no climbers passing us on a return journey, and our guide explains that's not the way out.

Instead, we turn perpendicular to the trail and launch down the southern face of Big Daddy toward the cracked white claypan below. High-stepping in the soft red sand, Asher calls out that he feels like an astronaut on Mars. He grips Mark's hand as they serpentine to provide some semblance of control over gravity.

At the base of the dune is Deadvlei, famous for its austere beauty. About six hundred years ago, ephemeral waters that flowed into the marsh during the rainy season stopped when the river cut a new course. The acacia trees that had filled this basin died, and because there isn't enough water to rot the wood, they still stand—blackened by the unforgiving sun. The combination of deep-ocher sand, pale-gray pan, inky acacia skeletons, and the brilliant azure sky make the vlei otherworldly. Astronauts, indeed.

Ronan directs a family photo shoot, and we capture a rare image of all of us together, frozen in time within our frozen surroundings. Even in the now-scorching heat, we want to linger, but our safari mates are ready to go, and our guide aims to secure a prime spot beneath the cooling branches of a tree

for brunch. We marvel with our fellow hikers over coffee, fruit, and bread.

Our final stop is a nearby canyon. While the rest of our group climbs down into the gap, the boys elect to stay closer to the truck, weary. After many weeks on the road and the long drive the previous day, we feel stretched thin, diluted.

Back at the outpost, we have dinner in a common room lit only by candles. Asher eats kudu, an ungulate he's seen grazing among the dunes.

Our tent cabin has an upper deck, and we go up for stargazing before returning "down-ladder" to sleep. In the US it is hard to find places far enough away from artificial light to really see the stars. In Namibia the closest light is hundreds of miles away. Our eyes adjust easily to the darkness, and the universe takes center stage.

We are totally alone, together, lying on our backs as the stars come into focus. We don't need to, but we whisper softly to one another. The boys point out satellites and meteors, and we try to identify the constellations, many of which are different from what we know at home. At twenty-four degrees south latitude, the universe is unfamiliar.

"Our eyes adjust easily to the darkness, and the universe takes center stage."

Choosing a Wonder Year

So, are you ready? Is a Wonder Year right for you?

We know it probably feels like there is no right time to voluntarily disrupt everything and embark on an extended family travel adventure. Your life is busy; your days are full. Work. Friends. Family. Laundry. Grocery shopping. Cooking. Doctor's appointments. Volunteering. Busy. Busier. Busiest. How in the world could you ever squeeze in a Wonder Year?

HELPING YOU DECIDE

Let's break it down a bit. We've come up with a simple three-question framework to help you examine your thoughts on this existential joyride so you can work through a decision process for choosing a Wonder Year. When you are ready, clear your mind of the chatter. Focus on your breath for a couple of minutes, take a walk, and unwind.

Question #1: What are your core values, beliefs, and priorities?

Ask yourself: What do I care about most? What do I believe is most important during my time on earth? Professional or personal growth? Financial security? Note that what you care most about now, as a person and as a parent, may be different from when you were younger. Be honest with yourself. Do you want freedom? Do you want a spiritual practice? Do you want security, adventure, or money? Do you want to shake things up?

Write about, discuss, or draw it. Sleep on it, and when you are ready, converse with your partner, friend, or journal. What is it that gives your life purpose?

This articulation of values will give you something to fall back on during your travels, a safety net of sorts. And if you are doing this exercise with a partner, you may find that the two of you have a shared vision. That's a great place to build from. If you realize you do not have a shared vision or common goals, it may be an indication that planning and executing an extended road trip together could be tricky. It's probably a good idea to have the conversation sooner rather than later in your process.

Question #2: What are the expectations that weigh you down?
What are the "shoulds" that tell you what "right" things you are supposed to be doing? Maybe you were brought up to believe you need to be the bread-winner or the stay-at-home parent. That you need to sacrifice. That life is supposed to be hard. Maybe you believe you are not worthy of the good life, that you don't deserve to take some time off. Can you identify expecta-tions that start from sources other than yourself? Just list and name them. We are not purporting to be therapists; it's your prerogative to go deeper if and when you want to. We're merely suggesting that it's helpful to identify these potential pressures and separate them from your innate desires. We want you to be able to put aside external influences and instead listen to your own voice so you can thoughtfully answer question #1.

What began as a 'wouldn't it be crazy' conversation condensed over several emotional months, filled with plenty of skepticism and excitement, sleepless nights, and animated debates, into an idea with mass. And the gravitational pull of the idea seemed natural . . . inevitable . . . and important.

—*Angela*

Question #3: Why are you considering a Wonder Year, and is anything holding you back?

When you tiptoe to the edge of your comfort zone and take a look, what comes up for you? Would you like to change something in your life, or are you searching for something new? Does your heart start to race a little when you think about taking a leap?

We have heard a lot of people say, "Oh, I would love to travel for a year, someday, when the time is right . . ." or "I wish we had done a trip like that, but now our kids are too old." We know it might be really hard to take this kind of step. But take a look at what is holding you back. Are you worried or afraid? Identifying what's lurking in your pit of uncertainty—concerns about education, employment, civil unrest, or public health—can help you devise a way over, around, or through it.

Now here's the trick: Tackle your fears by creating a contingency plan. That way, you can quiet your worries and take them out of the equation. You can break out of the what-if loop that keeps you stuck in place. You'll no longer need to ask, "What if we are making a huge mistake?" or "What if something happens and our house is rented and we'll have nowhere to live?" or "What if we can't find a new job—OMG what will we do?" A contingency plan could include putting aside reserve funds to support an unplanned return home, arranging with friends or family for you to live with them if necessary, or nurturing professional relationships throughout the year to keep future employment opportunities alive. We'll cover this more in the next chapter.

Now that you have reflected on the possibility of a Wonder Year, let's begin to envision what it may look like for you and your family.

Chaco Canyon, New Mexico

Knowing there'd be no state troopers in this rugged, parched region, we let Johnny, our nine-year-old, help drive the twenty-four-foot RV over thirteen miles of dusty, bumpy, deeply rutted road to Chaco Canyon, New Mexico, a UNESCO World Heritage Site. Chaco Canyon holds the ruins of a vibrant civilization from between the ninth and twelfth centuries and is considered the ancestral homeland to many Native American tribes—including the Hopi, Zuni, and Navajo. We arrive after dark, and Johnny and Charlie stay up late, sitting on the roof of our camper oohing and wowing at the Milky Way and a meteor shower that stripes the massive midnight sky.

Johnny had read about how the Chacoans used astronomy and the paths of the sun and the moon in their design of dwellings, a technique known as astroarcheology. Visiting Chaco Canyon during a major celestial event—the spring equinox—would deepen our connection to this curious place known for its alignment with the heavens. We wake early and hike from the campground to Casa Rinconada, a layered complex of rocks and ruins. The rising sun shines on an east-facing wall, casting golden light on ancient orange sandstone. Our cold toes tingle on the earthen floor while we three smiling visitors stand in the glow of history.

As we wander in and around the site, Johnny leads us into an underground room called a kiva, used by Chacoans for meetings and worship. The kiva has a firepit, a wind block, and a sandstone bench around the entire perimeter of the round room.

Later that afternoon, back at the campground, we notice Johnny sitting comfortably, cross-legged, on the ground by himself, moving pebbles around. He had brushed a canvas of ground and collected a pile of small stones. He carefully forms an outer circle and layers pebbles to form the rock bench. He then creates a mini firepit in the center and makes a pebble wind block. "I wanted to create my own little room, like the kiva," says Johnny boy, who never thought he was any good at art or history.

◀ The fascinating building designs of the ancient Chacoans mystify visitors and scholars alike.

Structuring Your Wonder Year

There are many types of family travel, and new approaches are evolving all the time with emerging technology, infrastructure, and innovative models of work and school.

As you will hear again and again, there is no correct formula. A Wonder Year may coincide with a school year, a fiscal year, or some other significant time frame in your family's rhythm. If you can't take off several months or more, you can prioritize family adventures and adopt a Wonder Year state of mind. It's not an all-or-nothing prospect. A Wonder Year has to make sense to you and your family.

To help get your gears turning on what your Wonder Year could be, let's consider a few key parameters:

Breadth or depth? Do you want to travel fast and go to lots of places? Count countries? Or do you want to travel slowly and pick a few places where you settle in, find an apartment, and try to fit in with the locals?

Home or abroad? Do you want to mostly stay in your home country and learn about and explore it more deeply? Or would you like to head overseas for an international adventure where the languages, foods, and cultures are different from what you are used to?

Take your home with you? Do you want to travel in a motor home, boat, or van where, like a snail, you have your home on your back? Or would you prefer to carry a pack and be mobile, moving about freely without an engine or anchor to weigh you down?

Fixed timeline or open ended? Do you have to return home by a certain date? Do you want to wait and see how your family does in motion before you decide if your trip is six months or three years? Maybe you do not have to decide any return date at all.

Getting clear on some of these priorities can help you focus your choices and move forward confidently. And don't worry, whatever you think now, it is probably going to change! But having a few decisions made sets you in motion.

Let's drill down a little further. Your Wonder Year could be:

- A six-month sabbatical
- Two years of full-time travel to six continents and thirty countries
- A one-year road trip through the US South in an RV
- Two months every summer for five years in a row
- Nine months in Barcelona with weekend explorations throughout Europe
- An around-the-world trip with a defined beginning and end
- A walk-out-the door-and-improvise-everything adventure

A Wonder Year can be whatever you choose; there are infinite possibilities. The consensus is this: Don't try to do everything! Put your right foot on what you love. Put your left foot on where you want to go. Now, do the hokey pokey and turn yourself around, and that's what it's all about!

A Conversation on Inclusivity

Travel builds relationships between people and with places. Unfortunately, travel and tourism are not always accessible, safe, and welcoming to all. The events of the early 2020s—the pandemic, social justice uprisings, calls for diversity and inclusion—elevated the conversation about inequities and prompted change in many sectors, including travel.[7] The travel industry, the media, stakeholders, and communities around the globe have committed to do better. As worldschooling families, we, too, have an opportunity and responsibility to educate ourselves and support efforts that diversify the faces, voices, businesses, and experiences of travel.

For some travelers from the US, getting a passport and putting together a trip is rather straightforward. The hardest part may be narrowing options for where to go and how to get there. The experience for others may not be simple at all. Families of color or LGBTQ+ travelers may be unwelcome or unsafe in some locations. Others may face discrimination when trying to secure a rental car or accommodations, or have difficulty finding a gender-neutral bathroom. Travelers with disabilities or allergies may have to overcome accessibility obstacles and navigate planning and logistical issues many could never fathom. People who wear certain attire may be stereotyped, harassed, or mistreated by virtue of their religious or spiritual expression. For some travelers, finding outdoor gear that fits their bodies or being comfortable in transit is a hurdle.

Subtle challenges or microaggressions are just as unwelcoming and problematic as more blatant acts of discrimination. Travelers might experience judgmental glances, longer waits for service, disparaging comments muttered under someone's breath, or shaming based on their appearances.

Businesses, governments, and nonprofit organizations have begun to examine how to change the travel industry, both inside and outside the US. Destinations and tour companies are diversifying their leadership, workforce, and advertising campaigns; they are examining their relationships with and impact on local communities; and they are evaluating how they include and meet the needs of all travelers. Advocacy and research groups are providing new ways to measure, track, and report on diversity and inclusion and are pushing for greater accountability. Domestic and international organizations are looking to promote the adoption of best practices and develop tools and the capacity to achieve responsible tourism that recognizes and works within the needs of local communities.

While the travel industry, governments, and institutions around the world are grappling with these important topics, this is just the beginning, and the outcomes are yet to be seen and measured. There's also a lot we can do as a worldschooling community in our capacity as travelers, parents, consumers, and allies.

Here are some actions we can take to promote inclusivity and diversity:

- ▶ Pay attention—be a vocal ally when you see injustice.
- ▶ Build tolerance and cultural exchange, which Astrid Vinje recommends in her blog, *The Wandering Daughter,* by noticing "What's different?" and "What's the same?" compared to home.
- ▶ When planning travel, use businesses that practice and promote inclusivity. Use your travel dollars to support airlines, rental car companies, accommodations, and other operators moving in the right direction.
- ▶ While on the road, get the scoop. Support the just and fair vendors and establishments.
- ▶ Tell, read, share, and like travel stories from diverse voices on social media.
- ▶ Follow accounts and hashtags that discuss hard issues as well as represent joy.

- ▶ Educate yourself and your family about history and social justice issues that expand or limit inclusion.
- ▶ Speak up—demand that the industry change.

The face of travel has never reflected the true diversity of people, but social media is helping to change that. Mary Solio, one of the earliest family travel bloggers of color, shares, "Back in 2011, there weren't many traveling families that looked like us. When Instagram came on the scene, people of color began to see other people traveling who looked like them. It brought confidence and helped get more diverse people out there." Today, platforms like Instagram, TikTok, and YouTube feature diverse voices of family travel. Social media can promote access and inclusion and connect travelers who may be looking for each other and for community.

Creating safe and welcoming travel experiences will take time, awareness, and the involvement of us all.

A Family Affair

There's one more important step. When the adults in the crew are on board and ready to start planning in earnest, we urge you to bring your children into the discussion. We loved involving our kids in the process. It was their onboarding to the great family adventure, and by virtue of being engaged, they felt valued. This was essential to our trip success and could be for yours, too.

I had the expectation and hope that we would totally check out for a year. I wanted to go away, change everything up, hit the road, and not look back. But travel rule #1: things change, and stuff happens. You cannot plan for a five-hundred-year flood hitting your hometown while you are away or your dog getting bone cancer or the outside temperature dropping seventy degrees in one day. So, while my quest was for a round-the-country loop, our travel path was redrawn into a four-leaf clover with three unplanned stops back home. How lucky for us! My presumption that contact back home during the year would somehow diminish or compromise the authenticity of our journey proved completely untrue.

——Julie

Final Note: Encountering the Reactions of Others

Okay, so you've done some soul-searching, stared down your demons, considered your time horizon, talked with your partner, and engaged your kids. Now you're letting yourself feel excited. It's actually going to happen! OMG! And then you tell some people your plan, and your sister-in-law says, "Must be nice. I could never do that." Or a snickering colleague says, "Have fun in divorce court." Maybe an uncle insinuates you are reckless for pulling your kids out of school.

Others may have opinions and question your choice. They might comment on your finances. Some will react with joy, but others might suggest you are irresponsible. Please remember that you don't have to apologize or justify your decision when you encounter those reactions. Stay true to yourself and your family's priorities, and absolve yourself of any guilt or need to explain.

Sarah De Santi, who has been worldschooling for many years with her husband, Massy, and three children, shared with us, "A friend said to me, 'You have the perfect house, the perfect car, the perfect life. You're going to change that? Why??' That's why. Who says this is perfect? It's only perfect because that's what society tells you. It's not perfect. We don't have time with our kids. We're so tired all the time that we don't enjoy each other. We don't really know each other anymore." Sarah said that choosing this lifestyle has given her back all the things she felt she was missing and more. And for her, *this* is perfect.

It's okay. You will find plenty of people who get it and will understand your reasoning and support your choice. We three coauthors are some of those people, and you will meet many more of them in this book and in the greater community of traveling families.

CHAPTER 2

The Money Questions

An investment in knowledge pays the best interest.

—Benjamin Franklin

I T'S THE QUESTION MOST ASKED in family travel forums: "But how do you *afford* it?" The short answer is this: it's different for every family. The longer answer is that it usually takes a combination of decisions and resources to fund extended time on the road. People sometimes assume that a Wonder Year is only for the wealthy, but that's absolutely not the case. We hope you'll be encouraged by all of the creative avenues we share here to turn your dream into a reality.

Financial planning is an essential component of making long-term travel work for your family. This chapter shares strategies for creating and managing a financially healthy and feasible Wonder Year. We know money can be a tricky subject, and we aren't here to tell you how to approach something as personal as family finances. Instead, we offer advice and share stories of how other families have done it so that you, too, can start to see a financial path forward. If your consumptive habits are lean, walking out the door might not feel risky. Others may need longer to prepare to feel ready to shake up their income-to-expense ratio. Like everything else about long-term family travel, you'll likely learn a lot about yourself and your family as you tackle financial questions and set priorities.

In this chapter we consider both sides of the equation: income and expenses.

An Initial Look at Budgets

There are several ways to build a budget for a Wonder Year. Some families start with their available funds and create a plan with that number in mind. Others dream up their trip and then raise funds to cover anticipated expenses. Some families save for years, building a reserve just as they might for college tuition. Still others are more comfortable financially and emotionally winging it—they trust that it will be what it will be and are willing to risk stepping into the unknown.

Our research found that Wonder Year budgets vary enormously. *Your* budget needs will reflect your family's values and priorities. They will depend heavily on what kind of travelers you are, where you choose to go, whether you travel fast or slow, your preferred accommodation types, and other cost/comfort/convenience trade-offs. It's often easy to think about a budget in terms of monthly expenses, but that's not true for everyone. You might instead choose to budget by a different length of time, or by phases when you will and won't be bringing in additional income. Some families decide on a per-diem budget, and if they go over it one day, they know they need to make up for it on another day to stay on track. Others start by sketching out the places they want to go and experiences they want to have, estimating in-country costs for lodging, food, and transportation to arrive at their ballpark estimate. The important part is to identify a target, stick to it as best as you can, and have a contingency plan for when you don't.

Budgeting decisions are driven by where travel falls in your family's priorities, and what you can and want to do to make it happen. Lots of families travel on lean budgets and find creative ways to make it work, so don't let the money questions stop you from pursuing your dream. Many are surprised to find life on the road can cost less than life at home and that they can reduce and simplify expenses when they aren't rooted in a single location. For some families, the opposite is true: their expenses are higher than living at home, and they must plan and adjust accordingly.

Worldschoolers exchange budget information often, so you can post specific questions for your circumstances in online forums and on travel blogs. We've found that the more detailed you are in your inquiry ("We're a family of four looking to rent a two-bedroom apartment in Tallinn, Estonia, for a month. A safe, walkable neighborhood would be great, but we don't need luxurious accommodations. We mostly cook at home but want to be able to eat out occasionally and visit local museums and cultural sites. Does anyone have suggestions for what a reasonable budget would be?"), the more helpful information you're likely to get. (See the resources section for more details on worldschooling forums.)

One final tip: don't feel as though your budget has to fund the lifestyles portrayed in the polished images of perfectly lit settings you might see on social media. Often, travel influencers are families who have dedicated considerable time, energy, and resources to developing a media presence and securing income through advertising and brand partnerships, and what is shared online doesn't reflect the experiences of the vast majority of travelers.

We'll come back to a full discussion of expense planning later in the chapter.

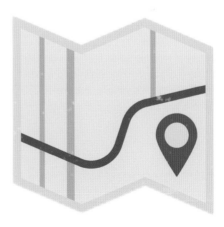

Moab, Utah

Moonflower Canyon is spectacularly situated against deep-red cliffs streaked with black vertical lines called desert varnish. Since it's on land that's part of the Bureau of Land Management and not actually a national park, dogs can roam and kids can climb freely. We're on the outskirts of Moab down Kane Creek Road, a popular route for mountain bikers and four-wheelers on their way to Amasa Back and Captain Ahab, two of the area's iconic trailheads.

We park in the lot and walk a few hundred feet to where campsites are nestled in the hillside or tucked under trees. We claim a flat site in the shade of a statuesque cottonwood, leave a couple of camp chairs, then head back out to get on our bikes. We never make it. Johnny is sucked into a vortex of youth—five kids ages six to fifteen are sitting at a picnic table, busily unwinding utility 550-gauge paracord in colors like hot pink, Day-Glo yellow, lime green, purple, and black. They are making DIY survival bracelets. Johnny slides right into the circle, and they show him how to measure the length, loop the paracord, and knot it to create a bracelet. The kids demonstrate how to fasten the finished bracelet and burn the ends to prevent fraying. Johnny picks his colors and gets to work with ten eyes and fifty fingers showing him the way.

This impromptu pod of traveling kiddos sits together for over an hour. Their finished bracelets, knotted with six feet of paracord, would be long enough when uncoiled to tie up a tarp, fix a snowshoe, hang a bag of food, make a sling, or lash some branches. One bracelet would be strong enough to hold 550 pounds of static weight.

On the way out of town, we stop at Walkers Hardware to pick up several yards of paracord. Johnny is over the moon for having made new friends and acquiring a new survival skill, and handsome Max gets a new orange-and-yellow survival dog collar!

"...sucked into a vortex of youth."

Funding Your Wonder Year

So, how do families fund their adventures? A Wonder Year often means simplifying your life and shifting your priorities and mindset. This can look different for each family, and there are many ways to support long-term family travel.

To make this all a bit more real, here are snapshots of how some families have made it work:

- The Gallagher family of four stayed for roughly three months at each of four budget-friendly destinations in Southeast Asia and Central America during their Wonder Year. Mom taught ESL online part time and set her own schedule, while Dad worked online thirty hours per week for a solar energy company based in Europe.

- The Martinez family of four began saving for their Wonder Year ten years before they left, and they earned additional income from renting their home while they were gone. Together, this provided a budget that allowed them to travel comfortably in Europe and Asia.

- The Edwards sold nearly all their assets, including their house and cars, invested the proceeds in safe, modest-return CDs and mutual funds, and lived off the interest income while they traveled. The amount they could comfortably and reliably yield each month became their budget. When they returned home, they were fortunate not to have accumulated additional debt, but they did incur the cost of reacquiring some of the assets they had initially divested to fund their adventure.

- Stella Barnes is a career coach who has a practice online. A single parent of an eight-year-old boy, she built her remote appointment schedule so she could work while her son took online classes. They returned home periodically to stay with family, see clients in person, and save more money for traveling.

- The Long family lived full time in their RV and traveled throughout the US and Mexico. Destrie led worldschooling lessons for their two boys while her husband, Derek, worked online as a software engineer to fund their adventures.

As you can see, there are many strategies families use to finance a Wonder Year. Let's take a deeper look at each of these, plus a few others, in turn.

SAVINGS

Make more, spend less. A familiar mantra that's easier said than done, right? Saving money is the most traditional, straightforward method for funding a Wonder Year. However, that doesn't mean it is the easiest. Families often save all year for a two-week vacation, so saving for a year on the road might feel insurmountable. If you are like the Higham family of the worldschooling memoir *360 Degrees Longitude*, you plan for nearly *ten years* and save for several.[8] That requires some considerable foresight and commitment to the idea when your kids are young (or not yet born!) so that you have time to save enough to go before they head off to college.

Setting a savings goal, especially if travel isn't something you've regularly saved for in the past, will likely require new trade-offs in your family. What expenses can you cut? These might require some big life choices such as living with extended family while you save or working an extra job. Or you might start smaller and cut out some extracurricular or social activities. Look at what is optional in your life and what you are willing to give up. Remember, you're making those trades so your family can follow the dream you share.

To help find motivation for sticking to your savings plan, spend time as a family talking about your travel aspirations. Read about places you hope to go, talk about what you want to do there, and pull inspirational photos and post them around the house. Create a sense of teamwork in your family as you work toward a common goal. Get your kids involved in cost cutting and doing the math: having dinner at home versus going out to eat. Solicit ideas from them on how you can further your savings, and include them in the moment as you make spending decisions ("I know you'd love to go to the water park today, but how about we add to our travel savings instead?"). Get creative in finding ways to motivate everyone in the family.

SELLING (AND DONATING)

Some people love their stuff and have every intention of returning to it after their Wonder Year, whereas others feel ready to let some (or all!) of their things go. If you're in the latter group, this section is for you.

Think about which belongings really matter to you—essentially, those that have sentimental value or can't be replaced. Then possibly add items that have long-term utility and would be expensive to replace after your travels. These might be the possessions you'll hold on to, then you can tackle the rest. Here are some practical tips.

- Create relevant categories such as keep/store, sell, donate, and trash.

- When selling, start early so you have plenty of time to manage the process and secure good prices. Selling can be a major time commitment, so be thoughtful about which items you list versus donate. Take good photos, price fairly, and respond quickly to inquiries for the best results.

- After you've identified what to sell, consider giving away other items to further reduce your possessions burden. Most areas have several local donation-based organizations, and some will even pick up larger items. And don't forget to take the related tax deductions, as any resulting savings can also be put toward travel.

- If you aren't keeping your remaining belongings in a dwelling when you leave, be aware of the potential storage costs. This may help you decide what is worth keeping.

The Moran family, who ventured to Central America from their home in Virginia, felt like they'd lost sight of some core beliefs as they worked busy jobs and grew their family. In the upward climb to attain "bigger" and "more," they had found themselves overloaded with stuff they'd never aimed to have, much of which they weren't using—or even seeing—anymore. Filling their house became a goal in itself, and they got caught up in it without pausing for serious reflection. So, when the question of long-term travel came up, in addition to raising travel funds, the thought of letting go of "stuff" was wildly appealing.

If you know you're coming back to the same place, you can leave some of your things with friends (tip: keep a list of who has what!). One of Annika's friends used her skis while she was away, while others benefited from her stand mixer and food dehydrator. Angela gave away almost all her clothes to friends; it was like a goodbye gift, and they enjoyed the free gear. Her friend Debbie wasn't willing to let her give away all of her best stuff and offered to list it on eBay instead. Every so often, she'd sell an item and send Angela a bit of surprise travel funds.

Be sure to involve your kids in selling and giving away your family's belongings. You can let them help sort personal items. Older kids can help with household goods, reflecting on what is really needed and what can go. They can also assist with the selling process and learn about finance, marketing, selling, and online transactions. It's a head start on worldschooling lessons! Plus, who can resist buying from a kid?

Many families find that their Wonder Year prompts them to reexamine how they want to spend their time and resources. It's different for everyone, and it is absolutely fine if you are someone who misses your stuff and is excited to see it all again. But you might also find that in this case, absence does not make the heart grow fonder.

All of that said, sometimes you might need something sentimental from home for your journey, too. Nadia Adnan Abdulrehman, who travels with her husband and two children, shared that her son decided to leave his favorite teddy at home because he didn't want to lose it on the road. They secured a stand-in teddy for their travels, but then *that* teddy became the favorite because it accompanies them on their family adventures.

ANGELA'S REFLECTION
Kids' Belongings

As we were closing out prior to our trip, I gave each of my kids a small container for any personal items they wanted access to during our travels. My older son didn't even fill his. Both kids had a surprising number of things they were ready to sell or donate, including things that had just been sitting on shelves or in boxes. Mark and I were happy to let them be sentimental about things they wanted to keep, as we were planning to have a storage unit close by.

When we unpacked our stored goods after our Wonder Year, our kids found they'd outgrown a lot of their belongings and were ready to part with them. So, we had paid to store a bunch of stuff that we were now ready to sell or donate. Lesson noted.

An even bigger realization was that their outlook on belongings had changed altogether. "Out of sight, out of mind" had rung wonderfully true, and it was revealing how little they'd missed our things. As we unpacked and our new house filled up, many possessions started to feel more like a burden than a bonus. We wished we had given away more things before our trip.

Don't underestimate your kids' ability to let go.

Simplifying

The process of simplifying starts with shifting your mindset—thinking about how you value time versus money, and experiences versus stuff. For some of us, belongings can give a false sense of something, whether it be pride, accomplishment, or wealth. But they can also weigh us down, take energy to maintain, and dilute our attention. People can get stuck in a cycle of purchasing items in hopes of obtaining a sense of leisure, idealism, and freedom. Ironically it is often those things that deny us the freedom we seek.

Letting go of your things might seem hard, but you may find it to be easier than you anticipated—in fact, many people are downright liberated by letting go. In *Minimalism: A Documentary About the Important Things*, authors and filmmakers Joshua Fields Millburn and Ryan Nicodemus challenge viewers to "imagine a life with less. Less stuff, less clutter, less stress, debt, and discontent. A life with fewer distractions. Now imagine a life with more. More time. More meaningful relationships. More growth and contribution and contentment."[9] How does this play out for you in your current life, and how would you like it to be instead?

INVESTMENTS

Some families use the financial markets to generate income for their travels. Money from savings or recently sold assets can comfortably sit in a bank account, or it can work for you by being invested. If applicable, examine any existing investments to determine how they might generate income for travel. If you plan to use this approach to help fund your Wonder Year, we encourage you to talk with a financial advisor to ensure you are comfortable with the associated risks and trade-offs. There are planners who help people at all income levels, and some charge only by the hour. Advisors can monitor economic trends and marketplace events with you and manage your assets, even while you're away.

LEVERAGING YOUR HOME

If you own your home, one of the biggest pretrip decisions is what to do with it while you're away. Some families choose to sell their primary residence, using any profits to help fund their travels. They might be planning to downsize or even relocate when they return. Or market conditions might be favorable for selling now and buying or renting a different home later.

Some families set out on open-ended journeys, blissfully sidestepping a plan for residential reentry. But many have a beginning and an end to their trip, and they expect to return to their current home, jobs, and schools. Unless you plan to move to a different residence after your trip is over, you'll most likely return to your current house, condo, or apartment.

Some people leave their home empty because they don't want to deal with the hassle of someone else occupying it while they are away. But renting out your house could generate significant income and go a long way toward covering big expenses while you are gone, such as mortgage payments and maintenance expenses, especially if the rental market is strong in your area. With planning and foresight, renting out your house can provide an excellent source of income while you're trekking in Nepal or snorkeling in Belize.

Long-Term Rentals

Long-term rental is the easiest for most people to manage, as there is less turnover and wear and tear on the property, and you can get to know your renters in a more meaningful way. If you plan to rent to a long-term tenant, here are some tips:

- Decide if you want to work with a property manager or management company. These businesses can help you list and market your property, handle background checks and financial transactions, and act as your on-the-ground resource for maintenance needs and emergencies. They typically charge a percentage of the rental income for their services, but the ease and peace of mind for you can be worth it. Many real estate lawyers will advise using a property manager as an added layer of legal protection, particularly when the owner is away.

- Alternatively, you might ask a trusted family member or friend to fulfill some of these duties while you are traveling.

- You might rent to someone you already know. One family we talked to rented directly to a friend, who also collected mail, paid routine bills, and cared for the property and pets.

- If you are listing and marketing the property yourself, research pricing trends and competition. Prep the property appropriately—will it be furnished or unfurnished? Figure out which property-listing websites get the most traffic in your area, and don't underestimate the power of well-lit photos taken from flattering angles. It may take some effort to find a qualified renter, and personal connections and word of mouth can go a long way.

- Plan for worst-case scenarios, and evaluate whether you can cover part of the mortgage if necessary. You should absolutely take a security deposit in case your renter unexpectedly stops payments or damages your belongings.

Short-Term Rentals

If you don't want to contract with long-term renters (maybe you have family members who want to stay in your home for part of the year, or you want to leave open the possibility of returning periodically or early), another option is to offer your space for short-term vacation stays, provided this is legal in your area. Given the increased number of transactions and turnovers, you'll likely want to contract with a property manager for this option. You can usually earn more on a nightly basis with short-term rentals, but it is more labor intensive. You can also look for short-term renters within the worldschoolers community, in which travelers often tell each other about their available properties and may even offer special deals to one another.

House Swaps

Taking the notion of offering your home to other families one step further, an increasing number of travelers are participating in house swaps. A house (or home) swap is exactly that—residing in another family's home while they live in yours. You create an online listing for your home with available dates, then look for places you're interested in staying and coordinate details with the other party for a temporary exchange of homes.

One pro of home swaps is that you may end up staying in places that feel more, well, homey. Additionally, there is a mutual responsibility for taking good care of each other's dwellings. House swaps can also cover the care of pets, houseplants, and/or gardens. There are several online services that facilitate matches. Working through these companies gives you the benefit of their assistance managing issues or concerns at both ends of the swap. (See the resources section for details.)

This is one instance when long-term travel might be less on your side. While finding a match for a two-week vacation swap is achievable, it might be harder to coordinate a significantly longer stay or many swaps strung together. If you are willing to pay for other accommodations to fill in the gaps, this could still be a good fit for you. Some house-swap websites use points systems to get around the issue of coordinating exact dates and could be a great option for families traveling long term.

HOUSE SITTING

If you don't have, or wish to offer, a home in exchange, house sitting may be a wonderful way to cover accommodation costs as you travel. In this arrangement, people offer reduced or free accommodation in their vacant home in exchange for care of their pets, livestock, gardens, house, or other property. House sitters also help keep the property safer, as an empty home is more tempting to thieves, and maintenance issues can otherwise go unchecked.

Just like home swaps, there are several websites that facilitate house-sitting transactions. In fact, *House Sitting Magazine* is a publication devoted to this lifestyle. First, consider whether house sitting is right for you, as it can affect the way you travel. You'll still have other travel expenses, including airline or train tickets, transportation costs for getting to and from the house, visas, car rental (although vehicles are sometimes included as part of the arrangement), food, and activities. You'll also have less flexibility, as you'll need to be in specific locations on exact dates. There are more responsibilities on the ground, and possibly less freedom to explore further afield, as animals and gardens can take up your time and require you to be home at certain times during the day. Essentially, you'll need to be house sitting first and traveling second. In fact, you might find that it feels too much like being at your own home, with a list of duties waiting for you every morning and evening!

That said, the potential upsides are many. House sitting might be a great option for *part* of your travel time—namely, when you need to stop for a longer period of time and catch up on remote work, schooling, or planning for subsequent travels. It can also be a wonderful way to feel more connected to a community, participate in local events, and make friends. This can be especially nice for families traveling with kids, as your hosts might even offer local connections, set you up with friendly resources, and have pets for you to love. And while some people might believe that traveling as a family presents a barrier to house sitting, in fact, many families house sit and find plenty of listings seeking their trusted services.

COUCHSURFING

Couchsurfing is yet another option for uber-resourceful families looking to reduce costs. Simply stated, couchsurfing is staying overnight in other people's homes for free. This can include visits with friends and family, but it often refers to residing with people you don't know before your stay. This approach may not be for everyone given potential safety concerns, but for those interested, a quick online search of "couchsurfing with kids" will provide a good starting point for the latest trends and resources. The website couchsurfing.com allows users to set up a profile and match with hosts—and fellow travelers, if you want to return the favor in your home.

USING POINTS AND MILES

Wise use of credit cards prior to and during travel can have many benefits, including accumulation of miles toward travel, accommodations, and cash-back rewards.

Credit cards that accrue rewards points or miles can help cover transportation costs. As soon as possible, start using cards that earn points. There may be bonuses for opening a new account, reaching certain levels of spending, or referring friends and family to the card program. There is often also a multiplier effect for travel-related purchases (for example, Chase United Visa points are multiplied when using the card to buy flights on United), so points can add up quickly.[10] Some people even close one card and open another to earn more new-account points, but don't forget to monitor how this might affect your credit score. Another word of caution is to shop carefully when it comes to interest rates and fees, which may be adjusted by the card company without a lot of warning.

When selecting credit cards, look for ones that are favorable to travel by design. Some offer better exchange rates on currency withdrawals and may reduce, or even eliminate, transaction fees at international ATMs, which can otherwise add up quickly. Others might provide travel or rental car insurance coverage as part of their services. Annika's card would have covered emergency evacuation from Nepal if needed (she checked)! Some companies, especially those associated with an airline brand, offer more luggage options for free on flights. You can also use card multipliers to keep paying the benefits forward while you are traveling.

Points can go toward booking flights, hotels, and other travel services. When you are booking regular vacations, it can often be difficult to use points given the demand for flights and hotels on popular dates, but long-term travel, when you are less attached to specific travel days, provides more flexibility for using what you've earned. Angela's family had miles earned via extensive work travel prior to their Wonder Year, and they used points to book flights to Africa and South America that were normally prohibitively expensive. Websites like The Points Guy and Miles Momma are dedicated to playing and winning the points game.

Okavango Delta, Botswana

I rub sleep out of my eyes and relinquish the covers that I'd been fighting my brother for all night. The muffled buzz of insects pauses periodically as I splash my face with warm water. My mom and I had decided on an early-morning excursion—rare for us night owls—to round out the afternoon boat and evening jeep safaris of the days before.

The sun is low, and the breeze blows enough to ease us into a day that's going to be extremely warm. Although wildlife is out and birds are chirping, there is a mesmerizing stillness to the world. The sky is chalky gray, one of the rare occasions during our time in often-sunny Botswana. A few minutes into our game drive, it begins to sprinkle rain, pattering against the canvas top of the vehicle.

The first hour remains drizzly and quiet. We see a few boar, tails raised in alarm as something approaches behind their den. A litter of Cape foxes plays with their mom in the dirt, just like puppies back home. A baby elephant with half a trunk crosses with its herd in front of us, and I wonder how the injury will affect its life.

Our driver comes to a sudden halt and bobs her head toward the right side of the jeep. There stands an impala, alone and shaking. Normally, game trucks will send impalas—who are prey for many animals—leaping quickly away. This one doesn't budge. She is immune to our presence, fully occupied with something far more important. As we look closer, I can see two tiny hooves hanging out from under her tail. I'm usually kind of squeamish, but I can't look away over the next hour as the hooves turn into legs and then a body and then finally a tiny impala face.

The newborn lays shivering slightly as the mother cleans it, then slowly raises its head. My mom and I watch as it stands, wobbling. It takes three comical, knee-knocking attempts to get to its feet. Its first steps are in search of its mother's milk, and I'm struck by how it knows where to find the meal.

Our guide is kind and patient with us, happy to stay as long as we want to watch, but mostly stares into the middle distance during the birth. I realize she's likely been witness to something like this many times before.

▶ A prized sighting of the endangered African wild dog; learning the difference between hippo and rhino prints.

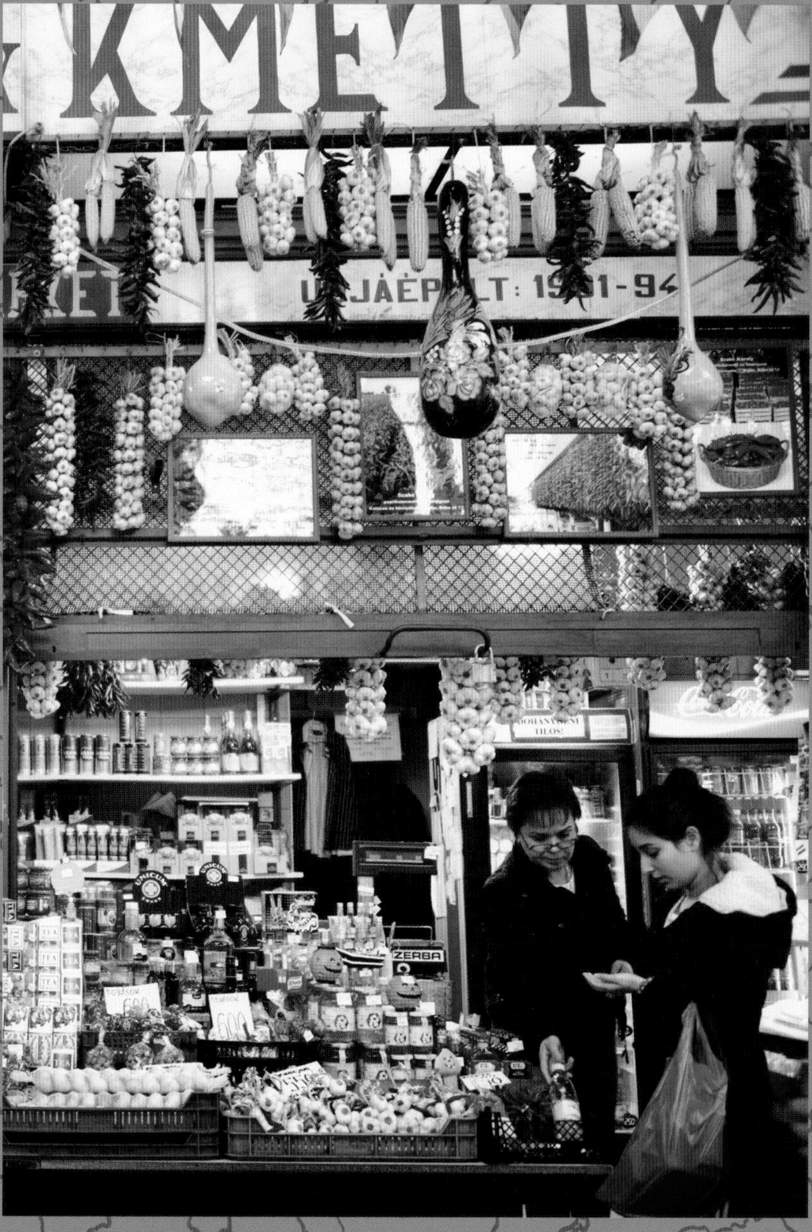
KMETTY
TILOS!
ZERBA

WORKING ON THE ROAD

We've looked at many means for building your travel budget. But it's not all about saving a buck or selling assets or finding every deal possible. Let's switch gears and talk about another way many families are funding their adventures: working on the road.

Location-Dependent Work

Some travelers work in roles that require them to be in a fixed location some of the time. Project-based work, seasonal roles, and consulting engagements such as campground hosting, teaching positions, or sabbatical research assignments often have clear start and end dates. Families staying in one place for a while often "live lean" during that time, saving large portions of their income toward future travel periods.

Taking Your Job with You: Digital Nomadism

As more work is getting done online, increasing numbers of employees can be location independent. Your employer might be interested enough in retaining you that they are willing to work out a flexible work arrangement for your current position. Consulting and contract work may give you the flexibility needed for living and working on the road. Online teaching and tutoring, selling goods, providing information technology services, and many other roles lend themselves well to this setup.

Skye White, a sports psychologist, continued to work with her most committed clients during her family's Wonder Year. She selected one day per week to meet with them online and coordinated family travel around that schedule. If you also plan to take your job on the road, just make sure you consider how you'll secure reliable internet access and coordinate meetings and deliverables across multiple time zones.

Taking Your Skills with You

You may have transferable job skills, as a teacher, doctor, fitness instructor, nurse, or arborist, that are needed throughout the world. Some families build their journeys around wherever the next jobs take them, using locally earned income to fund slow travel and immerse themselves in new communities. Sites such as Workaway allow hosts to recruit workers who can babysit, garden, cook, build, or provide other services in exchange for accommodations and wages, and often both parties benefit from the cultural exchange.

Travel as Your Job

There are travelers who thrive on writing about and photographing their adventures. This content might be turned into blog features, and some families are able to sell advertising on their websites, generating income. An even smaller subset are able to establish themselves as social media influencers, posting about their experiences and securing sponsorships from well-known brands. While this may sound like an alluring pursuit, keep in mind that it takes time and consistent effort to be able to generate reliable income from it.

There are many ways to earn money on the road, and one important aspect is to determine how it fits in with the rest of your Wonder Year experience. You'll need to figure out how to make the time and space for work and how this will impact the whole family as you live together . . . around the clock. When there's no office to go to, well, then there's no place to hide, and you, your partner, and your kids may have to negotiate ways to make work time work out for everyone.

Jobs People Take on the Road

The types of jobs held by full-time travelers are phenomenally varied, and remote work options continue to expand. We were surprised by the diverse and creative work that worldschoolers are doing on the road. Here's a list we gathered from literature, interviews, and personal connections to give you a sense of what might be possible for you.

- Yoga teacher
- Dance teacher
- ESL/Foreign-language teacher
- RV technician
- Blogger with revenue-generating content
- Online tutor
- Midwife and birth educator
- Online bookkeeper
- Web and graphic designer
- IT programmer
- Tour guide
- Hypnotherapist
- Repair person
- Alternative healer
- Event planner
- Personal trainer
- Nutritionist coach
- Jewelry designer
- Clothing designer
- Social media manager
- Lawyer
- Interior designer
- Financial advisor
- Nonprofit administrator
- Campground host
- Copywriter
- Occupational therapist
- Online music teacher
- Geophysicist

- Translator
- Functional medicine practitioner
- Virtual assistant
- Book author
- Freelance travel writer
- Online school administrator
- Online membership salesperson
- Educational consultant
- Day trader
- Digital content creator
- Career coach
- Health coach
- Rental property owner/operator
- Affiliate marketer
- Online course creator/teacher
- Digital product salesperson
- Travel agent
- Pet sitter
- Health insurance salesperson
- International realtor
- Professional chef leading tours
- Renewable-energy consultant
- Artist

Income Taxes

If only full-time travel allowed us to take a break from paying taxes, too. Nope. If you are earning any type of income during your Wonder Year, you still have tax obligations. Here are some considerations for US citizens traveling full time.[11]

- You are responsible for paying federal taxes each year, no matter where you are in the world and how your income is earned; taxes are based on worldwide income.

- This is true even if you don't live in a fixed place and are traveling full time.

- Tax and filing rules are usually the same, whether you are physically in the US or abroad.

- State taxes are more complicated, and you are generally required to pay state taxes for your state of residence. Many states require you to file a nonresident income tax return, even if you are overseas or traveling full time; be sure to check the rules for your home state.

- If you plan to reside in a single other country for most of your Wonder Year, be sure to research the Foreign Earned Income Exclusion law primarily aimed at US expats.[12]

- If you are staying in the US and traveling to multiple states, review the laws for each state where you earned income, as requirements may vary.

- If you have a family business, own an LLC, or operate under another framework while working on the road, keep track of your expenses; some may be tax deductible.

- Some expenses associated with volunteer work, such as food and lodging costs, may be deductible as well; keep track and consult your tax advisor.

Given the unique circumstances of each family's Wonder Year, we recommend looking closely at the potential tax consequences of your trip or consulting with a tax accountant *before you go* to review your needs and plans. We talk more about taxes in chapter 3 (Closing Up Life at Home).

BORROWING

If your savings and income streams don't provide you with the necessary funds for your Wonder Year, you could consider taking out a personal loan or line of credit. This might be especially relevant if you are trying to travel during a specific window of time, such as a work sabbatical or prior to your kids reaching certain ages. Personal loans can be a viable way to meet a near-term travel goal, as long as you approach them with a thorough understanding of their implications.

First, don't borrow money unless you absolutely need it. Review your finances and be willing to tap into savings before taking out a loan that includes interest, which will cost you more in the long run. You might also consider using credit cards, which have additional offerings for purchase protection, rewards points, and other benefits. One option is to use a low-interest-rate credit card while you're traveling, then consolidate this debt into a personal loan after you return home. You won't borrow more than you need, and the debt can be converted into a repayment schedule that factors into your budget. Online personal loan calculators can help you determine payment amounts and schedules based on the terms of your loan.

Banks compete for loan business, so shop around. Compare interest rates, processing charges, turnaround times, repayment schedules, and one-time fees. Be sure to read the fine print in your loan documents. And most importantly, only borrow what you know you can repay—don't risk living beyond your means. Travel is important, but funding it shouldn't make you stressed, anxious, or financially overcommitted after you return.

Tumbuk, Nepal

The woman places the *kata*, a stiff ceremonial scarf, over Kai's head. He knows to bow his head and put his hands together in a prayer position to receive the blessing of the kata. Then we shuffle together for the photo, our family in the center, flanked by Tumbuk community members.

Twenty-five years earlier, my husband spent time at the Tumbuk monastery and made lifelong friends. One year earlier, Kai and his siblings sold chai at various events around Colorado to raise funds to help rebuild the community center after the devasting 2015 earthquake.

After the photo, we walk around the dormitories surrounding the monastery. We stand and look inside at wooden scaffolds that appear to be holding up the roof. Deep cracks run sideways through sienna and mustard–colored stucco, cross diagonally over intricate, hand-painted Buddhas inside; lines in the exterior walls branching like spiderwebs make me think twice about the safety of entering to look at statues or to sit quietly in the prayer room.

We walk past the foundation of the old community center, the one that was reduced to rubble and repurposed, as much as possible, into the new structure we're here to welcome. The destruction makes us quiet.

A young woman, rosy-cheeked and wearing a bright headscarf, beckons us inside the new building for a cup of chai. She points to the new stove in the kitchen area and gives us a thumbs-up with a big smile. Wooden planks, stones, and lintels have been removed from the old structure and reconfigured to make the new one. Like pieces in a puzzle, planks painted with images of conch shells or the Buddhist deity Green Tara lie next to a brand-new one from the mill. A rebuild, but not a clean slate.

▶ Celebrating Sherpa culture with old friends and new.

Volunteerism

Volunteering can be a powerful way to engage with local communities, provide services to others, and create meaningful experiences for your family. And if planned with some forethought, it may help defray room-and-board costs or offer a chance to recalibrate during your journey. That said, many volunteer programs charge fees to participants, so this activity may unexpectedly land in the "expense" rather than "income" category of your travel budget. It usually shouldn't be counted on as a significant or reliable source for covering costs, but families often have other important reasons for choosing volunteerism during their travels. These firsthand experiences can be educational and leave lasting impressions that influence your family's perspectives and help some kids identify their priorities and life direction.

Stephanie Tolk and her family did a four-week Workaway in the Czech Republic. They lived in a small town with kids of similar ages, and the skill Stephanie's family brought was fluency in English. They were not paid, but room and board were covered, and they were immersed in the local culture. Most importantly, they made lifelong friends.

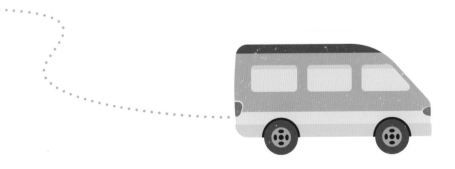

The Expense Side of the Equation

We've spent a lot of time addressing how to bring money *in* for travel. Let's also talk about how money will go *out*.

Full-time travel necessitates a shift in priorities and spending habits. Many families are surprised to find that, although they are bringing in only a fraction of their usual income, they are able to make it work because expenses are lower and their spending habits are relatively simple to change. They naturally buy less when both luggage and living space are limited. They also realize that although sacrifices are sometimes necessary, the benefits gained are worth it.

That said, travel expenses shouldn't be underestimated. Amanda Dishman, who lives and worldschools full time on a boat with her partner, Alex, and two daughters, cautions that while a Wonder Year can be done on a frugal budget, it may mean not being able to participate in as many worldschooling experiences as you'd like. Amanda and her family pay close attention to their expenditures and feel strongly that a "Just go travel" message needs to be tempered with sound budgeting practices.

Every family's expenses will be different, but at a minimum, you'll want to consider and plan for these categories:

- Expenses back at home (dwelling, storage, insurance, pets, etc.)
- Transportation
- Travel-related matters (immunizations, visas, and the like)
- Accommodations
- Food
- Medical (prescriptions, supplies, emergencies)
- Educational programs and activities

Some good news: a lot of expenses you are accustomed to at home may go away while you are traveling, including utilities, water use, vehicle maintenance, summer camps, sports programs, babysitters, music lessons, gym memberships, other recurring fees (like monthly subscriptions), and the ubiquitous costs of convenience.

Here are some tips for reducing costs on the road, several of which will be discussed more in chapters 4 (Charting Your Course) and 5 (Family Travel Logistics).

- Be flexible with your transportation plans—sometimes you can find significant savings just by adjusting things by a few days, taking an earlier departure, or adding a connection.

- Look for less expensive accommodations. There are many, many options for places to rest your heads, including campsites, free land, long-term rentals, house sitting, hostels, couchsurfing, and more (see the resources section for more details). Visit those far-flung family and friends you've been missing.

- As you prepare for your trip, you'll read it again and again: pack light. In some countries, the cost of checking a bag can be nearly as much as the price of your plane ticket. Paring things down can save money.

- Similarly, don't purchase too many items for your travels. Many families find that they overprepare and bring things they simply don't need once they are on the ground.

- Cook at "home"; this can yield big savings. Kids' finicky appetites can make restaurants a low return on investment, and eating out can quickly put a big dent in your budget. You can often enjoy local cuisine by visiting markets and preparing food on your own. Similarly, pack meals for full-day outings.

- If you're traveling internationally, consider buying a local SIM card for your phone and paying as you go. In many cases, this will lower your costs quite a bit. If you need cellular coverage, using your plan from home can quickly rack up significant charges.

- Be aware of what you are paying to manage your assets. Are you paying market rates for your property manager? Can you prepare your own taxes using software?

- If you are working while traveling, note anything you are using for business purposes that you can claim as a tax write-off (cell phone, Wi-Fi, etc.).

- If you took out loans for travel or any other reason, check into adjusting your payment schedule based on income.

- Take public transportation. Not only can you save some coin, but you'll also meet more locals.

- Be aware of tour and activity costs. There are excursions—snorkeling/scuba-diving trips, delicate ecological sites like glaciers or animal sanctuaries—you should only visit with a guide. For most other places, you'll be able to put together your own itinerary for significantly lower cost. Perhaps your children can do research online and be your guides. Choose activities that don't charge fees, like hiking, browsing farmers markets, visiting natural sites, or exploring a city on foot. Museums often have free admission days, and hotels might offer complimentary kids' camps; you can also find online travel guides that provide self-directed tours.

- Track your expenses. It's easier to understand what you measure, and recording your expenses can help keep costs down. A working budget is also a great teaching tool for kids, as we'll discuss in chapter 7 (Worldschool Education).

As full-timers, you can travel during the off-season when transportation bookings and accommodations cost notably less. It's possible to be a lot more flexible with dates given that you aren't scheduling as tightly around work or school commitments, so you can shop around for transportation and lodging deals (this also makes things less stressful, as you aren't fighting the crowds). In addition, you won't need to budget for vacations!

Contingency Planning

In addition to your plan A, we encourage you to have contingency plans in case the world deals you an unexpected blow. Doing a bit of scenario planning in advance and having a backup plan can provide peace of mind up front, and potentially welcome relief if it's ever needed.

Lee Strongwater, a financial advisor and partner at Colorado Capital Management, provides a few specific pieces of advice for long-term travelers:

- Build a medical safety net fund, with consideration for what your insurance will and won't cover. Hopefully, you'll never need it, but it's smart to be ready for the worst-case scenario.
- Budget for living expenses after you return, to cover the time you may need to spend looking for employment, a new home, or other essentials.
- Things most likely will cost more than you think. Pad your budget accordingly.

Final Words of Encouragement

Remember, it doesn't have to be all or nothing. If you can't travel full time (yet!), take shorter trips, read about far-off places, save your "someday" ideas as inspiration, host exchange students, and incorporate a worldview into your education plan. And, although easier said than done, we encourage you to do your best not to compare your experience with that of other families. Every experience is unique and any Wonder Year can be amazing. Keep your values in mind, and make the most of your version.

Now that the money hurdles (hopefully) feel more manageable, let's tackle some other aspects of getting your Wonder Year off the ground.

CHAPTER 3

Closing Up Life at Home

All things are ready, if our mind be so.

—William Shakespeare

SOME PEOPLE NEED TO PLAN THINGS to the nth degree. Others leave it to the gods. Regardless of your traveler DNA, embarking on a Wonder Year is a veritable plan-a-palooza! Managing all the details can feel daunting, and it definitely will keep you busy for a while. But it absolutely can be done by anyone, whether you have years to prepare for your journey or you are leaving in a few months. By walking you through the planning stage, we hope to show you that not only is it manageable but it can even be engaging and fun for everyone in your family.

In the next few chapters, we'll share the nuts and bolts for planning your family's Wonder Year. We'll say this up front: it might feel like a lot. Our goal in these chapters is to be comprehensive so that families can find the things that apply to them. If something is not relevant to your particular adventure, we wholeheartedly encourage you to skip it!

As you move from the philosophical *why* questions of your Wonder Year into making it a reality, three categories of to-dos will naturally emerge: 1) closing up life at home, 2) designing your journey, and 3) managing travel logistics. We'll address the first category in this chapter and the next two in the following chapters.

Leaving home for an extended period of time is quite different from departing on a two-week vacation. Entire portions of your life need to be closed down, or at least temporarily paused. On the flip side, being away from home for longer may mean you need to take parts of your life with you that wouldn't normally be needed on a short holiday.

Your Residence

Figuring out what to do with your current residence is likely one of the first decisions you'll encounter. If you rent, will you depart when your current lease is up, and if not, are you able to sublet the property? Check in with your landlord to discuss options. If you own your home, do you plan to keep or sell it? If selling, you'll want to contact a real estate agent or begin preparations for self-listing. As discussed in chapter 2, if you'll be renting out your home for the short or long term while you are traveling, start exploring ideas for marketing, listing, and getting it ready to show. You may need to research property managers or work out an arrangement with a trusted friend to deal with emergencies. You'll also need to make arrangements with local services (utilities, trash, internet providers, etc.), just as you would when relocating.

JULIE'S REFLECTION
The Road Back to Simplicity

Packing a recreational vehicle for a year was anything but straight-forward. We called 1-800-GOT-JUNK? We donated to Goodwill, arc Thrift Stores, Western Disposal, and the Center for Hard to Recycle Materials. We gave away junk at our neighborhood junkengrooven. There was still junk left over. We had two yard sales and a stuffengrooven, and there was still stuff left to deal with.

Then we hatched a plan: pack the RV, and whatever was left would be stored for the year.

We developed a scrupulous decision algorithm: First, do we need it? Second, does it fit in the RV? Do we need to bring a salad spinner on the road? A zester? A pillow? Two pillows? Does Charlie need his golf clubs? Do they even fit? Does Julie need yoga pants, or can she wear running shorts for triangle pose?

It was all about figuring out what trade-offs we were willing to make.

When Johnny was born, we used cloth diapers and glass jars. I prepared organic acorn squash, red chard, and golden beets, and I froze rainbow vegetable blocks in ice-cube trays. We took long walks and read *The Lorax* and other classic children's stories.

Then, before the very hungry caterpillar ate three plums, it happened. A mound of paper products appeared in our living room: paper diapers, paper towels, paper tissue, paper plates, paper placemats, paper wipes. It wasn't just paper either. A pack and play, a swing and play, a swing and pack, a wall swing, a hall swing, a night swing, a chair swing, a singing swing, and a swinging thing. One single-use or plastic product at a time, I realized I had traded off my prebaby sustainable, waste-free lifestyle for the sake of convenience and ease.

Oh, the guilt; oh, the exhaustion. Oh, the rolls and rolls of new normal.

Now we had come full circle. Packing into a house on wheels that was twenty-four feet long and seven feet wide brought me back to my environmental senses. In a small space, convenience and durability are not opposing forces. Sometimes we have the false impression that the earth is vast, that resources are limitless, and that it doesn't matter how much single-use shit we buy at Target. But it does matter. It matters a lot. The earth is our mobile home, and it is not that big. Our choices matter. Even for our precious wee ones. So, did I need to pack paper towels into the RV?

I know some paper towels can be composted, but in the end, we went with reusable bamboo cloths, and I enjoyed the mayhem in becoming a less stuff-y version of myself!

Work

Although it isn't always possible, most people try to leave work behind when they go on vacation. But a Wonder Year isn't a vacation—it is long-term travel. Will you be working for an organization during your time away? If so, you'll need to sort out details with your employer. It may mean a change in scope, responsibilities, or reporting relationships, and it helps to start those conversations early. You'll also want to start thinking through the logistics and technical requirements for working remotely and talk with your family about how that will impact where you go, when you go, and how you spend your time.

If you are quitting your job to take your Wonder Year, you'll need to decide how much notice to give your employer (and maybe how to keep your plans quiet in the meantime). Instead, maybe you'll ask for an extended leave of absence, work sabbatical, or other special arrangement. Regardless of your proposed plan, most employers will appreciate you coordinating with them as early and as flexibly as possible. If you own a business, you might need to find someone you trust to manage it while you're away, or at least be on the ground to coordinate with you while you travel.

Allie Rockwell quit her nursing job to travel. Her husband, Geo, owns a gym and spent many months preparing his lead manager to take over day-to-day operations during their Wonder Year. Geo did weekly staff Zoom calls from the road to make sure everything was on track while he and his family enjoyed their RV travels around the United States. As his comfort that everything was going well increased, the family went further afield into Mexico and Belize.

School

One of the most significant steps in closing up the home shop is arranging for the education of your school-age kids while traveling. In the US, decisions about education requirements are governed by each state. In all fifty states you have a right to withdraw your kids from school to travel, but the specific rules for doing so will vary from state to state, including reporting procedures.[13] It's important to know before you go whether you must educate for a set number of hours per day and/or days per year, notify administrators of academic progress, submit to any testing requirements upon reentry, or adhere to other rules.

In some states the process is simple, with few requirements. In others, you may have to register your traveling child as a "homeschooler" for the time you are away. (School districts and states likely won't know the term *worldschooler*, so you won't find that word on any documents or forms.) If your family already homeschools, you may be aware of the legal requirements. If you're new to the process, check in with your school, the district, or the state for details. Research your state homeschool law as a starting point. If they are not returning to their home state after travel, some families also investigate other states' laws to determine whether residency elsewhere would be advantageous to their worldschooling plan.

Because education is such a key part of a Wonder Year, we dedicate an entire chapter to it (see chapter 7). The takeaway here is to understand your rights and responsibilities before you depart. And regardless of the rules, we encourage you to reach out to the homeschool point of contact in your school district, a current teacher, or one who teaches the grade your child will enter upon your return. Good suggestions and relationships can emerge from this proactive outreach.

Nosara, Costa Rica

Kai stands tall on the porch of our Costa Rican rental in his best blue shorts, new flip-flops, and red-thread necklace frayed and bleached by the Central American sun. The thread had been blessed by a *rinpoche* (abbot) six months before in a Buddhist monastery in Nepal, and we had each worn ours ever since. Kai is about to present his third-grade "shelter project." He did a bit of online research but completed most of the project based on firsthand experience, having spent a week in a Sherpa house in Khumjung, Nepal, with family friends. His experience was his source.

Before him is a gathering of friends: some old friends have come from Colorado for a spring break meetup, some new ones from his language and surf day camp. And us, his now ever-present family.

On a piece of plywood, Kai has reconstructed a traditional Sherpa home from pebbles, glue, modeling clay, scrap wood salvaged from a nearby construction project, and paint. Before we left the US, I had asked his teacher for the project handout and carried it with me during our travel. We found a stationery store for supplies, and Kai handwrote a report on a two-sided piece of binder paper and is now presenting to the informal audience of twenty or so. He speaks with authority and fields questions about the outhouse, the guard dogs, and the reason for the green roof.

His spring-break friend, Leo, had just presented his own project back home on the teepee, and after Kai's presentation, shares other shelter reports from their class with Kai. The boys compare notes, speak about the pros and cons of different materials, look at the homes around them, and both agree that the Costa Rican straw *palapas* (dwellings with thatched roofs) and porches are best.

"Before him is a gathering of friends..."

Sports and Extracurriculars

If your kids participate in sports or other extracurriculars, you'll want to create a plan with their coaches and instructors that identifies how your kids will (or won't) devote time to these activities while away and how they can return to their programs. Some activities allow for ongoing learning and/or training during a Wonder Year—you might bring along your daughter's soccer ball or your son's roll-up keyboard—while others may need to be suspended. It may mean that your child returns to a different team or level, separate from friends they'd been participating with, and you'll want to talk about that together. On the other hand, the additional time and flexibility of a Wonder Year may allow for deeper, more focused attention and practice than is usually available at home.

Angela's son, Ronan, was months away from achieving his black belt in Kuk Sool Won when their family launched their Wonder Year. Not wanting to disrupt his progress, Ronan created a plan with his instructor for practicing while away, then attended classes and completed testing when his family visited home during their travels. Annika's children, who each play a stringed instrument, did music lessons via Zoom from the banks of the Mekong River.

The key is to make sure everyone—kids, parents, and instructors—is on the same page regarding the impact of absences from routine classes and programs. You'll also need to figure out the related financials, especially if the sport or program requires lead time to suspend or terminate membership payments.

Pula, Croatia

It's raining hard when we arrive in Pula, the ancient narrow streets made even more difficult to navigate by a lagging GPS that consistently reads our position a block or two behind where we actually are. We double-park and set the hazard lights for a quick coffee stop at a café filled with loud, red-eyed fishermen who've already returned from the sea with the day's catch. The stop allows us to orient ourselves to the town's grid so that the uneasy sense of dislocation subsides. Unfortunately, the rain does not.

Back in the car, as the windows fog up, an atmospheric tension is building.

"Do you think I'd have been a good gladiator?"

Asher, age ten, is asking the most important question of his day. His brother reacts with a performative laugh, which Asher ignores.

Pula is a very old city situated on the southern end of the Istria peninsula, in a well-protected deepwater bay. It has documented human settlements as far back as eleven thousand years ago, but we're more interested in its recent Roman past. Our destination is the famed Pula Arena, an amphitheater constructed by the Romans in their first hundred years as an empire, and one of the six largest and best-preserved arenas in the world. Archeological scholars have estimated it could hold more than 23,000 spectators. Pula and its amphitheater are a UNESCO World Heritage Site.

These are the kinds of facts we share with the boys leading up to the visit. Cold hard facts that fail to acknowledge what they're really interested in.

"Dad. Do you think I'd have been a good gladiator?" He isn't going to let me avoid answering the question.

"I think you're a very kind person," I say. "But I suppose, if you *had* to fight, you'd be a good, fair one."

There is a long, ponderous silence before he responds. "I think I'd be a good gladiator. I'm very good with a sword."

After several loops around the old city, I find a tight parking spot along one of the roads that slopes up to the arena. The rain is still pattering loudly under the sycamore trees outside the car.

"How wet are you willing to get, guys?"

No one says anything in response, but Asher's door opens, and he pops out onto the slick cobblestone walkway with two wooden swords in his hands. We'd bought them in the gift shop at the Bayeux Tapestry in France roughly

Imagining the roar of the crowd.

a month prior. He'd been awkwardly carrying them on trains, buses, and boats to bring them to this spot. Their handles are already worn, but their blades remain unmarked.

Although the arena's age and pristine condition should earn it some reverence, in honesty we show up as boys with swords. The security guard eyes us suspiciously as we pay our kuna and enter the arena. Our off-season visit means the crowds are light and the rain has scared everyone else away, so we're alone in the stadium. Asher hands me a sword as we stand in the center of the arena floor, then he steps backward, counting out paces: ". . . seven, eight, nine, ten!"

"You ready, Dad?"

Two wooden swords clack together, and two thousand years of history surround a father and son playing pretend. As Angela and Ronan watch from the spectator seats, the gladiators fight to the "death."

Belongings

In the last chapter we talked about how to sort your personal belongings before embarking on a Wonder Year. After you've decided what you'll keep, you'll need to figure out where to store anything you aren't taking with you. You might have movers pack and take it to long-term, remote storage, which is often less expensive than local self-storage options. The latter may work better if you'll need access to your belongings during your Wonder Year. Angela's family returned to their storage locker several times, exchanging seasonal clothing and returning things they were tired of carrying. If you're lucky, a friend or family member might offer some extra room in their basement or garage. You might even be able to leave some items in your home, either in a locked area or accessible for your renters' use.

Give yourself time to sort out your vehicles, too. Some families sell their cars for travel money and to eliminate insurance and maintenance costs while away. Others lease or lend them out. If they won't be used, vehicles will need to be stored somewhere secure, either at your residence, a storage facility, or possibly in a friend's driveway or garage.

Financials

Review your other financial payment records and responsibilities to determine what needs to be addressed before your departure. These will be specific to your family but might include the following:

- Car insurance (if you're planning to park and leave your vehicle or lend it to a friend)
- Health insurance (if you're moving to a different plan while you travel)
- Cell phone and internet services
- Monthly subscriptions for TV streaming and satellite radio services

- Gym memberships
- Instrument and hobby equipment rentals
- Home and lawn maintenance
- Anything else with a recurring payment or on autopay—perhaps a quick look at your bank account and credit card statements will help you review other financial obligations

Additionally, you may need to consider how you will handle taxes and tax filings during your Wonder Year. This might include gathering documents earlier than normal, taking them (or photos of them) with you on your travels, and/or arranging for a friend or tax preparer to assist you while you're away. Another option might be deferring your tax filing until after you return. The IRS allows taxpayers a six-month extension if you need more time to file, and it grants extensions automatically if you complete the proper form on time.[14] Be sure to check your state tax laws and department of revenue for additional guidance, as some states accept the federal extension while others require a separate form.

Mail

The USPS will hold mail for up to thirty days, then it must be picked up or forwarded.[15] Many people use a trusted friend or family member to receive, sort, and forward their mail. There are also virtual mailbox service companies that will receive your mail, send you a scanned copy of the envelope, and ask if you want the interior to be scanned as well. Many of these services can mail you the hard copies or forward your mail and packages in bulk. As of this writing, these services cost between $25 and $60 (USD) per month depending on the volume and number of scanned items you request.

Some people use a PO box to receive and hold mail, but contents must be picked up periodically or the postal service may discard it.[16] Also, sensitive items like a driver's license or ATM card might need to go to a physical address. In the US you can have mail sent to the attention of General

Delivery at a local post office (make sure the closest branch offers the program) or UPS store. Poste restante is a similar service available at some post offices outside the US, or mail can be sent to hotels, campgrounds, businesses, or new friends willing to receive it for you.

Voting

US citizens can vote in federal elections via absentee ballot when they are away from home. If you are a US citizen overseas, you can request an absentee ballot online. Be ready to share your voting residence information (the address in the state you last resided in or that you use as your home address while traveling). You can receive a ballot by email, fax, or download link, depending on your home state. Note that you must submit a new request each year to vote in US federal elections.[17] Absentee voting is also available in state elections; check your home state for valid reasons for voting absentee, key deadlines, and instructions for requesting and returning your ballot. Tip: all of these processes can be great worldschooling opportunities, so involve your kids as much as you can.

Pets

We all love our pets, and one of the most important—and sometimes one of the hardest—questions you may face when planning for long-term travel is how they will be cared for. It's tough enough to find trusted care for your pets when you go away on vacation, much less a Wonder Year! Here's the good news: it is doable. All three of our families had pets to consider when planning our time away, and we can happily report that we each returned with, or to, healthy and much-loved four-legged friends.

Fortunately, there are many avenues for finding pet sitters. Family or friends may be willing to take your pets in, even for a longer time frame, in support of your adventures. They might even be happy to reside in your

home with them, providing house-sitting services, too. Either of these choices works particularly well if your animals already know the sitter. It may be the most comforting option for you, as you'll have a direct line of communication to the sitter, and you'll know your pets will be well loved.

You might also look at professional boarding options. This can be quite expensive, so consider asking for a volume discount. Boarding can also be stressful for your pets, especially as you'll be away for such a long time. An "in-between" option may be professional pet sitters who offer boarding services in their homes. Ask pet-owning friends for recommendations, or see if your veterinarian's office can refer you. We've had great luck with online services such as Rover that match vetted pet sitters with families seeking care. If you choose this option, make sure the sitter and your pets have plenty of time to get to know each other before you embark on your journey.

Depending on your circumstances, it's possible you may have to look at rehoming your pets. This might apply if you will be away for several years or if you have no return date at all. Only you will know what is right for your family—we just encourage you to start thinking and talking about it early on so that everyone has time to prepare.

What if you want to bring your pets with you? This option can be great if you are traveling via RV or camper van. It could also work for those slow-traveling abroad. Some ambitious pet lovers even find a way to country-hop with their animals. Be sure to check transportation rules and immigration and quarantine regulations for any country you want to visit with your pets.

Julie took her dog along on their RV adventure; Annika had friends host her menagerie of creatures in their homes; and Angela leveraged a combination of almost every option listed above for her mutt!

Now that you've considered the myriad ways you'll need to close out at home, let's look ahead to what many consider the fun part—how you'll spend your Wonder Year.

CHAPTER 4

Charting Your Course

The purpose of life, after all, is to live it, to taste experience to the utmost, to reach out eagerly and without fear for newer and richer experience.

—Eleanor Roosevelt

A GREAT FIRST STEP TOWARD creating your Wonder Year is to talk as a family and figure out guiding principles for the journey. Together you can identify your overarching goals and the values you want to incorporate into your travels.

Finding Your Compass Heading

To get started, here are some questions:

- Do you have family goals such as exploring your heritage, maximizing your time in nature, or better understanding traditional farming methods? Do you want to learn Spanish together or take that ski bum season you've always longed for?

- Do individual family members have pursuits or things they wish to learn or accomplish while traveling? How do you hope to spend your time together? How will you balance together time with need for time alone?

- Where is your comfort zone, and what experiences might reasonably push the edge for your family?

- How much do you want to plan ahead versus leave space for spontaneity? (The ages of your kids might inform how much flexibility you'll have in the moment.)

- What is your planning horizon? How much time do you have to prepare before your Wonder Year launch, and once on the road, how far in advance do you want to sort out your plans?

- How do you feel about the environmental footprint of your travels? How do you want to manage it?

- Do you want to learn to live with less? Do you want to pare down or find a comfy home base where you can have more gear and spread out a bit?

- Will you be incorporating paid work into your travels? Would you like to volunteer, and if so, what contributions do you hope to offer?

- How will you measure success and know the experience is worth the effort? What will make your Wonder Year feel complete?

Some of these aspects might become the scaffolding around which you build your trip, or they might simply be fodder to get you excited and motivated. They certainly can inform your itinerary, which we'll explore next.

Where Will You Go?

So, how do you choose where to go when the possibilities seem endless? Here are a few ideas to get you thinking about the kind of adventure you'd like to take.

WISH-LIST DESTINATIONS

What have you always wanted to see and experience? Do you have inspirational travel photos posted on your computer or fridge? Are there places that are just calling your name? Spin the globe. Choosing your destinations is a great time to involve the whole family. Being curious about a place will make your kids all the more engaged once you're there.

The Vinjes had each family member pick the top three countries they'd like to visit. In the first year of their travels, they went to one of each person's top three. Their young son had chosen "the beach" as one of his countries, which gave them a lot of flexibility for their final destination!

MULTILINGUALISM

You might plan some or all of your itinerary in order to learn a new language or reinforce a second or third one. Are your kids taking language classes at school and you'd love for them to converse with native speakers? Adults, too, may see great value in language immersion.

PREFERRED ACTIVITIES

Think about how you like spending time as a family. Do you prefer being outdoors? Camping, biking, or trekking can drive an itinerary. Are you drawn to water? You might build your trip around kayaking, surfing, or diving hot spots. Maybe you are more of a big-city crew, with a love of museums and restaurants. Building in some of your family's favorite activities can help keep everyone engaged.

SEASONAL CONSIDERATIONS

Research the best time of year to visit your high-priority destinations. Some places will work any time of the year; others might have peak times for desirable weather conditions or seasonal flora or fauna: wet or dry salt flats in Bolivia, butterflies returning to San Juan Capistrano, monsoon seasons in Southeast Asia, or the fall foliage in New England. Or there might be festivals, events, or cultural celebrations you want to attend, such as the Thai New Year celebration water fights or Day of the Dead happenings in Oaxaca. Prioritize key events and anchor your trip around their locations.

SUSTAINABLE TRAVEL

The choices we make about travel—destinations, transportation, accommodations, and even souvenirs—have an impact on the local environment and people. Asking questions and being aware of how our presence in a place affects the local community is a responsibility we can all embrace (we'll talk more about this later in the chapter). And it's not just about doing the right thing; many travelers we interviewed noted that their most memorable experiences had a strong local flavor.

Dianbai, China

We cannot unsee it, the environmental devastation.

We are in Dianbai, in China's southern Guangdong province, strolling barefoot on a wide beach. To our right is a berm sculpted to protect the juniper forest uphill. Between us and the berm is something I've never seen before—a beached garbage patch, a foot-deep hedge of plastic waste that runs parallel and inland from the beach and continues as far as the eye can see. We cannot pretend it away. Chunks of carpet pad, plastic spoons wrapped in fishing net, caps, shells, plastic bottles, shoe soles, green leaves, large Styrofoam bricks, and sharp sticks. Taken as a whole, it's a being. Dissected into individual pieces, it's a cautionary tale.

Chinese couples on holiday walk a safe distance away from the garbage patch, looking out to sea and dodging jellyfish. The sky is neither cloudy nor clear but instead something in between, polluted.

"Mom, why don't they clean it up?" my daughter, Lucy, asks with urgency and alarm.

"I don't know, sweetie. Maybe it just keeps coming."

"Is that some of the Great Pacific Garbage Patch that broke off?" Lorna asks. I wonder if it is. We've been studying the problems of garbage. We hear about the Great Pacific junk gyre, but rarely do we step onto it during a beach walk. My kids take in the expanse of this garbage.[18] I wonder just how far this goes.

"Well, what's just east of here?" I ask. I'm stalling. I don't know how to cushion their souls from this sight. I feel like it's not a PG-rated walk. Lucy and Kai grab my hands.

We put our shoes back on and explore as we would a tide pool. I think about how much of our environmental impact is out of sight back home.

"Philippines is east of here!" suggests Kai, proud of his geography knowledge.

"Hong Kong?"

"Hawaii."

"All of us," says Lorna. "All of us are east of here."

This is not a problem for them; it's a problem for us. All of us.

▶ Marine litter from the South China Sea.

FINDING COMMUNITY

More Wonder Year families are arranging their itineraries so they can connect with other traveling families at schools, summits, hubs, pop-ups, and informal gatherings. Sparks fly when worldschooling kids connect with each other! We'll talk more about this in chapter 7 (Worldschool Education) and chapter 8 (On the Road).

OTHER LENSES

Here are some other ways you might create your itinerary:

- Around homestays (see page 114), home swaps, or volunteerism

- Via around-the-world air travel, which often requires that you travel in only one direction: east or west

- Off-season all the way to maximize easier bookings, lower costs, and fewer crowds. One downside: you may find accommodations, sites, restaurants, and tours closed for the season, or you may encounter construction and repairs underway.

- Country collecting: some travelers want to visit as many countries as possible. Just make sure you keep it meaningful by taking time to really appreciate the local people, places, and culture.

- By theme: you may wish to choose a worldschooling theme as you go. Angela's family studied World War II while in Europe and selected some of their destinations, including Berlin and Normandy, in order to visit battlefields and museums. The Shin family goes in search of animals in the wild. We discuss this further in chapter 7 (Worldschool Education).

- Educational programs: alternative schools, experiential programs, and immersive experiences geared toward worldschoolers are rapidly proliferating, offering families the opportunity to enroll their children and build itineraries around their attendance.

- Personal history or connection: some families like to visit their ancestral homes or retrace their forebears' migration paths.

- Friends and family: extended travel can offer the chance to visit those you might not often see, or to stay with them for longer periods of time than is usually possible. This can also provide a nice break from being alone on the road, give the kids friends or cousins to play with, and save some money, too.

- Convenience: sometimes you just have to choose what is easy and makes sense—a good stop between two of your favored destinations, or somewhere inexpensive to spend a few nights. If you have the right attitude, you can almost always turn these sojourns into wonderful opportunities.

ADDITIONAL ITINERARY CONSIDERATIONS

Travel Advisories

Before finalizing your plans, check current safety conditions, travel advisories, and warnings for the places you are interested in visiting. The US Department of State website is an excellent place to start, with tour companies and travel blogs providing additional insight about real-time safety considerations.[19]

Seeing the Sites

When you first commit to extended travel, six, twelve, or eighteen months might seem like a long time. Once you fill it with your planned itinerary, you might realize that there will never be enough time to see everything you want. In the places you visit, please try to let go of the notion of covering everything. No matter where you are or how long you're there, you'll still have to choose the things you *most* want to do. For example, don't try to see every temple in Siem Reap, and don't regret it if you missed a certain one that your cousin mentions later on Facebook. Savor what you are fortunate to experience, and release the rest.

For those places you don't want to miss, be aware that booking lead times for hot destinations and activities are picking up. As our society has become increasingly mobile and more travelers are hitting the road each year, some national parks, museums, tours, top-rated campgrounds, and other popular attractions are newly requiring advance bookings, and reservation lead times have gotten much longer. Nearby accommodations and transportation may also be affected, so monitor what you'll need to book in advance versus on the ground.

Planning versus Winging It

Try to find balance between planning before you depart and figuring things out while you are on the road. Sarah De Santi shares this: "When you're planning, you don't know everything that's there. You only see the tourist stuff before arriving, but once you're on the ground, you can really see all there is to experience with your family." Leave room for some spontaneity and changes of plans, while of course keeping in mind the cost of adjusting or canceling reservations.

Annika's family left their last month open. In the end, they decided to spend it in California reconnecting with family, and each kid did two weeks of summer camp! They were excited to be with their peer group again while Will and Annika had some precious couple time to end the year. The month also helped the family become slowly reacquainted with the United States before they headed home to Colorado.

ANGELA'S REFLECTION

Space for Spontaneity

Our family left the last six weeks of our South America trip completely unbooked, as there were several destinations we could explore, and none of them required booking far in advance. But Africa—which we originally thought we didn't have time to visit—kept calling to us, and we suddenly realized that flying from Santiago to Cape Town was quite an easy journey (relatively speaking, by this point in our travels). So instead, we ended our Wonder Year in South Africa, Namibia, and Botswana—a region that ended up being one of the highlights of our entire trip.

Scheduling Downtime

One of the most important pieces of advice we can offer is to leave downtime in your itinerary. As much as you think you want to cover a lot of ground and see as much as you can, travel fatigue is a very real thing. When you are traveling full time, occasionally it can start to feel more like work than play, and sometimes you'll need a vacation from the traveling. In addition, you'll likely need days set aside for future travel planning, laundry, cooking at "home," and catching up on worldschooling lessons.

Angela's family didn't include enough downtime as they traveled throughout Europe, and after three months, everyone was exhausted. They had to seriously regroup back in the US, and on their next leg to Australia and New Zealand, they were sure to include periods of time when they had absolutely nothing planned besides catching up on math lessons and playing card games.

Sustainable and Responsible Travel

Travel has the potential to be a force for good in the world, but it can also cause harm by destroying the very resources travelers have come to experience—the natural, cultural, and community wonders of the world.

The United Nations (UN) Environment Programme and UN World Tourism Organization define sustainable tourism as "tourism that takes full account of its current and future economic, social and environmental impacts, addressing the needs of visitors, the industry, the environment and host communities."[20] Sustainable travel is a natural corollary to worldschooling, as it aims to nurture attitudes and awareness in our children so they are motivated to contribute positively to our world.

You may hear terms like *ethical travel, green travel, ecotourism, responsible tourism, regenerative* or *transformative travel,* and more. While there are some nuances in definitions, the sentiment is shared—together, let's grow a travel industry that protects people, places, and the planet.

Sustainable travel can do the following:

- Promote economic development and job creation.
- Support appropriate investment in infrastructure, revenue generation, and incentives for local empowerment.
- Reduce poverty.
- Catalyze educational opportunities for marginalized groups.
- Seed global connections.
- Build tolerance and peace.

Here are some positive ways you can promote sustainability while traveling:

- Measure your travel footprint using tools like the EDF Travel Carbon Footprint calculator.
- Seek out businesses—hotels, restaurants, and transportation companies—that disclose and demonstrate their water, energy, and waste management practices; commitment to conservation and animal welfare; plastics reduction efforts; employee benefit programs; and other responsible practices.
- Choose a diet that is environmentally friendly, minimize single-use packaging, and buy locally produced fruits and vegetables where possible.
- Be savvy and learn to detect greenwashing—when a company purports to have sustainable practices but in fact their actions do not match their claims.
- Look broadly for sustainability opportunities in nature and in cities. You can walk, take the bus, rent bikes, and shop locally.

- Learn about Indigenous Peoples and their history.
- Create travel content for your blog or social media that tells truthful stories and includes diverse voices.
- Ask locals about what's going on in their region.
- Support the small mom-and-pop shop that is doing the right thing but not tooting its own horn.
- While there is no universal seal or standard of a "sustainable" destination, there are certifications that may indicate that a company is moving in the right direction. Keep in mind that it takes time and money to pursue these certifications, and many small local operators or businesses do not have the resources to invest in a certified "stamp of approval." (See the resources section for more information.)
- Talk to other worldschooling families, expats, and locals before you book, reserve, pay, or otherwise use a business, lodge, outfitter, or guide. There are outstanding local operators who are committed to sustainability, cultural preservation, and regenerative practices. By working with these businesses, we put our dollars toward supporting progress; building local capacity; promoting conservation; and helping put an end to exploitative, unsustainable practices.
- Perhaps the most important step is to think about where your travel dollars are going. Is your money supporting the local economy? Or is it supporting destructive practices or development? Who is benefiting, and who is bearing the burden?

If you are curious to learn more or do more, tap into the momentum and incorporate sustainable travel into your worldschool education. To get started, check out the list of sustainable travel organizations in the resources section.

Sustainable travel has been around for years. What's exciting is the mainstreaming of the movement and the availability of new data, metrics, resources, partnerships, and models. There is room for everyone in this mobilization—the destinations, guides, travelers, owners, operators, regulators, policy makers, local and international businesses, and content creators. The travel and tourism industry, tourists, and influencers have an opportunity to contribute to the kind of growth that builds positive, lasting impact. Let's do our part to ensure our children and generations of children around the globe can experience the beauty of our shared home.

Getting There

Oh, the places you'll go! Sure, but how will you get there?

There are a number of considerations for deciding between the many modes of transportation you'll take during your Wonder Year, including time, cost, and environmental impact. Often, time and cost are a trade-off, but as we've already mentioned, when traveling long term you may find you have more flexibility when considering how to make the most of your days and dollars.

The environmental impact of car, train, boat, and air travel is an important consideration for many traveling families. Air travel produces greenhouse gases from burning fuel, which contributes to climate change. Shorter hops contribute more per mile than long-haul flights, as taking off uses more fuel than cruising. There is a wide variation among per-passenger emissions for many airlines, so if you plan to travel by air, do some homework about the greening of transportation.[21] Train, car, bus, and small-boat travel may have a considerably smaller carbon footprint, while cruise ships often fall into a similar category as flying.

TOURS

One of the questions you may wrestle with is whether to take any organized tours. Packaged tours can be great for destination selection, logistics planning, educational value, and local sensitivity. They can also be a good way to meet and bond with other travelers. However, many company-guided, multiday tours are designed for people on shorter trips, and Wonder Year families may feel that paying extra money for a guide or escort is an unnecessary expense. Some worldschoolers prefer not to be locked into a group itinerary, especially when traveling with younger kids, and instead find that they get comfortable quickly with managing these aspects of travel on their own.

That said, there are some places where you can travel respectfully, safely, and feasibly only by using organized tour companies and guides. Guides hold the keys to some of the richest experiences in the world, whether they are single-day excursions or multiday journeys. A few examples include the following:

- Extreme adventures: rafting the Grand Canyon, hiking Amantaní Island on Lake Titicaca, glacier trekking in Patagonia

- Wildlife viewing in places like the Galápagos, Brazilian Pantanal, and African savanna

- Countries like Bhutan, Cuba, and China, where guides are legally required or practically necessary for getting off the beaten path

- Some cultural tours to sacred, religious, or ancestral locations

- "Behind the scenes" visits to sites and cities, such as the Vatican and other holy places

- Specialized knowledge: art, history, or culinary tours, such as the history of enslaved people in Savannah, food in New Orleans, or politics in Budapest

When we needed guides, we found that local independent operators—hired on the ground at quite reasonable prices—offered some of the most insightful and educational experiences of our respective Wonder Years. They can often be sourced online or at your accommodations, and even many taxi drivers can double as guides.

Ho Chi Minh City, Vietnam

It's clear from our arrival at the airport in Saigon that Mr. Nguyen is a military man. His stature, handshake, and carriage all suggest a lifelong mastery of mind and body. He looks us directly in our eyes when he speaks; he walks with purpose. And he's taking us to Ben Duoc in the Cu Chi district for a history lesson.

The drive is long enough to afford time to talk with Mr. Nguyen, and he joins us for lunch along the lazy Saigon River. He leans in close to Ronan as we eat, glancing back over his shoulder. "You're American, yes?" he asks. "Good. Then there are things I can share with you about this region that you won't hear from others." His gaze returns to our family.

"Who wants to go down in the tunnels?" Mr. Nguyen asks.

Asher and I raise our hands. The tunnels of Cu Chi are a significant memorial of the Viet Cong's successful campaign against the American soldiers during the war; more than 45,000 Vietnamese people died protecting this underground base. Entire hospitals, armories, dining halls, barracks, and kitchens once existed across four levels beneath the jungle floor, a network stretching more than 150 miles. The crude weapons used by inhabitants—punji sticks; spears; and hand-dug, booby-trapped pits—were things kids could make in their backyards. Our boys' slender bodies just fit down the leaf-covered mud hatches originally used to pop through and surprise invaders.

Mr. Nguyen points at a spot about a hundred yards away and says that is where we'll reemerge. He then disappears down a flight of stairs cut into the red clay earth. Tunnel rats were specialized US soldiers who performed deadly search-and-destroy missions in the twisting burrows of the Cu Chi fighters' base, sneaking into holes like these, each armed with a .45, a flashlight, and a bayonet. We had an iPhone.

"Did they clear these tunnels of *all* the mines?" Asher asks Mr. Nguyen.

"Yes," he replies. "They don't find new ones very often anymore."

In the dark shaft, there are no lights. No handrail. It is hot and claustrophobic—we have to crawl on our bellies for much of the journey.

Mr. Nguyen is far ahead of us in the pitch black, encouraging us through a burrow no more than three feet in diameter. "I'll get you out. Do not worry," he says, seemingly reading our thoughts. "I know the way."

Mr. Nguyen shares the inside story.

We can hear the smile on his face as he reassures us from the gloom.

"Are you scared?" I ask Asher.

He stops shuffling along on the hard-packed clay ahead of me and replies after a long pause, "Are you?"

There is a glimmer of light off in the distance, and we relax a little bit, but

Mr. Nguyen stops and says, "Give me your camera and I'll take a picture of you. Does it have a flash? Yes? It will work then."

Asher and I wait for Mr. Nguyen to crawl back to our position, turn around, and snap the photo—all the while looking at that sliver of sunlight at the end of the tunnel.

TRANSPORTATION

Air Travel

If traveling internationally, you might need to determine which direction you plan to fly around the globe—east or west—and then start figuring out your specific route. But not everyone sees the world by going "around" it. You might decide to use a location as a home base for your travels. Some families might build a Wonder Year around a foreign work assignment or sabbatical base location.

"Round the world" (RTW) tickets have gotten a lot of media attention over the last decade and can be a good option for some families. They are most useful to those who want to establish their key destinations early and who don't plan to make many adjustments along the way. These tickets resolve your airline bookings up front, relieving you from this duty while traveling. They also eliminate uncertainty around your air travel expenses, locking in this cost so you can focus on other budget line items. If you have airline miles to use, booking RTW tickets can save you a lot of dough, and on the flip side, if you are purchasing your flights, they can help you *accrue* a lot of miles.

However, RTW tickets do have some downsides. They're not always the least expensive or the easiest to plan around. RTW tickets often have rules to which you must adhere, including a set number of stops per continent, time constraints, or one-directional travel only. Probably the biggest limitation is their lack of flexibility. Having all tickets locked in ahead of time removes the opportunity for spontaneity as you travel. Part of the wonder in a Wonder Year can be not knowing exactly where you'll end up or for how long you'll stay. You might fall unexpectedly in love with a destination or dislike one so much that you're ready to move on sooner than planned. RTW tickets often restrict or charge hefty fees for changes in destinations or dates, putting a dent in going with the flow.

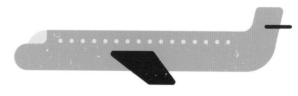

Here is some general guidance for all kinds of airline tickets:

- Conduct online searches in incognito or private mode! Your computer logs your other searches in its cookies, and airline algorithms can and will use this info to tweak the prices you are seeing.

- Use search engines to shop across many airlines at once. Since these sites change over time, find out what the smartest travelers are currently using.

- Get savvy with your flight segments. One-way flights can be less expensive than multistop tickets, so it may be advantageous to string together multiple single-leg journeys. If you are flying to an expensive destination, it might be cheaper to book that as a connection and just get off early. Just make sure your luggage doesn't go on to the final destination without you.

- When allowed by the airline, consider booking your ticket using another currency in which the rates may be cheaper.

- Unlike many other bulk purchases, airlines often charge more for group tickets than for individual ones. That's because they have tiered pricing (a set number of seats available at each price), and their booking algorithms aren't set up to split up group pricing as tiers sell out. In other words, if you are booking for your family of five in a single reservation, they may not price three tickets at the US$250 tier and two tickets at US$325 tier; all five could be charged at $325 each. It's often best to purchase a ticket for each person in your family separately, or at least play around with the quantities to ensure you are all paying the same amount in a group booking.

We'll talk more about air travel in chapter 5 (Family Travel Logistics).

Train Travel

Many families find traveling by train downright pleasant. While it does take longer than flying and stops can be somewhat limited, it offers some nice advantages over air travel. It is almost always less costly than flying. Typically, there are no baggage allowances or extra fees, so you are limited only by what you can carry. Strollers and other assistive devices are often allowed on board, too. Wiggly kids (and adults) can get up and walk in the aisles and between cars. You can enjoy panoramic views as well, often of scenery you can't experience otherwise. Trains also frequently arrive and depart near the centers of cities and towns, offering easy jumping-off points for your itinerary and negating the need for airport transfers.

Train travel can be wonderfully conducive to Wonder Year adventures, too. You can relax and enjoy the ride without worrying about the longer journey. Plus, trains offer awesome opportunities to worldschool. Some trains have Wi-Fi, and seating might include table space (as long as you show up early and grab a good spot), so kids can spread out to do schoolwork or other activities.

Here are some tips if you plan to travel by train:

- Ask about classes of service and discounted kids' fares and/or family rates, which are offered on many routes.

- See if train-pass programs are available in regions where you plan to spend a lot of time; these are often quite flexible and cost-effective.

- Consider overnight journeys to save on accommodations while traveling between destinations. Some sleeping berths even include a private bath.

- Bring food and drinks. While some routes offer gourmet dining, most are snack services only, and the options can be limited.

- Know that on some routes, a higher class of service may mean a higher level of security, with greater attention paid to ensuring only ticketed passengers and their belongings are on board.

Bus Travel

Probably the biggest advantage of traveling by bus is the relatively lower cost in comparison to air and train travel. Buses also give you a chance to experience the way many locals travel. They can work well for spur-of-the-moment itinerary decisions, as their networks are typically more extensive than other modes of transportation. And unless you plan on hiring a car, buses are often the *only* means of travel to remote locations.

However, bus travel can be tougher on kids, who must stay seated and/ or wear seat belts for the duration of the trip. They can also be rough on those prone to carsickness. Views, services, and entertainment options are more limited, and not all buses have table space, restroom facilities, or air-conditioning. And although strollers, wheelchairs, and assistive devices may be allowed on board without extra fees, it may be more difficult to navigate these on buses than on other modes of transportation.

Safety statistics for buses are highly variable, so check records for the companies and routes you plan to use. Google it, post inquiries on travel-related sites, or ask around. The leading cause of death for healthy Americans traveling abroad is traffic accidents,[22] and many of these occur in countries where roads and infrastructure are in poor condition and traffic laws and enforcement are weak. Guidebooks often don't provide enough detail about road safety, so the US Department of State website is again a great source for local road travel information, advisories, and warnings. You might also consider registering with the Association for Safe International Road Travel, a nonprofit organization that provides a wealth of online resources.

Try to book with experienced, reputable companies that are willing to share safety records. Don't be afraid to ask questions of your tour operator or bus driver, and speak up when you see behaviors or conditions that are unsafe. It is generally advised to avoid bus travel at night, when the danger is higher due to poor road visibility and sleepy drivers.

Car Travel

Cars can offer the ultimate travel freedom. Even though they sometimes make for a longer journey, you can stop to explore sites and take breaks as you wish. You can also travel point to point between accommodations, eliminating the need for connections and transfers. As with trains, you may find the opportunity to worldschool along the way—reading signs, navigating via maps, or even doing spelling lessons or wordplay games aloud. If you plan to rent a car outside the US, make sure each driver has a license, international driving permit, and insurance that covers rental in the country you're traveling. Travelers with disabled-parking permits may want to check their validity in other states and countries.

Or consider ride-sharing services, which keep money in the local economy and may cost less than renting a car. These businesses also offer the ease of traveling point to point without the hassle of parking. In the US we're familiar with Uber (also available in many other countries) and Lyft (offered in Canada, too), and almost every country has its favorite ride-hailing service. Check online to find current and trustworthy ones for your destination. Download the apps (often available in English) before you go, and find out whether you can order a larger vehicle for your family size or luggage. Figure out if you need to arrange a ride in advance or can walk to the curb, position your cute kids in front, and raise an arm. There are many ways to hail a cab in other countries, so do a bit of reading ahead of time so you don't accidentally communicate something embarrassing—or even offensive—by how you wave your arms!

Some families find that for extended stays in one region, it can be more economical and/or convenient to purchase a car on arrival and sell it on departure.

Bike Travel

Adventurous families might consider traveling some or all of their Wonder Year by bike. Several families have captured their experiences in blogs that offer advice for those considering a cycling adventure. You might ship bicycles to your destination or buy them on the ground and donate or sell them at the end of the trip. For those who don't want to go it alone, tour companies such as Grasshopper Adventure Tours and Backroads offer interesting itineraries, good safety records, and helpful support services along the way.

Boat Travel

Boat travel with kids can be a lot of fun. In addition to full-day water excursions, consider boat trips to explore areas best reached by water. River cruises can be a relaxing way to visit port cities without having to find new accommodations and move all your gear between locations. Ferries are like trains on the water—great for worldschooling and sightseeing, with nowhere to be other than where you are. And it's often fairly easy to arrange a visit to the bridge to meet the captain; don't be bashful— tell a crew member you are worldschooling and would love to learn about navigation equipment, mapping, or marine weather forecasting.

Some traveling families even live on their boat full time, using it for both travel and accommodation similar to RVs and vans on land. Amanda Dishman (see page 59) lives and worldschools on a catamaran with her partner, Alex, and their two daughters. She says that despite the small living quarters, she loves being able to pick up and go, and finds it to be "one of the last truly free ways to live." And she means free as in freedom, not cost; marinas, cruising permits, and visas are all pricey aspects of the lifestyle.

RV and Camper Van Travel

Recreational vehicles (RVs) and camper vans provide a unique way to experience a Wonder Year, and indeed, many families build their entire experience around this lifestyle. RVs and vans offer both a place to live and a way to move around, an appealing combination for an increasing number of full-time travelers—especially those who want the same bed every night. Others go back and forth between their RV, van, or camping tent and other accommodations, depending on where they're headed and if they need a bit more space for a while. More than a million Americans, many of them families with children, live full time in RVs.[23] With the rise of digital nomadism and increased familiarity with educating kids at home, this number rose considerably during the pandemic and is likely to continue to grow.

There are many considerations for living on a boat or in an RV or van, including choosing the best new, used, or rented vehicle for your family's needs, financing and insuring your selection, maintaining your traveling home, finding storage when not in use, and keeping or selling it after your Wonder Year. The purchase of a home that moves with you is a significant one, and we encourage you to do your due diligence and secure warranties and/or inspections. You do not want to spend thousands of dollars only to find out there's a leak in the water line or faulty electronics that you did not know to check. Our resources section, as well as many websites and books, provide guidance about these topics, and we advise checking them out for the most up-to-date information about this lifestyle. There are now even consultants who will help you find, inspect, and purchase the perfect rig!

Julie's and Angela's families each lived in an RV for part of their Wonder Year, and both enjoyed their experiences immensely. While it can be an adjustment to live together in small mobile dwellings, the simple, minimalist lifestyle holds much appeal, and don't worry—you'll get used to rubbing elbows while brushing your teeth. If nothing else, it's great not to have to pack and unpack repeatedly as you travel. RVs also make for excellent traveling classrooms, with space for worldschooling materials and built-in tables or desks to complete work. Mobile lodging can give kids a sense of "home," often with their own dedicated space inside, plus responsibilities for packing, cleaning, maintaining, and beautifying the rig. Another big win is the opportunity to reside in ports, campgrounds, parks, and open spaces that provide unparalleled access to the great outdoors. After all, your home may be small, but the world is your backyard.

Many of us equate RV travel with domestic excursions, but you can travel by RV or van in many parts of the world. If there's a place you want to visit, look into campsite and off-grid options—some countries have excellent camping infrastructure, whereas others are quite limited. You'll need to decide if you are going to rent or purchase a vehicle at home and transport it internationally, or instead will travel to your destination and rent or purchase a rig there. If you are sending your vehicle overseas, you will need to comply with export regulations on the domestic side and import requirements on the other, including a clean title and proof of ownership and insurance. There are companies that specialize in shipping recreational vehicles and helping with the necessary paperwork.

In addition to the usual border crossing procedures, be prepared to share where you're headed in your rig and how long you'll be staying. If you have any pets on board, make sure you have the requisite documents for their entry. Clear your refrigerator and pantry of items that are likely to be prohibited, such as fruits, vegetables, and plants in soil, and plan to do your grocery shopping after you have crossed the border.

Living on the road in another country is part of the fun, but make sure you know which locations are going to work for your rig. Consider the local conditions, road safety, Wi-Fi availability, cost and types of fuel, and traffic. And do your homework to make sure your big RV fits through that little tunnel in the hills of Tuscany!

Sharing final tips before the downstream rapids.

Rogue River, Oregon

Three weeks after I turned nine, my parents and I take a four-day river trip on the wild and scenic stretch of the Rogue River, in southwest Oregon. Wild and scenic rivers are free flowing (have no dams) and protected for their remarkable scenic value. There was a wildfire in the Kalmiopsis Wilderness, which had been burning for several weeks. We'll have to paddle through the fire zone on the first day. A number of trips have already been canceled due to the wildfire, and we have to figure out if we are going or not.

The trip organizers and guests make the decision to go, but on the condition we have a very long first day, about eighteen miles to travel, so we can get through the whole burn area and camp in a safe bank of the river.

Everyone is quiet when we put in early the first morning. I think we're all a little nervous. The river water smells fresh and piney, but the air is warm and smells like ash. We see smoldering logs and debris on the riverbanks. Luckily, it starts to rain midmorning; we can hear the crackling logs, hissing soil, and raindrops tapping on the water. It feels primal, like it could have been the 1800s.

We get to our camping spot on the bank by late afternoon. Phil and Mary, the guides, instruct us to have everything well organized and packed so that if there is a flare-up, we can depart downriver quickly. That evening, the sun looks hot pink through the thick smoke, and the air is still.

This is an odd start to the trip for sure, but I've learned you have to push through your fear sometimes, and once you are immersed in the adventure, it will be amazing. And it is. The next morning, I get my kayak roll working really well, smoothly flipping my capsized boat back up using a paddle sweep across the water and a strong hip snap. The kayak roll is a necessary whitewater skill so you don't have to "wet exit" and risk losing your boat or paddle, slowing the group down, or ending up in sketchy water. Phil tells me I'm ready to paddle in my own boat, and I paddle all the class III rapids on the Rogue River that day and the next. Pretty big water for me! I help make crepes for dinner, get my toenails painted (a good river-rat practice), and hang out with the hilarious crew. I dunk in the cool water in the evenings and see sturgeons and other fish. I even see a juvenile black bear on the third day. Paddling on a river during a wildfire is like being in a sanctuary. It's beautiful, and I feel brave.

Map Your Route

Show your kids how your route is shaping up. Then start to fill in locations between your anchors. There may be some push and pull between costs and priorities. You might need to choose some budget-friendly places to visit to balance your other selections. Can you mix your transportation options between locations? If you are open to visiting places closer to your anchors, you might be able to go by car or train and save considerable cost. Get creative and make trade-offs as you see fit, knowing you are crafting your own adventure.

Accommodations

If you aren't bringing your mobile "home" with you, you'll need to figure out where to lay your lovely heads. Accommodation options are plentiful, so it can help to think through your family's criteria before you start making bookings. Some factors might include the following:

- Budget: Some families set a daily accommodations budget, knowing they can flex up or down per night depending on local costs and options.

- Location: Do you want to be near tourist attractions or off the beaten path? Are you interested in a particular site or neighborhood?

- Length of stay: Many families find they are able to negotiate down the per-night price for weekly or monthly stays; you might consider this in your itinerary planning and then reach out to properties to inquire about options.

- Amount and type of space: How many beds do you need, and will you be sharing bedrooms or have a separate one for the kids? Do you need a kitchen, a quiet work area, or outdoor space? Do you want a private bath, or is a shared one okay?

- Comfort level: What is your tolerance for roughing it versus desire for the comforts of home? Can you handle spiders in a campground so you can sleep under the stars? Can you wear the same clothes four days in a row so you don't need to do laundry at each stop?

- Amenities: Do you want meals included with your accommodations? Fast Wi-Fi? A front desk you can go to for assistance? Are any other services essential for your family?

- Other assurances: What is your tolerance for risk versus cost on other aspects such as cleanliness, safe locations, and noise level?

You'll also need to decide whether you are booking all, some, or none of your accommodations ahead of time. While there's comfort in knowing where you will sleep, you might enjoy the flexibility of finding places once you've arrived and can move around or change dates. Some families find better pricing by booking in advance, whereas others are able to secure last-minute deals once on-site. Still others like to see accommodations in person before committing to a stay.

Some thoughts on several accommodation types:

HOTELS

Hotels and inns are often the most straightforward to book because you are dealing with a large company or local business owner, and third-party booking sites may make it even easier. Offerings are more standardized, and customer assistance is usually available on-site. Some families we've spoken with note that when they need a break, getting a hotel is nice because many things (food options, laundry, excursion planning) are offered or taken care of for the guest(s). The key downside is usually cost, as duration discounts aren't common, and many hotel rooms don't have kitchens that allow you to cook at "home" and save money.

HOSTELS

It's a myth that hostels are just for twentysomethings. Few facilities have an upper-age limit, and families can mix in nicely. Some even offer dedicated family rooms with their own bathrooms (which are otherwise usually shared). Hostels are often well located near bus and train stations, and they are great for making connections and getting the scoop on local places to see. They can be quite low cost compared to other options and often have kitchens and laundry rooms, providing further ways to save money and meet other travelers in shared spaces. Potential downsides are the relative lack of privacy, noise levels, and increased risk of theft.

HOUSE/APARTMENT RENTALS

For families planning to stay in one place for a while, the advantages of long-term house/apartment rentals are many. They allow you to unpack your bags, settle into your own bedrooms, and have a kitchen to save on food costs and accommodate special diets. They can also feel more like a home and allow you to really connect with the community by visiting local groceries, shops, and parks.

Longer-term stays can help you slow down a little, stretch your budget, and avoid travel burnout. They're typically more cost-effective than per-night accommodations, sometimes dramatically so. Owners may be willing to negotiate pricing for longer stays, so don't hesitate to send a message on Vrbo, Airbnb, or private listings.

HOMESTAYS

Home swaps and house sitting are accommodation options we covered in chapter 2. Homestays are when you stay together with local residents in their homes. Stays can offer the opportunity to live like the locals, observe and partake in their cultural and family traditions, and enjoy their traditional foods. Participants may get to practice language learning, ask questions, build relationships, and hopefully make new friends. Homestays are often booked through third-party organizations; search online by destination and read reviews to ensure you are working with someone reputable. Then go in with open minds and enjoy the experience.

OTHER LODGING OPTIONS

In addition to homestays, there are other economical accommodations that help you connect with the local culture, such as mountain-trekking huts, Bedouin tents, monasteries, camping along pilgrimage routes, and jungle treehouses. These, too, are usually coordinated by third parties.

If you are feeling even more adventurous, you don't have to limit yourself to online reservations. Although the safety vetting and oversight filters will be missing from your search, renting accommodations directly on the ground, without the internet, can save you money. And you just might find a hidden gem.

CHAPTER 5

Family Travel Logistics

Give me six hours to chop down a tree and I will spend the first four sharpening the ax.

—Abe Lincoln

NOW THAT WE'VE DISCUSSED where you're going and how you'll get there, let's walk through some more detailed travel logistics.

Travel Documents

PASSPORTS

To travel internationally, you must bring the right documents, including up-to-date passports. Without them you could be denied boarding, or even worse, entry into the country you're intending to visit. Make sure you allow plenty of time in your planning phase to get all family members a valid passport.

Passport rules vary by country and change often, so research them thoroughly for each destination you plan to visit—*before* you leave home. Some countries require that your passport be valid for six months *after* your departure date. For US residents, passport initial application and renewal instructions can be found on the USPS website.

Some additional tips:

- If you or a family member needs a passport, you should start the application process at least three to four months before your initial departure.

- If you need a passport sooner than the lead times quoted by your passport service office, you can pay additional fees for an expedited passport.

- If you need a renewal while abroad, you can visit the local embassy. It may be able to offer a faster turnaround time. Keep in mind that you won't be able to cross any borders until you receive your renewed passport.

- There are many third-party companies that will help you navigate the passport application process and obtain any visas you require (for a fee).

- Make sure the names you use to book travel match *exactly* the names on your passports. If you've recently gotten married or divorced or changed your name for any other reason, ensure the name on your passport is how it appears on your travel documents.

- Travelers can select male (M), female (F), or another gender identity (X) as their gender marker on passports; this identifier does not need to match the gender shown on supporting documentation like birth certificates, state IDs, or previous passports. No medical documentation is required to change the gender marker on passports.[24]

- Put a unique sticker on the cover of each family member's passport—this is a great way to identify quickly whom each passport belongs to, without having to flip through to find the ID page.

Make a photocopy of each family member's passport and other key documents to keep in a separate place while traveling in case the original is lost, stolen, or damaged. Put a scanned digital copy on your laptop or in cloud storage. While these can't be used in place of the original, copies can give you a head start in replacing a passport.

In addition to passports, a limited number of countries require that parents present an unabridged birth certificate for each of their children up to age eighteen to gain entry or secure a visa. Concerns about child abductions have made government officials around the world wary when only one parent is traveling with a child, and sometimes even when both parents are present. If traveling as a single parent, in addition to your passports and your child's birth certificate, you should bring written, notarized consent for travel signed by all living parents or legal guardians. Check destination-country rules online. Customs and border agents take these rules very seriously, and we've personally witnessed families getting turned away at international borders.

Calatafimi, Sicily, Italy

Angus, our Worldwide Opportunities on Organic Farms (WWOOF) host, pulls up to the station in Calatafimi at our planned meeting time. A white-haired Brit, he's all business as he throws our bags into the back of his Peugeot. We race the five miles over potholes and gravel to the home he shares with his Sicilian wife, Catarina.

We are volunteer laborers, and we'll be harvesting Catarina's family's hundred-year-old olive trees in exchange for room and board in their centuries-old limestone villa. Fuchsia bougainvillea dot the washed exterior; row after imperfect row of mature olive trees line the rolling green hills. The south-facing terracotta patio is perfumed by the scent of lemons and oregano and overlooks Catarina's heirloom garden, bursting with artichokes, arugula, cauliflower, chard, basil, tomatoes, peppers, and kale. Grapevines, prickly pear, and fig trees fence the garden, a vestige of the area's Greek, Phoenician, Arab, and Spanish culinary roots.

One-third the age of a typical WWOOFer, Johnny is given chores fit for a celebrity. First, he brushes and pets the three dogs. Then he climbs a couple of trees to test the readiness of the olives, turning his fingers into rakes to sweep the fruit off robust leafy branches. Finally, he goes to the garden to harvest ingredients for *pasta alla Trapanese*.

I watch as Catarina grabs a handful of almonds from a large glass jar, throws them into a blender, along with fresh tomatoes, peppers, garlic, basil, a dash of salt, and a generous pour of last year's olive oil, and pulses the pesto to perfection. Then Angus, Catarina, our family of three, four other giddy WWOOFers, Rafaeli the groundskeeper, and three local friends sit down at the long wooden table. We pour glasses of Nero d'Avola, and we all enjoy a slow meal on the eve of the harvest.

▶ Our hands become softer as the olive harvest goes on.

VISAS

You'll be able to enter some countries without a visa or obtain one upon arrival. For others, you'll need to obtain a visa ahead of time so that you have it in hand when you arrive. Embassies and consulates will have the most current information for each country; for US-issued passport holders, this information can be found at the Department of State's website. A couple of other recommendations:

- Make sure you bring additional passport-sized photos with you. Many countries require one or two for entry visas and/or trekking permits. Trust us, you don't want to get stuck using the grossly overpriced (and often painfully slow) airport photo booths, or worse, be turned around at a border due to not having a photo.

- For each country in your itinerary, research visa and immigrations "insider tips" online before you go. These will often provide info about how to navigate the process, whether you need to pay in cash (and whether they prefer US dollars or local currency), and how to avoid scams at the border.

Visa applications typically require information on your planned length of stay and departure date, and they often require documentation showing your plan for exiting the country (such as proof of a purchased plane or train ticket for onward travel). If you plan to stay in a country for an extended period, a tourist visa might not be possible. You should always check visa rules if you'll be spending more than three months in one location.

Special note: The Schengen Area is a European zone of countries that have abolished internal borders, allowing its citizens to travel from one country to another within the region as if it is a single country. In general, the residents of non-Schengen countries need to obtain a visa to visit. Websites are available to help travelers track their lengths of stay and visa rules within the Schengen Area.[25]

INTERNATIONAL DRIVING PERMIT

If you plan to drive in a foreign country, you'll likely need an International Driving Permit (IDP), often and incorrectly referred to as an International Driver's License. An IDP is a document you use *along with your valid home driver's license* that allows you to legally operate a motor vehicle while abroad. You can get an IDP at most AAA offices, and it is typically valid for one year after issue.

Make sure you understand the local rules of the road for all countries you'll be visiting. Also, research whether your credit card provider and/or insurance company covers car rentals overseas, particularly if you've made changes to your policy prior to travel. Annika's auto insurance company wouldn't cover a camper van in New Zealand, so her family had to buy local insurance for that portion of their trip.

OTHER DOCUMENTS

There may be other documents from home you'll need on the road. Depending on your circumstances, these might include a power of attorney, which is a written authorization that allows another person to act on your behalf, including giving them authority to conduct financial transactions, sign legal documents, or make health care decisions if you cannot do so. Some families find it helpful to identify a trusted helper in their home base who can help coordinate or execute needed duties and transactions on their behalf.

NOTES ON CURRENCY

These days it's typically easiest to simply pull money from ATMs once you've arrived at a foreign destination. Watch out for foreign transaction fees, which are often imposed by both the ATM owner and your own bank. Check for debit cards that bypass some or all of the home-bank expenses, and do some homework to know the best places to retrieve money locally in the country you plan to visit. Load your bank info and credit cards into your digital wallet to make things even easier.

There will be times when you need funds and won't have them. Your credit card won't work, or a vendor will only take cash or digital-wallet transactions (and transaction vendors, such as Venmo in the US, vary widely by location). A good tip is to carry along a bit of US cash from home. A US$20 bill goes a long way in many countries when local currency isn't readily available.

Airport Security

If you are considering a Wonder Year, you may have already navigated through airport security with your kids. Here's some good news: if your Wonder Year includes air travel, your kids will probably get *very* good at it.

Here are a few ideas to help make the process easier on everyone:

- Practice your security-line process. Even young kids can know which items they'll need to remove from bags and backpacks and how to pack them in a way that makes doing so quick and easy.

- Be prepared to encounter different security rules across countries. In some places it's fine to bring your camera tripod as a carry-on, but in others it is seen as a potential weapon that must be checked. Research or ask for rules before you are in line. Some countries have quirky regulations—in Laos, you must deflate a football to pass security; and in New Zealand, expect your hiking boots to receive a downright intimate inspection.

- Consider whether investing in programs such as TSA PreCheck, CLEAR, or Global Entry, which help speed the security process (Global Entry has the added benefit of expediting US customs screenings), would be a good investment for your family. These programs are currently located in many airports and continue to expand.

Customs and Immigration

Getting through customs and immigration (C&I) with kids may test your patience, but it isn't difficult if you know what to expect. If you haven't navigated C&I anywhere before, know this: you can't miss it. After exiting your flight, you'll be led, cattle-style, directly there. Move along as fast as you can to get in line, as queues can become long. You'll need to choose the right line to enter, most often based on your citizenship. Have two documents ready: 1) everyone's passports, open to the photo page and 2) your customs declaration form, one per family. This form is often given to you on the plane—fill it out there, before you begin juggling kids and luggage.

The customs agent may ask you and your children a few basic questions about your travel, such as the purpose of your trip, where you will be visiting, and how long you intend to stay. An important note for long-term travelers, especially those without fully set itineraries: some countries require you to show evidence of ticketed travel for leaving the country *as you enter*. Check online to find out if your destination requires you to demonstrate your confirmed departure plan and which documents (such as train, bus, or plane tickets) they'll accept. After you pass through, you can claim your bags, exit customs, and continue to your connecting flight or local transportation.

Also, be aware that in some locations, customs officials may attempt to separate family members from each other during the process. While this might be a normal part of the procedure, it can be disconcerting. Do your best to stay together, but if you can't, try to stay calm and keep an eye on each other.

Border crossings by road have a bit more variability depending on where you are passing to and from. At a minimum, expect to show identification and other travel documentation—many countries publish helpful checklists and document links online. You might also need to share information related to any pets, purchased goods, and cash. Border wait times can be long, so if you aren't excited about sitting in a queue, try to avoid crossing at peak times and stations.

Speed Bumps

We guarantee that some logistical linchpin is going to be changed, rerouted, delayed, or canceled. If you've paid attention to our humble traveling guidance thus far, you will not be surprised by our recommendation: be prepared for anything. Have in your backpack some time fillers: a couple of books, snacks, a deck of cards, a ball to kick or toss, a camera, maybe a local map. You may be delayed for an hour, or two days, or a week. Have fun and go with the flow, knowing you have time on your side. Also, get familiar with your travel insurance eligibility criteria for claims, and ask the airlines for lodging and food vouchers to help cover unexpected costs.

Technology

The proverbial double-edged sword, technology is something we can't live with and can't live without. Most full-time travelers find that a reliable connection supports many needs: working on the road, sourcing online education, making reservations, navigating, keeping in touch, maintaining records, providing entertainment, and more. We encourage you to reflect on two key facets of long-term travel and technology: access and use.

ACCESS

Since 2020 we're all a little more adept at remote transactions, online meetings, virtual classrooms, and video chats. The interconnectedness allows for location independence that helps make a Wonder Year possible.

It's hard to imagine the utility of technology while traveling until you need it and don't have a connection. A reliable tech setup will likely be among the handiest of tools in your traveling toolbox. Perhaps you've already figured out a system that works for you and you have your hardware and accessories. If not, you'll want to look at computer equipment requirements, Wi-Fi connectivity options such as hotspots and other portable devices, cell phone plans, or SIM card options that best meet your needs. There are even GPS phones that keep you connected off-grid—they're great when you're in remote backcountry or way downriver. Also, consider which of your family's streaming services are worth keeping—access varies by country, so don't assume your home services will work everywhere you go.

USE

One thing that is similar between travel tech and home tech is the importance of setting expectations for your family's use. Is FaceTiming friends every day cool with you? What about checking in with grandparents? Are three hours a week of Khan Academy too much? What if your daughter loves photography and shoots beautiful wildlife images or shots of public markets, then wants to spend hours a day editing and posting to Instagram? What about video games? Are they okay to play during long waits? On rainy days? All of this is for you to decide, and it's great to talk about it and get aligned as a family before you depart—but expect your policy to evolve once you're out there, too.

You might also play around with using old-school analog methods like guidebooks, maps, board games, and field guides on your trip. Indeed, many families look at their Wonder Year as an opportunity to break the grip of screen time and try in earnest to limit social media, video games, and other technology-dependent ways.

Insurance

While we don't want to dwell on all that might go wrong during a Wonder Year, things can, and sometimes do, happen. Our advice is to be prepared, and insurance may be part of your plan. When researching insurance options for full-time, long-term family travel, it is helpful to consider these categories:

TRAVEL

Travel insurance is what you typically think of when purchasing coverage for vacations. In addition to canceled flights, flooded hotels, travel delays, and lost baggage, it *might* cover medical emergencies, but not preexisting conditions or long-term care of chronic conditions. Read the insurance policy fine print on what are covered expenses and what are eligible claims. Keep your policy number and date of purchase handy.

PERSONAL BELONGINGS

You may want to protect your belongings against damage, theft, or other loss, such as a broken camera, stolen wallet, or misplaced phone. Some insurance policies will cover your belongings no matter where they are located, providing additional protection for the items you've stored at your home base. Others have exclusions, so read your policy's details.

MEDICAL

This is the type of policy you'd have back home for any medical needs, including routine care, illness, and injury. If your insurance came through your employer and you are taking a leave of absence or have quit your job, you may be able to extend your medical insurance through the Consolidated Omnibus Budget Reconciliation Act (COBRA) program or other temporary continuations of coverage. However, many health plans do not cover you abroad, so you may want to protect yourself with another type of policy. As with travel insurance, take time to read about the covered claims, especially regarding preexisting conditions and emergency care.

EVACUATION AND REPATRIATION

Most medical policies do not cover emergency evacuation or transport back to your home country, unless specifically noted. You may need to purchase this type of coverage separately. Some travel credit cards include this as a benefit.

Not all policies cover everything above, and you may need to search for more inclusive plans or purchase a combination of policies to protect your family fully. We aren't endorsing a particular provider, and you'll need to figure out what works best by comparing offerings, costs, and reviews. Here are some other considerations to keep in mind:

- There are many, many choices for insurance, and you may want to use a broker to help you shop around.

- Purchase insurance as early as possible. Although you can buy a policy up until the day you leave, you can't get travel insurance after something goes wrong. You'll want to be protected in case any of your Wonder Year plans go awry before you even leave home.

- Pay close attention to coverage limits, and insure your family enough to cover major catastrophes.

- Insurance for RV and camper van rentals may not be covered by standard credit card or auto insurance policies. Inquire about other transportation exclusions.

- Check to see if certain types of items (jewelry, electronics) are excluded from the list of covered personal belongings or if categories have any dollar limit. You can sometimes purchase supplemental insurance to get a higher amount of coverage.

- On that note, ask for a list of anything *not* covered so there are no ugly surprises once you are on the road. If you are unfortunate enough to be in a situation where you need insurance, the worst thing is to then find out that your policy doesn't cover it!

- Ensure your plans offer twenty-four-hour emergency services and assistance. You don't want to call for an evacuation from Bolivia only to reach a voice mailbox.

- If your family participates in extreme adventures, such as bungee jumping or hang gliding, inquire about coverage for those activities (or at least know when you *aren't* going to be covered). Supplemental insurance may be needed.

- Whatever policies you purchase, make sure they cover where you're going. Some plans exclude certain countries or regions.

- Keep a copy of all policies on hand when you travel, and use customer service numbers to check in before you seek medical care or other services.

Somewhere in the Amazon, Brazil

They tell us not to take anything out of the jungle. It is our last day at Pousada Uacari. Situated at a tight bend in the Japurá River, a wide feeder to the Amazon about a mile away, it is a place so remote that its location was described to us simply as "two hours by boat from Tefé." Our small room, at the end of a narrow wooden walkway, floats atop the river on enormous Styrofoam pontoons. It contains four single beds and a small bathroom with a shower that pumps recycled river water from a rooftop tank. Our countless roommates—roaches, spiders, and lizards—make us grateful for the bed nets that Mark tucks around the boys and me each night before crawling under his own.

The day before, Asher had speared a river piranha, and we ate it sushi-style for lunch. We'd ventured out in a narrow aluminum canoe for an evening paddle surrounded by giant caiman watching us from the water, all eyeballs and teeth. I'd been sucker-punched in the face by an airborne fish attracted by our boat's headlight in the pitch black. Gathering on the floating dock back at

the lodge, we had stayed up late to view a total lunar eclipse, munching popcorn like we were watching Earth's biggest blockbuster movie. We would have liked to sit at the edge of the dock and cool our feet in the water, but we didn't dare.

We are fine to take nothing home with us. Even touching anything is risky business.

Our trackers meet us early this morning for a hike across a peninsula lying between the main river channel and an intersecting tributary. They are three local tribe members whose family roots run deep into the basin. Carrying blue jugs of water and red backpacks with white crosses, they have machetes hanging at their sides. We all do our best to bridge Portuguese and English, and with earnest intent, hand gestures, and lots of smiles on both sides, are able to communicate fine.

Our hike an hour away by canoe, Ronan spends the journey deciphering birdsong and monkey howls. Storm clouds gather above the forest canopy, bathing the jungle in a grayish-yellow light as we slide our boat onto the bank. Disembarking into shin-deep mud, it's clear that the land has spent most of its

◄ A different kind of bed and breakfast.

year underwater. Leaves with no crunch cover dank earth dotted with stagnant pools of water. There are thickets of thorny shrubs and beautiful orchids perched in the crooks of spreading branches.

There are no trails, and I hang a few paces back, watching my boys bushwhack their way through the dense vegetation. Everyone but Asher and our lead tracker, João, who are the same height, have to bend forward as we walk. The river fades from sight, but we can still sense the low hum of its flow as we trek to an enormous kapok tree taking center stage in the marshy glade. Its roots stand taller than all of us, and vines drape around its trunk, creating eerie spaces to walk through. Ronan spots a line of giant ants carrying larvae from one home to another. A guide shows Asher the tracks of a large jungle cat.

Captivating creatures abound, but we're in search of one in particular: the elusive sloth. Travelers from around the world come here to spot them, and we haven't seen one all week. The boys are especially excited by the possibility of finding this exotic, smiley soul.

It's Ronan who spots one first. Tapping João on the shoulder for confirmation, he points to his own eyes, then holds up two curled fingers. It is a mother two-toed sloth with a baby wrapped tightly around her back. After that, sloth "hide-and-seek" comes more

quickly, and we soon locate several, so well camouflaged that they blend into the mass of leaves above. Our guides eye a three-toed male slowly returning to the heights of a giant fig tree. Sloths live in the trees and come down only once each week to poop in an ever-growing pile on the ground. Now on his unhurried return climb, he is so close above our heads that we can see the gnats buzzing around his exposed face.

One of our guides points to his watch—time to go. We hack a new path through the jungle to the boat, where our gear is already loaded for the long trip back to Tefé. At the port, we heave our bags to the taxi driver on the other side of the gangplank and pile into his small car. Inside the tinted windows with the air-conditioning on max, the heat is staved off, but the smell is thick, ripe, and overwhelming—something like rotten fruit.

After we've been dropped off at the airport and are waiting in line, I notice Asher holding his nose. "That taxi smelled pretty awful, didn't it?" I ask.

He squeezes his nose tighter, shakes his head, and with his other hand, points at Mark.

Our heads lower to Mark's "mud"-coated hiking boots. He was the one who had stood directly under the sloth.

"Dad, you took something out of the jungle . . . , " Asher says, with a grin spreading across his face.

Safety Considerations

This section focuses on the safety of your *stuff*. Personal health and safety is covered in the next chapter.

BELONGINGS

Things can go missing on the road—especially phone chargers and anything you might hang on the back of a bathroom door! Here's some advice we like to keep in mind when we travel:

- In general, it's best to leave your most valuable items, such as jewelry or irreplaceable treasures, at home or in a bank safe-deposit box. For those you do bring, leave them at your accommodation. Use the safe in your room or locked drawer at the front desk to store passports, travel documents, extra cash, jewelry, and electronics.

- When you're moving between destinations, don't put valuables in checked luggage or in the storage compartment of a train or bus. Keep them in your carry-on, and keep that bag close to you. Stay attuned to valuables at security checkpoints, too.

- When they're available at hostels and transport stations, use storage lockers. Bring a padlock or two on your trip.

- If you carry a bag, consider cross-body bags or backpacks, which are harder to grab than shoulder bags. Secure your bag to your leg or chair when you sit down. Choose an unassuming or even beaten-up bag that doesn't scream that you have valuables inside.

- When you carry higher-value items with you, keep them on the front of your body in a pouch or money belt, and make sure your bag stays completely closed. When you need to get cash or cards out, be aware of the activity around you.

- Don't have your kids carry anything valuable, including their own electronics. Talk them through an age-appropriate version of the suggestions above.

- Use social media with care. Posting your pictures or where-abouts during travel can leave you more susceptible to theft at your home base.

There are lots of special bags, gadgets, and anti-pickpocket gear you can buy, but even more important is to be street smart and diligent. Read about security risks and common scams for an area prior to your arrival. Be alert, and walk with confidence and purpose—you'll be less of a target if you act like you know your way around.

We've covered theft, so let's take a moment to talk about loss. Families on the move are managing a lot of stuff, and it's easy to lose track of items. Help each family member develop a system for keeping track of everything. Here are a few ideas: label and photograph items before departure, use packing cubes, and create checklists. Run through scenarios before you go, and always take a final look behind you when you leave.

FINANCES

In addition to copying and storing important documents safely, there are many other things you can do to keep your financials secure while traveling.

- Let your bank and credit card companies know about your travel plans.

- Know where you plan to retrieve foreign currency, carry multiple cards with you for backup, and spread them between adults.

- Check ATMs to ensure the card reader doesn't look tampered with, and switch machines if you have any doubt.

- Set up transaction alerts to monitor charge activity while you travel. If something doesn't look right, contact the issuing bank.

- Bring a list of phone numbers for your bank and card companies that you can use outside the country.

TECHNOLOGY

Here are some guidelines you can follow to keep your devices and data safe while traveling.

- Make a note of everyone's laptop (and tablet) model and serial number, and leave this information at home. Back up your system and data, and keep them somewhere safe, too. While you're on the road, perform regular backups to the cloud, a service provider, or external hard drive.

- Update your antivirus and firewall programs before you depart—it's best to limit software and app updates on unsecured networks while traveling, as they can expose you to malware.

- To help prevent information theft, set strong passwords, use a password manager, and trust only secure Wi-Fi networks. If you must use unsecured connections, don't enter sensitive information.

- Consider getting a virtual private network (VPN) before you leave, which acts like a filter so that anything you do online is more secure.

- Limit the use of Bluetooth, and turn it off after use so that it isn't used to lift your information.

- Consider using RFID-blocking wallets or bags to protect cards and passports from skimmers.

Hopefully all of these beware lists haven't scared you away. Now you have everything you need to get packing.

Packing

"How did you figure out what to pack for your whole family?" is one of the most-often-asked questions about our respective Wonder Years.

We've provided you with an extensive list of things you *might* need for your Wonder Year in appendix B. The important thing to know is that there isn't a magical set of items that every family will need. It depends a lot on where you're going, the climate, the activities you'll be participating in, where you'll stay and what those accommodations offer, your personal hobbies, how much weight you are willing to carry, what you can buy on-site, and what you are most attached to from home. You definitely won't need everything listed in the appendix, and it's just as important to determine what you *won't* bring along.

In addition to what to bring is the question of what to bring it *in*. How will luggage and packs be distributed between family members? Do you need wheels? Backpack straps? Here are some considerations for how to choose your luggage:

- Can your child(ren) carry their own?

- Will you be walking along rough roads or walking up many staircases? If so, consider straps on your bags to provide support.

- Will you be maneuvering many airports with littles by foot, or do you have one in a stroller/car seat? Consider how things can roll together.

- Does the idea of the duffel abyss, with items tossed in willy-nilly, make you itchy? Consider a hard-shell suitcase with zippered compartments and easy organization. Or use compressible packing cubes, perhaps color coded by family member.

- Do you prefer to check bags or have carry-ons? Is it cost-prohibitive, inconvenient, or risky for your group to check bags? Then you need to maximize everyone's carry-ons. Even the youngest will need to carry their share.

- If you're settling into a van or RV, will you also be doing over-night excursions? You might want foldable weekender bags.

- Do you need waterproofing? Consider a trash bag or a water-proof duffel or suitcase, or for a backpacking trip, a pack cover.

Kyla Hunter's girls each carried their own backpack and could bring as many stuffed animals and treasures as they wanted with the caveat that they had to pack and carry those items themselves. No exceptions. Her daughter, Calais, brought a backpack full of her favorite rocks. She didn't complain about the weight because it was her choice.

A few final packing tips:

- Weight matters, especially with kids. If you find you aren't using things, ship them home—the cost for doing so quickly pays for itself in convenience (and probably even dollars, given the cost of checking bags). You don't have to bring everything with you—purchases can be made at your destination. Some-times they are much cheaper on-site.

- Help your kids load their backpacks with items for traveling days. This might include books, toys, stuffed animals, games, stickers, and snacks.

- Carry a daypack in case you get stranded somewhere. See appendix B for suggested items.

- Some countries have luggage-forwarding services where your bags are sent onward to your next destination while you are in transit. Costs vary widely. Some families find it's worth it, espe-cially as they are navigating the world with littles.

CHAPTER 6

Health and Personal Safety

If no one ever took risks, Michelangelo would have painted the Sistine floor.

—Neil Simon

PART OF THE ADVENTURE YOU'RE CHOOSING is knowing that tricky stuff may happen. Being away from home—and thus, away from usual sleep schedules and diets—may make some travelers prone to illness. Frequently changing time zones, beds, food, water, and weather can be tough on anyone. But while sensationalized articles eagerly cite all the things one can "catch" while traveling, in truth, with good preparation, you can comfortably and confidently take your family almost anywhere.

We coauthors agree that our kids were all healthier on the road than at home. Minus one very surprising public vomiting incident in a Peruvian airport, Angela's kids didn't catch any viruses during the two years they traveled full time. Annika's family seemed to have stronger immune systems from more sleep, fresh air, and together time than the hectic pace at home. A jellyfish sting, a first period in the Himalayas, and a case of laryngitis just added to their family memories. Julie's family also experienced a year of good air and good health. Apart from Johnny's twenty-four-hour bug in Zion National Park and Julie's epic backcountry fall, their family had no other colds, contusions, or cramps. While one may chalk this up to luck, it's just as likely that a travel lifestyle with more time and less stress makes for more physically resilient humans.

People asked us, "How did you stay healthy? What immunizations did you need? Are there places we should avoid?" Your concerns, and those of your loved ones, might also be amplified, given our experience during the pandemic. If this is one of the major mental hurdles for your Wonder Year, we want to help you think through some questions and provide you with actionable steps so you'll be prepared, and feel confident enough to handle almost anything that comes your way. You can also take comfort in knowing that people are out there to help.

In this chapter we take on the most common health and safety concerns for traveling families. You'll find that certain parts are specific to international journeys, because some concerns are localized. While it may sound a bit scary, we believe that an ounce of preparation will go a long way toward comfortably managing any concerns once you're on the road. And hopefully you'll end up not needing any of this advice!

Staying Healthy on the Road

BEFORE YOU GO

Prior to your Wonder Year, check in with your family's physician(s) to ensure clinical exams and lab tests are up to date. Even if there's nothing of concern, this will allow you to make arrangements for any prescription medications you'll need during your journey. It's also a good idea to carry a recent paper prescription for medications or glasses/contacts, if anyone in your family wears them.

All countries have varying health risks, and depending on where your travels take you, your family may need certain vaccinations to enter some places. We know there are disparate beliefs around vaccinations, and it is not our goal to debate that here. We simply encourage you to know the rules for wherever you are going so you aren't surprised. Some countries require proof of specific vaccinations prior to entrance, especially if your passport shows a history of spending time in high-risk areas. A list of recommended and required vaccines, by country and area, is available at the Centers for Disease Control and Prevention (CDC)'s travelers' health website and the International Air Transport Association (IATA) website.

Some health insurance plans offer travel medicine specialists who can provide vaccine and preventive medication recommendations based on your intended itinerary and personal medical history. If this service is available to you, consult these specialists as early as possible. Most immunizations should be taken at least four to six weeks prior to travel.[26] Others may require a series of injections, spaced apart according to a set schedule. The longer you plan to travel, and the more high-risk places you plan to visit, the farther ahead you may need to allow for all required vaccinations. For some families, these group vaccination visits might be the first tangible signs that their trip is really going to happen!

Depending on your itinerary, you and your kids might choose to be vaccinated against meningitis, rabies, typhoid, yellow fever, Japanese B encephalitis, malaria, COVID, and/or other diseases. Detailed travel vaccine recommendations for babies and toddlers are further described in many resources online, including the CDC website. Regardless of age, make sure you take your kids' immunization records with you wherever you go.

ACCESSIBILITY AND SPECIAL NEEDS

If you or a family member has a physical disability, arrange for mobility aids and equipment in advance of your travel when possible, and check the rules regarding service or support animals if you travel with any. These are more difficult to do once you're on the road, where language barriers and inconsistent policies may come into play. If your family has known medical needs, you may want to scout ahead of time for the medical facilities in each of the areas you'll be visiting. It's also a good idea to check insurance coverage for any necessary medical equipment in the places where you're going.

Families traveling with special needs can find a growing number of disability travel specialists (see a few in the resources section) to help them locate accessible lodging, transportation, recreation, tours, and other travel resources. The CDC provides information for immunocompromised travelers. The TSA's special procedures page outlines information to help people with disabilities or medical conditions. Many airports have more accessible security lines and other accommodations, and you can find this information by searching their websites.

NEURODIVERSITY

There are many worldschooling families with neurodiverse kids. Two of us each have a neurodiverse child. If you do, too, we hope to assure you that with some planning and realistic expectations, a Wonder Year can be possible for your family, too.

Some families have told us that the relaxed schedule and lower-pressure travel logistics help ease stressful experiences that could otherwise affect their child. They are able to schedule days for downtime and rest breaks with greater flexibility, finding a rhythm that works for their families. Many bring along supports for sensory needs and find that they have more time for pursuing their children's interests at a pace that works for them.

That said, full-time travel isn't without its stressors, many of which can be more challenging for neurodiverse kids. Changes in routine, altered sleep schedules, new foods, and intense sensory environments can all be difficult to manage. You know your children best and what they can navigate, and hopefully you can leverage some of what already works at home. There are also books and other resources devoted to traveling with family members who are neurodiverse.

Lindsay Vandermyde, family traveler and mother of a neurodiverse son, suggests starting your travel with short-duration trips close to home. If all goes well, you can then increase both distance and duration. And remember, these can all be a Wonder Year—whatever length of time your family can manage.

PHYSICAL FITNESS

Travel puts you on the move. No matter what, you're going to get a lot of functional activity. It might not look like twelve reps of squats or three sets of pumping iron, if that's what you're used to. But just being out in the world—walking, carrying, packing, sightseeing, walking, and more walking—will likely get you well over ten thousand steps per day. The nature of family travel keeps you mobile, so just keep on keeping on.

If you intend to do any longer hiking or backpacking trips, you will need to get used to carrying some weight, test out your equipment, make time to acclimatize, and be prepared for moving in inclement weather. Schedule accordingly and give your family time to train, especially if altitude is going to be a factor. If you have time, you might have the ability to train in the field, building your mileage and readiness.

You might pack a travel yoga mat and grippy socks, a tennis racquet, running shoes, or swim goggles to continue doing the things that keep you fit and happy. Some families incorporate physical exercise into their daily lives. You and your kids might create challenges for each other, like working up to fifty push-ups a day or competing to see who can hold the longest plank. Find what works for you and have fun with it. Visit playgrounds, hike some trails, and trek through cities. No gym required!

MENTAL HEALTH

It's not only your bodies that benefit from moving around. Through our experiences and interviews, we know that a Wonder Year can provide profound mental health benefits, too.

Long-term family travel can help you connect, reduce stress, increase resilience, provide purpose, and even enhance your creativity. You might be leaving a stressful job, relationship, or situation behind. A Wonder Year can offer a clean slate, fewer demands, and quality time with your people that leaves you feeling more centered.

However, for some people, travel can make matters worse. Challenging travel situations, homesickness, loneliness, loss of work and purpose, too much together time, and tight spaces can aggravate existing conditions or create new ones. Teens can be particularly vulnerable to feelings of isolation and discontent.

Allie Rockwell's daughter struggled with anxiety before they left. At first it was exacerbated on the road by not knowing where they'd park their van or by driving through military checkpoints in Mexico. As parents, Allie and her husband wondered if they'd made a huge mistake by choosing this lifestyle. Little by little, with time and lots of family discussion, their daughter's anxiety became better managed. She realized that she was comfortable not knowing exactly where they'd sleep each night and how they'd spend their days.

Talk with health care providers before you depart, and leave room for your kids to express concerns or difficulties related to your travels. If you need further support while away from home, there are many health resources available online, including therapists with expertise in helping traveling families.

ROUTINE CARE

At home you likely have a health care regimen set up for your family: annual physicals and lab tests, regular dental cleanings and orthodontist visits, and the like. Being away will put a (likely welcome) dent in that routine, which warrants some planning before you depart.

There are probably a few things you can get done before you go and then pause while you travel. Annual physicals (and the medical forms for school and extracurriculars that accompany them) can be scheduled before you leave, especially to suss out anything you'll need while on the road. You might do a final dental checkup and cleaning for each family member, plus specialty visits such as dermatology, gynecology, or immunology. If you are inclined to keep your regular schedule instead, you can plan ahead and book appointments at your destinations. You'll likely find familiar resources in locations with large expat communities.

There may be specific medical needs that warrant a stop back at your home base. Angela's family built their domestic travel segments around required orthodontic visits in California for their son. They made it work, but the logistics were definitely tricky, and other families might consider postponing braces until after they return!

REPRODUCTIVE HEALTH

While all family members need to maintain their health while traveling, there are a few extra considerations for people who menstruate.

- Travel can trigger changes in menstruation patterns and side-effect severity. Changing time zones and eating different foods at irregular times can worsen period cramps, and remedies may be hard to find, so bring along what works for you.

- Foreign menstrual products may be different from what you're used to, and finding your favorites can be difficult and expensive (note: menstrual pads in the Himalayas are pricey!). If you aren't up for figuring this out on the road, bring supplies from home.

- If you're on a prescription contraceptive, bring enough to last the duration of your trip.

- If pregnant while traveling, you will have special considerations. Make sure you research transportation modes, destination risks, medical care pre- and post-delivery, where you'll give birth, and related citizenship questions.

- Travel experiences—including sitting for long durations of time, hot climates, and damp clothes and swimwear—can be triggers for urinary tract infections (UTIs) and yeast infections; we suggest you bring treatments or a prescription from home so that you're prepared in advance.

"We decorated each of our campsites
with conchs, cockles, seaweed, driftwood…"

The Florida Keys

We are three snow-loving Coloradans spending the month of December barefoot and sticky in South Florida. It doesn't take long for us to fall in love with the minerally feel of salt water, pastel-pink skies, any cold beverage with fresh lime, and that brilliant color of sunrise on ocean water that is impossible to name. We park-hop down the 125-mile chain of islands, eventually crossing all forty-seven bridges, which make up the Florida Keys, reserving tent-only sites in the campgrounds. The extra schlep from the rig to the more secluded tent-camping site is always worth it to us.

We use the sun (and shade), the tides, and US National Park Service Junior Ranger activities to structure our time, and we find a worldschool rhythm that is perfectly informed by wherever we are—boating through gnarly, rooted forests of coastal mangroves; trying out underwater photography at John Pennekamp Coral Reef State Park in search of sea fans, brain coral, urchins, anemones, and schools of scaly rainbow parrotfish. We learn about hurricanes, climate change, and invasive species.

We decorate each of our campsites with conchs, cockles, seaweed, driftwood, and the occasional piece of turquoise sea glass or fried egg jellyfishes, which look like eyeballs. We smile a lot, get really tan, and my curly hair becomes curlier every day.

About halfway down the keys on the "Highway That Goes to Sea," we come to Long Key State Park and score another fantastic walk-in campsite right by the water. That evening after dinner, we sit by the water, toes dipping in, hands whooshing across the fine white sand, when I feel a sting, then another, and another. I jump up and try to brush off whatever is biting, but I can't see 'em! I shake wildly as my eyes puff up and everything itches. I get in the tent and I still feel 'em. Johnny boy saves the day—he grabs a headlamp, hops on his bike, and races to the rig for the first aid kit. No surprise: I need a double dose of Benadryl. The next day, we carry on, appreciating that the tiniest Florida pests—those ever-present no-see-ums—have a bite way bigger than their imperceptible bark!

Health Concerns

In this section we walk through potential concerns you may encounter on the road. We also offer strategies and resources for staying healthy once you are in the thick of your traveling pest parade. Our aim is not to overwhelm you here; we have erred on the side of thoroughness only so you can easily find the issues that might apply to your family. You'll know best when to research them further.

INSECTS AND INFECTIOUS DISEASES

In addition to immunizing against disease, or if you are a family that doesn't routinely vaccinate, you'll want to have a solid plan for navigating infectious disease risks where you travel. Diseases spread by mosquitoes, including West Nile virus, dengue, yellow fever, malaria, chikungunya, and Zika, are common in many parts of the world. Tick-borne illnesses, such as Lyme disease and babesiosis, are also prevalent, particularly in some parts of the US.

A key aspect of prevention is to help your kids avoid getting insect bites in the first place. Some people swear by natural approaches such as garlicky foods or citronella, either in candles or creams, to keep bugs away. Other families may prefer chemical intervention. Use insect repellent (specific recommendations for repellents by age of child can be found online, and the Environmental Working Group publishes consumer guides for bug repellents, sunscreens, and other consumer goods on its website), and cover skin as much as possible by wearing long sleeves and pants. Permethrin can be applied to clothing as an extra deterrent—spray it on ahead of time; protection lasts through several rounds of laundering. Another line of defense is to sleep in screened rooms and under bed nets wherever possible—you can even purchase lightweight nets that are easy to pack and bring with you. Stroller nets and face nets that fit over hats are also available.

Additionally, it's important to know that anyone is at risk for malaria, a serious and potentially life-threatening infection. If you are headed to an area where malaria occurs, talk with your doctor about antimalarial medications or vaccines. These drugs are not 100% effective, so it's still necessary to heed precautions against bug bites.

MOTION SICKNESS

Motion sickness is common, especially in children. It is caused by repeated, unusual movements sending strong and sometimes conflicting information to the brain, disrupting the vestibular system that provides a sense of balance and stability. Motion sickness can be triggered or exacerbated by anxiety, unfamiliar smells, or multitasking (reading, watching a video, or looking at a map) while on the move. Symptoms include nausea, disorientation, dizziness, sweating, headaches, feeling cold, and fatigue. These typically go away when the journey is over; however, some people might still feel a sense of movement hours later when trying to fall asleep, or even longer.

The best way to stop motion sickness is to stop moving, but that isn't always possible when you are a family that is, well, on the move. It's helpful to focus on prevention techniques, including eating light prior to travel, staying hydrated, breathing fresh air, avoiding strong smells, positioning yourself so that your eyes are attuned to the movement, and avoiding reading or other similar activities while in motion. Kids who struggle with motion sickness might benefit from closing their eyes and listening to an audiobook or even sleeping en route. For the worst cases, your physician may be able to recommend natural treatments like acupressure wristbands or prescription medication like scopolamine patches. Before embarking on your Wonder Year, try to take various forms of trips as a family to find out who might be prone to motion sickness and test any recommended remedies.

EAR PAIN

Many adults and even more children experience ear pain during air travel. The rapid altitude changes experienced during takeoff and landing in an airplane can mean the air pressure in your ears doesn't have time to equalize to the outside air, stretching the eardrums and causing a sense of fullness, discomfort, or pain. Children are more susceptible due to a still-developing anatomy, compounded by the fact that they get more respiratory infections than adults do.[27] Younger kids may react by crying or tugging at their ears. While usually more annoying than concerning, this discomfort can become more serious and result in ongoing pain or hearing loss. Adults can usually equalize this pressure by swallowing or yawning, but kids don't have the same instincts, so they may need assistance. Many families keep pacifiers, gum, or breath mints handy because the suction in the mouth can help pop ears, or at least provide a distraction.

JET LAG

The pain is *real*, folks.

It's bad enough to deal with jet lag as an adult. But managing it with kids can be downright rough. Here's the good news: Since you are traveling long term, you might not be flying across enormous distances all at once. You may be able to break up your journey or plan things so that the time changes aren't so drastic. Most importantly, you might have more flexibility to take time for you and your kids to recover. These are some other ways you could prepare for time-zone shifts based on your family's needs.

- Start shifting bedtimes in the days leading up to your travel, a bit more each evening.

- Take an overnight flight if you think everyone can get more rest. Set your watches to the new time zone, and try to sleep as if you're already in it.

- Dress comfortably and bring cozy blankets and pillows on the plane—anything that will encourage the kids to head to "bed."

- Stay hydrated. It will help your body adjust and feel less funky.

- Once you arrive at your destination, spend time outdoors, in the sunlight. Follow the light and the dark, and your family's circadian rhythms will soon stabilize.

- Don't schedule much for the first day or so after arrival; this will give your family time and space to acclimate without pressure. The general rule of thumb is that it will take one day of adjustment for every time zone crossed.

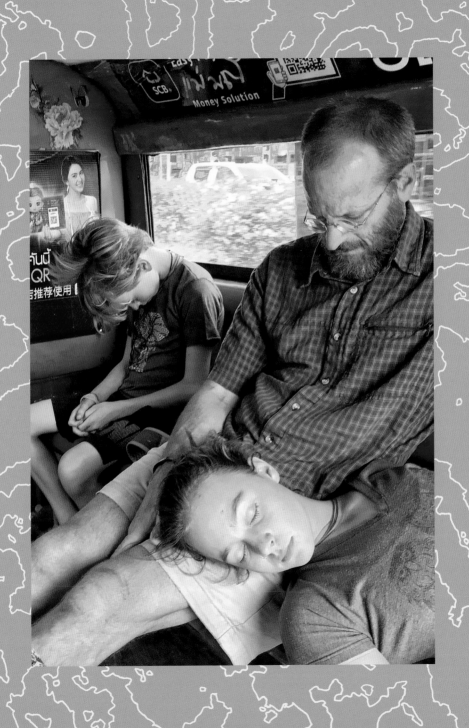

- Expect some possible discombobulation, clumsiness, disrupted schedules, and upset moods during your first days on the ground. Parents may need to be even more attentive than usual to help keep everyone safe.

ALTITUDE SICKNESS

Altitude sickness, also known as acute mountain sickness (AMS), typically occurs at altitudes over 8,000 feet, but some people can experience symptoms as low as 6,300 feet above sea level.[28] AMS is caused by reduced air pressure and lower oxygen levels at high altitudes. Symptoms include headaches, nausea and vomiting, loss of appetite, dizziness, fatigue, and mood swings. If your child develops more severe altitude sickness, they might be confused and have a pale or blue complexion. They might also have difficulty walking, experience shortness of breath, or develop a cough. AMS is not something to take lightly, and if you are traveling to higher elevations, you need to study its effects and be prepared.

Here are some ways to help prevent altitude sickness:

- Acclimatize. This means ascending over multiple days to give your body time to adjust gradually. With long-term travel, you can often work this into your itinerary, enjoying time in each subsequent, slightly higher location. Avoid flying directly into high-altitude cities such as Cusco, Peru and La Paz, Bolivia. Guidelines based on destination altitude are available online.

- Adhere to the climber's adage: "Climb high, sleep low." Explore higher elevations during the day, but return to lower altitudes to sleep. Your breathing slows during sleep, so the risk of AMS is higher overnight.

- Stay hydrated, avoid alcohol, and eat lots of carbohydrate-rich foods.

- If you or your child has had AMS in the past, talk with your doctor about medications that might help. Some work best when taken in advance of high-altitude travel.

People acclimatize at different rates, so make sure everyone in your family has adjusted before going higher. Experts say there is no correlation between overall physical fitness and the risk of altitude sickness.[29] Even if you and your family do everything "right," anyone can still develop altitude sickness at any time. A person experiencing symptoms should never go higher until the symptoms have gone away. Altitude sickness can be more difficult for children, as they may not know how to communicate their symptoms. Be sure to research prevention and treatment methods before your journey, and talk with your family physician about any concerns.

GASTROINTESTINAL ISSUES

It's often a myth that you can't drink the water outside your comfy domestic dwelling. In fact, many places in the world have excellent water quality. That said, gastrointestinal (GI) upset is among the most common illnesses experienced while traveling.[30] You'll need to understand water sanitation and safety issues relevant to the places you are headed, and this information is often easy to find online.

We've all heard the advice about drinking bottled water in areas where water safety is a concern. Some other good things to know:

- To lessen the environmental impact of plastic bottles, you might consider boiling water or bringing your own water filtration or treatment system. Annika's family carried UV-light filters that attached to their water bottles for a minute of active swishing to make any water drinkable.

- In some areas, local water is placed in used water bottles, recapped, and sold. Always make sure your cap has the original seal.

- Have your kids brush their teeth using safe water, and remind them not to ingest water in the bath or shower. If you have small children, watch out for bath toys ending up in little mouths.

- Eat foods that are cooked and served hot or that you can peel yourself. Be aware that fruits, vegetables, and salads may have been rinsed in contaminated water.

- Avoid ice cubes, as they are usually made from local tap water.

- And of course, wash hands often.

Symptoms of food poisoning or GI upset can include cramps, nausea and vomiting, sweating, skin flushing, and diarrhea. These can be serious in kids due to the risk of rapid dehydration. The best treatment is usually to imbibe plenty of fluids. While there is often no need to take medicine for GI issues, many families travel with a prescription broad-spectrum antibiotic for each traveler and some rehydration powder, like Pedialyte, just in case. Ask your doctor if you think this could be helpful, especially if anyone in your family is prone to stomach bugs.

FOOD ALLERGIES AND PREFERENCES

There is growing acceptance of, and willingness to support, people with dietary restrictions due to health concerns, religious reasons, and/or personal preferences. Airlines, cruise lines, and lodgings are all stepping up to accommodate these needs via expanded menu offerings and the creation of separate areas for storing and consuming food. Many airlines have eliminated common allergens in their snacks, and some even offer a "buffer zone" around customers with allergies to prevent exposure from other passengers' foods.[31]

If finding suitable food is a concern, you might consider bringing nonperishable items in food containers as backup. If you use them, bring EpiPens from home. You can also create laminated cards detailing food allergies in the local language and show these at restaurants and gatherings.

There are even companies that offer free, printable allergen translation cards. If the issue is severe enough, you might consider limiting travel to areas with medical infrastructures adequate to support your family's needs.

OUTDOOR WATER SAFETY

Time spent in water can be one of the great joys of traveling. A few thoughts to help make sure that things stay fun:

- If your kids aren't yet swimmers, start swimming lessons before you leave. Depending on their ages, you may be able to get them water-safe before your trip, an investment that will save you worlds of worry.

- Even if your kids are comfortable in the water, it's important to remain cautious, just like you would at home. Drowning is a leading cause of death for those who travel abroad, and kids should be closely supervised at all times.[32] Life jackets aren't readily available everywhere, and even when they are, tour operators and local staff don't always encourage and monitor their use. Make sure you ask about availability, or bring your own. Inflatable water wings are also a great packable option.

- Watch out for local creatures; they can be fun to learn about but may carry risk of a bite or sting. Make sure you know what might be lurking in the sand or water and how you would treat any ouchies, should they occur.

- And then there are the creatures you can't see—fresh water can harbor protozoa, bacteria, or viruses, and some experts recommend that children never swim in unchlorinated, nonsalted water. Depending on the circumstances, you'll need to decide how to balance those risks with your own sense of adventure.

What to Carry with You

Angela's family likes to be prepared. When they were traveling in their RV, they carried a robust safety kit that included not only first aid items but also food, water, warming blankets, and safety flares in case they became stranded. When traveling internationally and only carrying their backpacks, they whittled their kit to the key essentials. You'll know best what your family needs to bring along, but here are a few ideas to get you started. For a complete packing list, refer to appendix B.

First aid kit. Many families prefer to travel with their own first aid kit. Some items to include are Band-Aids, blister tape, antibacterial or tea tree ointment, Aquaphor, and gauze pads. In addition to first aid supplies, you may want to bring a few key over-the-counter medications, including Benadryl for allergic reactions, ibuprofen for inflammation and pain, Orajel for tooth pain, and probiotics and antidiarrheals for gastrointestinal upset.

Prescription medication. You'll want to bring any prescription medications along with you, as many countries do not permit pharmacies to fill (or refill) prescriptions that originate outside their borders. As long as they are in clearly marked containers, you probably won't have trouble traveling with them. If you'll be traveling internationally for extended periods, you can often make special arrangements with your prescribers and insurance company to fill several months' worth of prescriptions ahead of time. In a pinch, you can make an appointment with a local provider to explain your medical condition, show your old prescription, and get a new written one that can be filled nearby.

Toilet kit. Carry some hand sanitizer, toilet paper, menstrual products, and a plastic bag to dispose of your trash.

Sun care products. Sunscreen is available almost everywhere, and unless you or your children require a particular brand, this is one item that's often more easily purchased at your destination. Try to purchase reef-safe products that protect marine habitats, and talk with your family about why this is important. Watch out for over-priced sunscreen at hotels and tourist sites, and instead aim to purchase it when buying groceries or other items in town.

Insect repellent. This can be a bit tougher to find, so you may want to bring repellent from home. Wipes travel well and are easier to get through security checkpoints than aerosol bottles.

Tip: It never hurts to take a first aid or wilderness first aid class before you depart on your Wonder Year. The Red Cross offers suitable classes for kids, too. It can be a family event—a kickoff for learning together. Basic first aid knowledge and a good first aid kit may be just what you need for that more adventurous outing.

Car Seats, Strollers, and Babyproofing

In some developing parts of the world, vehicles might not have seat belts. When booking local tours or transportation between locations, you may want to ask ahead about vehicle safety restraints. Angela's husband, Mark, insisted on a replacement van to Sapa, Vietnam, after their initial one arrived without its promised seat belts. Given that the driver then operated the second van at warp speeds, Mark was glad he'd insisted on them.

If you are traveling with small children, you might want to bring your own car seats, as they may not be available in many countries or be compliant with US safety standards. That's certainly more to carry, so you may have to get creative with your packing. Strollers can be cumbersome, too, and some families might opt for kid-carrying (slings, backpacks) in lieu of another wheeled vehicle. Only you know what is best for your family when trying to balance convenience and safety with the amount of gear to haul. Just be sure to research checked and carry-on baggage rules ahead of time.

You may be staying in many places that aren't as baby- or childproofed as back home. Always check the operation of doors in your accommodations (take it from a friend who once woke up to his younger kiddo sleepwalking out the hotel-room door) and ask for lower-floor rooms if that's helpful. You can also bring along a small rubber doorstop to help prevent unwanted entry or exit.

Many major cities have rental items—from strollers and car seats to books and toys—that can be reserved online and delivered to your accommodations. Some places even offer babyproofing prior to your arrival. These services may be less expensive than hauling along your gear, so consider researching offerings at your planned destinations.

Tip: Bring along some duct tape! It's great for covering outlets, padding sharp corners and edges, and securing other risky items out of reach of kids' hands.

Toileting around the World

How do they poo in Kathmandu? You'd be surprised by all the different ways we can interpret something as universal as toileting.

In some countries, people squat over a toilet seat that is flush to the ground so that no body parts ever touch a public surface. In others, toilet paper is considered unhygienic. Instead, they use a bidet and their hands to get clean. Sometimes privacy stalls only go up to shoulder level, so you might be looking a stranger in the eye while you're doing your business. Yet other countries have high-tech toilets where you can choose bidet water temperatures, seat-heat settings, air dryers, and your favorite accompanying music.

We are creatures of habit, and sometimes these differences can be . . . unhelpful to the process. So, bring supplies to make it more comfortable, like toilet paper, soap, and hand sanitizer. Some families are committed to reducing their environmental impact and travel with a washable bandanna.

Expect the unexpected. Everything is an adventure. The only universal imperative is to wash your hands.

Seeking Medical Care on the Road

Okay, so you've prepared, and then prepared some more. You've packed a first aid kit, brought along medications, and done your best to avoid hazards along the way. And yet—something happens anyway, and you need to find medical care on the road. Maybe urgently. How do you find it when you're far from home?

- First, keep basic medical information for each family member in your daypack so you'll have what you need if you must take a trip to the emergency room or village doctor. Include a summary of each person's medical history, such as a list of ailments, allergies, and current medications.

- If relevant, wear a medical-alert bracelet or pendant for specific conditions.

- You might even want to get a letter from your doctor detailing your family member's medical requirements, in case this information is necessary for treatment. If bringing paper copies isn't convenient, take photos of the documents with your phone.

- Carry a list of your family physicians and their contact information, in case you need to reach them for guidance. When one traveling friend got sick in South Africa, the first thing she did was call her doctor's office back home to get medical advice. Her situation was an emergency, and she was glad to have the contact information readily available in her phone.

Domestic travelers can usually use traditional means for finding a doctor on the road. If you are traveling overseas and one of your family members needs medical care, you can do the following:

- Reach out to your health insurance company for assistance. Many insurance providers have an emergency phone number you can call for advice and referrals to local caregivers. This also helps start the coverage process when you are seeking care outside your home country, especially for services that require preauthorization.

- Contact the local embassy for a list of international physicians. Be sure to specify if you need English-speaking providers or translation services.

- Ask a local, especially if your need is urgent and you don't have time for a phone call. Rely on your rental host, hotel staff, local restaurant employees, or tour providers, who are accustomed to helping travelers.

- Research or inquire on expat websites. Rely on local English speakers who are in the know.

- Sites like USEmbassy.gov and other apps can help connect you to physicians and hospitals in your area, translate drug names, and provide a list of local emergency contact numbers by country.

- Splurge on a nice hotel if someone is sick. Sometimes concierge services cover medical help and might even arrange for a house call by a doctor.

- We really hope it doesn't come to this, but if anyone needs an IV or a shot, you might offer a crisp $20 to the health care worker and ask that a new needle be opened in front of you. That's why you keep some cash handy.

Weminuche Wilderness, Durango, Colorado

Charlie, my hubby, stays back with Max, our dog, while Johnny and I go on a multiday wilderness excursion with our good friends Kaitilin, David, and their kids, West and Zoe. With full backpacks and scuffed hiking boots, our crew disembarks from the Narrow Gauge tourist train in Elk Park, a grassy subalpine meadow along the Colorado Trail. The gray smoke clears, and evidence of the steam engine disappears down the Animas River gorge. It is quiet and the air is fresh; I feel my ribs expand with an exaggerated inhale and audible exhale.

We drink a bunch of water and share crunchy peanut butter Clif Bars, pose for a selfie at the Weminuche Wilderness sign, and then hike three miles in and twelve hundred feet up to the base of Vestal Peak. We camp in a ponderosa pine forest that smells like vanilla and offers shelter from the afternoon monsoons. A mama moose stares at us from across the emerald-green beaver pond.

On the third day of our adventure, Kaitilin and I wake up early to go for a short run. It is freezing at 6:30 a.m., and instead of walking to warm up, we start running from the get-go. Fifty feet into the single-track trail, I stumble on a jagged ledge and fall hard, instantly feeling the sting of bone on rock.

Kaitilin helps me back to camp. She and David wrap me in their sleeping bags and wake the kids. They eat maple-brown-sugar oatmeal and huddle with David while Kaitilin makes a sling out of a bandanna and holds my pasty hand. Johnny, West, and Zoe (all under ten) are like little chipmunks, scurrying about and whispering to each other as they stuff sleeping bags back into their sacks, roll up the tent flies, collapse the poles, and count each stake they pull from the ground. They redistribute my gear to everyone else and hand me an empty pack, along with a mug of hot chocolate with extra mini marshmallows. They tell me it's going to be okay. I tell them the same.

We hike back down to Elk Park, board the train, and freak out the other passengers with my bloodied pants and splinted arm. In Silverton, at the end of the line, we meet up with Charlie, who transports me immediately to the Durango hospital. I have emergency surgery for a compound fracture of the right elbow and get a bunch of stitches in my hip. Johnny has since declared he wants to study emergency medicine and be a mountain guide. West and Zoe still love the wilderness.

▶ Without cell service in the Grenadier Range.

Personal Safety

It's common to feel more vulnerable on the road than at home. After all, you're in unfamiliar surroundings and can't rely on your normal routines. You'll be going to new places, interacting with new people, and doing new things—sometimes dangerous things—and it's easy to imagine potential risks and pitfalls. Annika describes this as "having my hackles up."

But for many travelers, that's exactly the point of being *out in it*. There's a delicate balance between being careful and remaining open to experiences, and there are ways to plan ahead so that you can enjoy being in the moment. Also, kids will pick up your cues; be aware of what you transmit, and encourage open dialogue.

STAYING FOUND

Kids like to wander and explore, and as worldschoolers we want to give them space and freedom when we can. To help keep track of their whereabouts, here are some tips:

- Know where you're going and help your kids get familiar with your destinations before you arrive.

- Teach them to freeze when they are lost or hear your voice from afar.

- Make sure everyone knows their identifying information—their full name, plus your name and cell phone number. If a kid can't relay this information, write it on their arm, have them wear an ID bracelet, or put a card in their pocket.

- Role-play asking for assistance.

- Have a contingency plan in case the family gets separated— choose a meeting spot and make sure your kids know who to approach for assistance.

- If your kids have cell phones, add key contacts to their phones and enable location tracking; show them how to turn on cellular coverage and make that expensive call if you get separated.

NATURE AND ANIMALS

Many kids like to pet animals. Unfortunately, any animal can be dangerous. In the US, it's common to see posted rules, signs, and physical boundaries that control for most of the risk, but that's not true everywhere. Teach your kids never to approach or feed wild animals, even if the animal approaches them and seems friendly, and talk together about safe distances. Help kids understand that the best thing they can do for wildlife is to stay away from them and not contribute to their harmful taming. If anyone in your family does experience a bite, scratch, or other animal-related injury, seek medical attention.

ANNIKA'S REFLECTION

Whistles to the Rescue

When I was a Peace Corps Volunteer, our country director gave us each a cheap toy whistle on a loop of thin climbing cord when we graduated from training and were about to head out to our sites. Before we left the graduation ceremony, she asked us to affix the whistle to our regular bag in some way, and she waited while we did so. I thought it was ridiculous, but I did it anyway. That fifty-cent whistle was only used once, but it was the most important "once" of my life. Whistles cross language barriers, attract attention, and deter potential malcontents; they also aren't dangerous, and children can use them easily. Consider putting one around each of your kids' necks.

NATURAL DISASTERS

Travelers should research a destination's risk for natural disasters before visiting. Travel alerts and disaster threat information can be found on the US Department of State website listed in the resources section. Events such as tornadoes, earthquakes, floods, and tsunamis can injure large numbers of people, disrupt local services, and catalyze the spread of disease, and it's wise to avoid areas during high-risk seasons. If you are in an area of risk, learn the local warning systems, evacuation routes, and gathering locations. Carry important identification and travel documents and a list of emergency contacts, and talk through your response plan as a family. If disaster does strike, pay attention to what the locals are doing and follow their lead.

POLITICAL UNREST

As with natural disasters, it's important to research current events and be informed about the likelihood of political unrest in your destinations prior to travel. Understanding the history, culture, and politics of your intended destinations is a helpful start, and you can gain additional perspective from the US State Department country reports and Amnesty International's annual report on human rights.[33]

Avoid known conflict zones whenever possible. Have a family response plan in place ahead of time, and if you do encounter protests once you are on the ground, leave the area immediately and seek safe shelter. Regardless of how you feel about the demonstration's aim, don't participate—as a visitor you may not fully understand its reasons or risks, and even attempting to photograph or record the events may be illegal or inflammatory to the participants. Confirm exit plans and identify transportation contingencies in case your first option gets shut down. To keep abreast of status changes, follow trusted news sources and your local embassy online.

Consider Your Embassy as a Resource

If you have a true emergency or serious safety concern, your embassy should get involved—quickly. That's its job.

The main purpose of an embassy is to assist its citizens who live in or are traveling in the host country. The embassy staff can usually assist you if you've been the victim of a crime or are seriously ill or injured, although the level of service varies by country. It's important to know that if you travel to a high-risk area, you may not have embassy coverage, so it's a good idea to research this in advance.

Always carry the contact information for the local embassy with you, and don't hesitate to call upon its services if you need it. In fact, many embassies prefer that you register with them upon arrival so they know where you're planning to go and can be on the lookout for any potential problems. Some request that you enroll in the Smart Traveler Enrollment Program (STEP) to receive alerts and make it easier to locate you in an emergency.

Final Thoughts

Another way to prepare yourself mentally and physically is by running through worst-case scenarios, maybe with your partner or family, and creating corresponding contingency plans. In his book *The Last Lecture*, based on his famous presentation, "Really Achieving Your Childhood Dreams," Randy Pausch calls this the "eaten by wolves factor."[34] You can run scenarios ranging from a missing passport to a lost kid. You can also think through what you'd do in various types of medical emergencies, which came in handy when Angela got altitude sickness in the middle of Lake Titicaca. (By the way, her kids love to tell that story, mostly because it gives them a chance to say Lake Titicaca repeatedly.)

CHAPTER 7

Worldschool Education

Education is the kindling of a flame, not the filling of a vessel.

—Socrates

I N CASE YOU WERE WONDERING . . . Yes, you absolutely *can* educate your kids on the road. This chapter will provide you with guidelines and gridlines, ideas, and inspiration. And if you're reading this from the road, we hope this chapter reminds you just how much experiential learning is already happening effortlessly.

As noted in chapter 3, you have the right to educate your children outside of traditional schooling. We've already shared the process for pulling them out of school, and now we want to whet your appetite with all the ways that you can *put them into the world*. This chapter provides a menu of options that will help meet your child's educational needs during a Wonder Year.

Here we open up the idea of education itself, asking you to consider your larger goals for your family. We walk you through available curricula, including DIY options, and introduce you to the worldschool community at large. Finally, we show you how to bring home what you have learned.

We've spoken with many parents at all stages of worldschooling, and strong sentiments emerge. Before parents leave, they often feel pressure to have their whole worldschooling plan figured out. While on the road, they worry that they're not teaching enough or that their kids haven't mastered the academic milestones. Good news, though: you already have the three most important ingredients for educating your kids: 1) you love and want the best for them; 2) with every question you ask and excursion you take, you model curiosity; and 3) having chosen to travel as a family, you recognize that the world is a very good teacher. Even more good news: most parents return home proud of all the growth they see in their children.

There are as many paths *to* worldschool as there are paths *in* the world. Some parents want more structure, academic focus, and alignment with traditional school standards, whereas others prefer spontaneity and freedom. Our suggestions are guideposts for you to create your own approach, knowing that the alchemy comes from diving in and interacting with each other, with learning, and with the world. Be prepared to pivot as you, your children, and your map will likely evolve.

Identifying the Terms

Here are some common terms you will encounter in this book and in online conversations about educating outside of traditional schools. Because this is an evolving space and the definitions are not written in stone, note that these terms are sometimes used interchangeably and are not mutually exclusive. It's important to note that this is a dynamic—fluid, even—landscape that continues to evolve.

Homeschooling: learning at home rather than at a public or private institution

Worldschooling: learning through direct interaction with the world

Roadschooling: a form of worldschooling that most often refers to domestic travel

Nature schooling: using the natural world as the primary classroom; sometimes called forest schooling

Gameschooling: a form of homeschooling that teaches concepts and skills through games like chess, cards, board games, and manipulative toys like Rubik's Cubes

Unschooling: using students' curiosities and interests instead of prescribed curricula to drive self-paced learning (more on this on the next page)

Hybrid schooling: Anything goes! You can blend any of the above.

Unschooling: Don't Let the Name Fool You

This is an increasingly popular form of education, and we want to delve a little deeper into it because many worldschoolers find themselves leaning heavily into unschooling. The word may sound extreme, but it does not necessarily mean *no* schooling. It's called *un*schooling because, as a form of learning, it does not try to mimic traditional classrooms with schedules and standards-based learning but instead lets kids follow their interests with great fluidity. Popularized by American educator John Holt in the 1970s, the premise of unschooling is that we learn better when we aren't forced to do so.[35] Unschoolers believe that *learning* is not the same as *schooling*. Proponents believe that the unschooling parent's job is to maximize their child's experiences in the world and to find the learning that is already happening, hear the questions of their blossoming youngster, and nurture that inquisitiveness. The parent becomes the collaborator, the guide, the witness, and the recorder. Families carve out time and space, and they expand the surface area between them and the world by exposing their kids to all kinds of people, places, and experiences. That way, the world becomes more readily accessible, and adventures become teachable moments.

Unschooling can be entirely open, or it can take on some structure. An unschooled Wonder Year might include monthly or weekly learning contracts (agreements between parent and student about program of study, dates, and assignments), interest projects, writing portfolios, fieldwork, direct instruction if desired, and other ideas listed at the end of this chapter.

Unschooling starts with the premise that we are all lifelong learners, and *schooling* is just one resource that aids education.

Real-Life Worldschooling Plan: Julie

I have always loved math and was not too concerned about helping Johnny with mathematical functions, word problems, and practical applications. We purchased the math books that fourth graders use in our school district and tried to work through them over the year. Learning the multiplication tables was important, and Johnny also practiced addition and subtraction in an applied way, pretty much daily as the keeper of the gas and mileage log while we were on the road. It became a practice to mark the starting and finishing mileage whenever we were on the go. We could calculate weekly or monthly totals and averages. We could check to see how our fuel efficiency changed at different speeds and elevations. Math went great, and eventually I got rid of the math books and focused more on real-life applications.

We also read a lot. Picking out books was a fun chance to dive into local stories, history, and characters. The hands-down family favorite was *The Captain's Dog: My Journey with the Lewis and Clark Tribe,* in which Meriwether Lewis's dog, Seaman, tells the story of the adventurous search for the Northwest Passage. Reading along while we were tracing Lewis and Clark's journey, with our own dog, was perfect.

Everyone also kept a journal. We bought Johnny a gorgeous journal before the trip, and while we did not enforce a daily entry, he wrote with fervor and heart, and to this day, he keeps his journal by his bedside to revisit.

An excerpt (reprinted with permission):

Johnny, age eight:

Right now I am in the top bunk of a cabon, wich is one of the four on [Hesketh] Island. I can see a rose boosh and in the background the ocean. I can hear the faint sound of the waves crashing. I am inside but allthoe I have been outside [all] of the day, I can almost smell the spray of the salt water. It is just backing off from high tide. Yesterday I cought my first two fish ...

And other than math, reading, and writing, we improvised, following Johnny's curiosity. We made a ritual out of the US National Park Service Junior Ranger program (many state parks have similar programs), an excellent, place-based resource that is focused on the local topography, ecology, geology, and culture. Completion of the work at each park earns a badge; Johnny collected twenty-eight Junior Ranger badges over the course of our year.

With our interest in sustainability and love of skiing, we created a module on the environmental impacts of ski areas and set up meetings with operators, managers, and environmental

staff from different organizations, including ski areas, ski manufacturers, local government, and environmental groups. We dug avalanche pits, studied snow layers, hung out with avalanche dogs, and learned about snowmaking operations and the new technology to minimize water use and maximize use of snow fencing. And we did a lot of "mountain fieldwork."

A typical day:

Johnny makes the family breakfast: scrambled eggs with spinach on corn tortillas with shredded cheese and salsa. We take a three-hour hike through an old-growth forest, learning to identify coastal hardwood varieties, fungi, and ferns. Stop for an hour diversion to test our balance on fallen trees, walking backward and forward, sideways, and on one leg. Hop, hope, listen. Get back to the rig. Study the analog map; decide to stay another day because it's so gorgeous and we have nowhere else we have to be. Johnny builds an elaborate rock sculpture/ rock-climber course for his RC vehicle. Julie makes bebe soup—veggie broth with kale and capellini, lemon zest, and Parmesan. We eat outside. We write a blog post, then read aloud. Johnny and Charlie go on a night photography stroll. Julie and Max (the dog) read some more and snuggle.

Creating Your Education Road Map

Some families know at the outset what their approach will be. Others have no idea!

We'll walk you through the following suggestions to help create an education road map. We begin with some logistical considerations that may help you narrow your planning. We ask you to think about your vision and values around education. Then we drill down into goals and objectives and look at options for how you "do" education. And finally, we show you how to delegate the teaching: a world of faculty awaits.

STEP 1: CONSIDER LOGISTICS

Every family has a unique situation with regard to their school district, their children's educational history, and other practical needs. All of these considerations should be looked at when tackling the educational logistics of a Wonder Year. It's best to address any specific requirements or constraints up front so you can leave and come back without disrupting or complicating enrollment status, academic credit, or advancement. Considering the following parameters can help illuminate options so you can build a workable game plan.

Enrollment Parameters

If your kids are in public school, you may simply need to register each of them as a homeschool student for the time period they are away. The forms don't include worldschooling as an option. Yet. So, in most cases, worldschooling families are homeschoolers in the eyes of your US public school district.

Be aware of the following:

- Homeschool laws vary by state. Check your state's department of education website.

- If worldschooling families follow the procedural and performance requirements, the vast majority of students can advance a grade (or grades) upon return. Another option is to pause grade advancement while you are away. There is no right or wrong approach.

- Your district might have requirements already spelled out on its website, or it may write an individual contract with you that includes quantifiable benchmarks. For example, your district might say that your child needs to pass a math exam or produce a writing sample. Your school might also ask you to keep a log of instructional hours or sign a document certifying that you will homeschool for a prescribed number of hours per day or week.

- School districts can be bureaucratic, and this process can be daunting! Remember, school administrators are guided by funding, ratings, and child protection, and that exceptions—which may seem perfectly reasonable to us—can feel disruptive to them. On the flip side, their suggestions and enthusiasm may give you some great ideas for your homemade educational adventures.

- Your school district may have an online learning option. You can also reach out to the principal or a teacher at the school to get their input, cooperation, and support.

For families with children outside a public school system:

- If you are already homeschooling your kids, you may need to research the implications of an address change or shift in curriculum.

- If you have a rising kindergartener or a student entering a new school upon return, you may need to think about when you want them to start and if you can register from the road.

- If your kids are enrolled in a private school, ask the school how to work within the law. In some cases, you don't need to do anything official with the state to homeschool.

- If you're relocating upon return from your Wonder Year and you do not know where your family will reside, you can conduct research from the road. Perhaps you can explore new possible hometowns and learn what might be expected.

- We highly suggest networking with other homeschooling families as you are going through this process (see the resources section for websites).

Practical Considerations

There are a host of other factors that can inform how you approach worldschooling. For example, you'll need to be realistic about how much access you will have to digital resources, Wi-Fi, and technology. Be sure to investigate the speed and capacity of Wi-Fi connectivity. Knowing what you will need for everyone's work and school, as well as what's realistically and reliably available at your accommodations, is essential. If getting off the beaten path and unplugged is your goal, then online education may not be the most suitable option for you, and we offer plenty of other approaches in this chapter. You might also consider your desire for English-speaking libraries and local tutors. Physical space is also a factor for some families. How much can you carry, and where will you store school materials as you travel? There may be dates or milestones that influence your academic approach, such as ACT or SAT dates, entrance exams, or placement tests. Keep these practical considerations in mind so you don't invest in options that are impractical for you and your family.

Finally, if you are working from the road, that can have a great influence on how you roll out your worldschooling plan. You'll need to think about leveraging the working hours, the Wi-Fi bandwidth, the desk space, and the locations where you may stay a while. A more free-standing curriculum plan, with accessible online tutors, may be more your style. As we noted earlier, the flip side is that work time for parents can naturally be schooltime for kids. Even if you fall into this camp, there's something for you in all these steps.

STEP 2: EXAMINE YOUR VISION AND VALUES

There are so many educational opportunities beyond what's listed in your state's learning standards. Is it important to learn long division? Absolutely! But the experience of visiting with a Native American elder or tasting fresh mangosteen at the Chiang Mai night market just might be the catalyst to ignite a passion for learning itself. Does your child intend to go to college? If so, this will shape their worldschooling curriculum, and they may have to navigate the application process differently. But worldschooling kids do it all the time, even if they've been on the road for most, or all, of their high school years. So, before diving into the nitty-gritty, let's consider your family's education vision and values, knowing they may look different before, during, and after your Wonder Year. This is big-picture thinking; we'll get to specifics as we move through the process.

Spend some time thinking or writing about these defining questions:

- What do you wish you did more of as a kid?
- What were the most powerful lessons you learned as a child?
- What do you want your child to know about the world?
- What do you think will matter most to their educational future?
- Is it important for you to have a plan, or do you like to be spontaneous?
- What do you wish you could learn about if you had more time?

Keep these inspiring values close to your heart as you begin to braid goals and objectives into your vision.

STEP 3: IDENTIFY YOUR GOALS AND OBJECTIVES

Goals can serve as the philosophical underpinnings of what you will do day to day—the principles that arc across the specific content that you'll teach and learn. On those days when you ask yourself why you're doing what you're doing, goals can be helpful as a compass heading.

Invite your kids to partner with you in making your family's list. Here's an example list to get you started.

We will:

- Make our own opinions about the world. Is it kind, beautiful, and safe?
- Interact with people who do not share our language, and discover our similarities and differences.
- Learn how to respond when we are outside our comfort zones.
- Pay attention to how the world views our own country, and begin to recognize our cultural biases.
- Become fluent in "I notice, I observe, I wonder . . ."
- Develop a deep understanding of the world.
- Make connections across subject areas.
- Think critically and creatively.
- Communicate and collaborate with others.
- Learn to analyze data, test assumptions, and draw conclusions.
- Develop street smarts.
- Explore future career paths.

Add more, subtract some, make it your own.

Let's take goals one step further and articulate education objectives. Objectives are the direct, tangible, specific activities that are born from your goals. They are often measurable achievements that your child can meet during your Wonder Year. Many school districts would love to see this level of specificity after you return.

Here's an example of an objectives list:

My learner will:

- Trace the alphabet in the sand.
- Follow fourth-grade math curriculum and complete fourth-grade Khan Academy.
- Research one curiosity every month, and teach others about it.
- Meet with an online tutor each Monday, and create a weekly study plan.
- Read for one hour each night with a parent or sibling, and make a list of books completed.
- Learn about foods, trees, and animals that are endemic to a region they'll be visiting.
- Make a travel brochure with good old glue and scissors. Or create a digital slideshow for each state, country, or national park visited.
- Write a paragraph using a topic sentence, three supporting ideas, and a conclusion about something meaningful.
- Write a compare-and-contrast essay about breakfast in Mexico and the United States.
- Complete four practice SAT tests.
- Know how to check tire pressure and oil levels, fill auto fluids, and understand each gauge on the dashboard for your vehicle.
- Meet someone new each day.

STEP 4: DETERMINE YOUR APPROACH

You might be saying to yourself: *Yes, yes. Alchemy, kindling of flames, and blossoming children, that's all well and good, but what do I actually* do? *How do these abstractions translate into what happens when I sit down with my kids, they're looking at me expectantly, and I need to be their teacher?*

For many worldschooling parents, this is the most overwhelming *and* the most fascinating pillar of their Wonder Year. Consider this discussion a menu of options to help design your worldschooling approach. Some families know from the outset that they want to purchase a full-year curriculum already prepared for a third or eighth grader. Or they are just looking for a math or writing supplement. Others build off of what their child would have been studying at home had a Wonder Year not been happening. Still others follow a theme, or globe-trot to locations where they have family members or friends. We will explore a rich collection of options for you to "try on" and see what fits—school based or not school based, structured or unstructured, print or online, prepackaged or do-it-yourself.

Packaged Curricula

Prior to 2020, there were several big-name education companies and organizations in the online curriculum business—Khan Academy, IXL, Outschool, Charlotte Mason, and Oak Meadow, to name a few. The COVID pandemic contributed to a huge transformation in this space as more educators and businesspeople tapped into the demand for online and prepackaged homeschool offerings.

Some public school districts offer remote options with free online curricula so that you can do self-paced public education from afar, while online private schools are popping up virtually everywhere.

Popular online sources directed specifically at worldschoolers include Outschool, Kubrio, Brave Writer, and many others. For learners on the younger end of the spectrum, Art for Kids Hub or MUZZY language programs are some examples of resources available through online platforms like YouTube.

For older students looking for college credit, consider "CLEPping." The CLEP test, administered by the College Board (a nonprofit organization that creates standardized testing and is best known for the SAT), costs roughly US$100 per test.[36] With over thirty tests available, this can be an economical leg up on a college degree or an inexpensive way to learn at the college level from the road. Modern States offers free online courses that help students prepare. The College Board sells study guides for US$10 each. Another great resource for older learners is a membership learning hub for creatives called Skillshare.

Deciding on a curriculum package or à la carte options, apps, resources, and content can get exciting and messy all at once. Our assessment is that the quality varies with off-the-shelf resources. You can find resource hubs that rate curricula, such as Common Sense Media's reviews and professional opinions on hundreds of options.

As you explore options, be sure you consider the fit with your learner(s). Maybe your Wonder Year is a time to try out something new, or maybe it's the time to go with what you know will work for your children. To help narrow the field, here are some additional factors and questions to consider in selecting an off-the-shelf curriculum that is right for your learner:

- Are there specific topics that your child requires?

- Do you want to limit screen time?

- Do you need to get your own work done? How much of your involvement is ideal?

- Do you want to be wedded to being on Wi-Fi at a specific time each day or each week?

- What's your budget? Remember, there are tons of free options out there like Khan Academy, Oak Academy, or educational videos on YouTube.

- Is there a trial period before you need to purchase?

- Does your child do better with independent or more social learning? Some programs offer synchronous learning pods. This provides group planning, goal setting, discussion, and social interaction.

- As mentioned earlier, do you have room to carry and store books?

Many families like the predictability, structure, and modularity of preset resources. You can make it work in so many ways. For instance, your child might be in second-grade math and first-grade spelling. Or you might use a print workbook for cursive and an online class for coding.

When using a packaged curriculum as the fulcrum of your approach, you can think of worldschooling as a set of massively cool field trips.

Theme-Based Curricula

There are many families who see a Wonder Year as a time to untether from academic prescriptions and structure and feel freedom in designing their own curriculum. If this do-it-yourself model is for you, consider these themes as brushstrokes on your blank canvas.

Subject-Driven Some families "take a page" out of what would have been their kid's school syllabus for the semester or year they are gone and turn it into the experiential equivalent. Traditional subjects can come alive in the world. Here are some ideas to consider:

- If your child would have been studying the ancient Mayans, you could check out the ruins and visit museums in the Yucatán.

- If your first grader would have been studying biodiversity, you could get down and dirty with living things in the Olympic Peninsula tide pools.

- Geometry in the cards for your eighth grader? How about some time on a sailboat or comparing arc length to arc measure at Arches National Park in Southern Utah?

- If your student's classmates back home are all learning about US government and politics, you could easily spend a month or two in and around Washington, DC, and not only read, study, and discuss government, but also see it in action: meet with your representative, go to the National Archives, see what groups are rallying in Lafayette Square, or do research at the Library of Congress.

To get subject-specific ideas, you can review your school district's website for curriculum details by grade. For a snapshot of expectations, you can pull up grade-level report cards to see what your child would be expected to learn during a year. You can also browse state standards by subject area or dive into the Common Core Standards, a set of national guidelines meant to provide consistency and maintain high benchmarks for all children living in the US.

Itinerary-Driven The places you visit or want to visit drive the discovery and provide the material for your educational journey. Maybe you've found an uber-cheap flight to Miami or you're incorporating a professional conference overseas. If you know that you will go to Argentina, for example, think about topics that naturally sprout from visiting South America. Is it the rainforest? Impact of colonialism? Tango? Catholic iconography?

Here's a list of what other families have done:

- The Langenegger family relocated to Guam for Chris, the dad, to do a four-year stint with United Airlines. Elissa, the mom, decided to worldschool instead of enrolling their fifth-grade son in a local school. They leveraged their family-of-a-pilot perks to worldschool across the South Pacific, with a deep study of local culture and history, sailing, navigation, and the effects of climate change.

- The Horton family studied the Renaissance while in Europe, using the lenses of geography, history, literature, and art. When they traveled to extreme latitudes like Iceland and Argentina, they wove together questions of global warming and receding glaciers.

- The Blew family was consciously working through the parents' destination bucket list. Their son was fascinated by art and architecture, so they seamlessly wove in an organic lesson plan wherever they went.

- While Jake's family was settled in Spain for his work leading banjo workshops, his daughter, Zinnia, became fascinated by the sea creatures that washed up on shore or found their way to the seafood markets. This spurred her research report on jellyfish, squid, and octopi.

Parents as Students

Remember that you are a learner, too. You've planned and saved for this opportunity; make the most of it. Maybe there's something that you want to practice or perfect over the year—a language, skill, hobby, or mindset. You can challenge yourself with the added benefit of modeling lifetime learning for your kids. Maybe that means trying any of the following:

▶ Read both a nonfiction and fiction book based in each city or country you visit. Think Anthony Doerr's *Four Seasons in Rome* and Shakespeare's *Julius Caesar* for Rome, Italy.

▶ Write travel articles and publish them on blogs or in print, as well as learn the tools needed to follow through.

▶ Learn to play a new instrument, like the harmonica (think travel size).

▶ Commit to journaling every day.

▶ Start a new travel-friendly hobby, like running, photography, yoga, or knitting.

▶ Take an online class side by side with your kid, such as calculus with your teen or French with your preschooler.

▶ Learn as much as you can about learning. Read books and online articles, or simply observe your kids and see what works.

ANGELA'S NOTES FROM THE ROAD

Bayeux, France

It is an early and unusually quiet start as we carefully navigate the narrow streets out of Bayeux, France. The village is our base camp for several days of exploration in the Normandy region and an opportunity to learn about its historical significance—from its founding as a Gallo-Roman city in the first century BCE to the rise of William the Conqueror to its liberation from the Nazis in World War II.

As Mark accelerates the sleek black Citroën station wagon across rolling pastures and past ancient stone barns, Ronan leans toward the front seat and, presumably out of concern that his brother is asleep, whispers a question.

"Why were there so many American flags hanging in the town?"

I hadn't noticed, but he is right. Bayeux is festooned with various national flags integrated with the cityscape—painted on the windows of restaurants and bakeries, strung along wires between buildings. The Tricolore, the Union Jack, the Maple Leaf—and the Stars and Stripes. I don't want to answer immediately a question I hadn't even thought to ask myself.

"Might have had something to do with the war, yes?"

He doesn't respond, and I don't press.

I see his gaze return to the landscape, still lush with late-summer green. This part of France reveals no horrors or tragedies upon its impassive fields and gardens but rather does only what it has done for hundreds of years—it feeds its people.

We visit Arromanches-les-Bains, a critical support position for securing and holding the deepwater ports of Le Havre and Cherbourg. We walk the German artillery battery at Longues-sur-Mer, the boundary between the Omaha (US) and Gold (UK) beaches, where the four 152 mm gun placements, in various states of destruction, now serve only as minor impediments to a local farmer. Ronan and Asher stand at the ridge of Pointe du Hoc, a position that reduced a US commando force of 225 to 90, and wonder aloud how that many soldiers could have climbed its steep bluff.

We finish at the Normandy American Cemetery and Memorial in Colleville-sur-Mer. In the museum, the deeply personal stories of those who lost everything during the assault prompt the boys to imagine their great-grandfathers fighting in this war and leaving their families behind.

196

Nine decades later, a peaceful day.

On the rise overlooking Omaha Beach, there are more than nine thousand remains permanently interred beneath white stone crosses and Stars of David. Our voices soften as we walk the grounds of this holy place, where young men so faithfully committed themselves to empathy, liberty, and sacrifice.

The ride back to Bayeux is silent amid the darkening sky. As we enter the central historic district on the way to our hotel, we drive past a café with a large American flag painted on the plate-glass front, and I turn around to look at Ronan in the back seat. As our eyes meet, I realize he has answered his own question.

Curiosity-Driven Passion and curiosity bring learning to life. You might have a daughter who loves architecture or a son who loves monkeys. How might you build this into your plan? What are *you* curious about?

Consider a yearlong inquiry of passion for your family that encompasses the places you go. For example, your primate-loving son might research monkey business in various countries by visiting native habitats, sanctuaries, and reading fiction and nonfiction books. This gives you a set of questions and observations to thread through the year across locations, cultures, and languages. Here are other examples to inspire you:

- The Simon family chose to research and visit the places where their ancestors were born. They traced family roots in Hungary and tried to understand the reasons for emigrating. This inquiry helped with both education and creating a Budapest itinerary that included the Jewish Quarter, the Dohány Street Synagogue, the Holocaust Memorial Center, and the Shoes on the Danube Promenade.

- Annika's family paid attention to plastics. How ubiquitous were plastic containers and bags? Were they recycled? Was there plastic waste in streams, on beaches? Was the recycling symbol the same in China as it was in Costa Rica? They even searched out the local dumps.

- Margot wanted to study fashion design, so her family used fashion as the basis for her educational approach and designed a curriculum that looked at international styles, textile supply chains, slow fashion, thrifting, silk in China, and lace in Croatia.

- Johnny, Julie's son, conducted a research project comparing American ice cream and Italian gelato. This, of course, required lots of fieldwork, tasting gelato in every town he visited in Italy, sometimes twice a day. He took a tour to see how gelato is made and learned about the importance of temperature, choosing ingredients, the science of flavors, and why some people like crunchiness and others prefer smooth. After the five-week study tour, he practiced making graphs and bar charts and illustrated a final project. His fieldwork has continued to this day!

- Conor loved playing viola. His family went to Mozart's birthplace in Salzburg and the Puccini Festival in Lucca for an immersive experience in music history, classical composition, and operatic performance.

- Julie and Charlie shared expertise in water and sustainability, Charlie as a hydrogeologist and Julie as a sustainability analyst. They used water as a continual theme in their roadschool curriculum. They kayaked. They took pictures of rivers, which they also located on maps, and learned about watersheds, headwaters, tributaries, confluences, dams, diversions, pump houses, and water rights. At every river crossing, they'd estimate cubic feet per second, a common measure of flow, and then check their estimates on the USGS Water Data website. A quick stop by a river could turn into a three-hour "lesson" with amazing people to meet—fly-fishers, river heroes, waterkeepers, and others.

You can help your children wrap their theme-based inquiries into a final project, such as a journal entry, a publication, or a portfolio to share with their school at the end of the year. Alternatively, you could just enjoy the conversation as it unfolds and not worry about a final project at all.

Bend, Oregon

I guess Johnny looks pretty approachable in his orange board shorts, dripping with river water, as he rinses off at the outdoor shower, when up rides a friendly guy on a bike.

Jakob the bike-riding baker: "What's up? Where are you heading?"

Johnny: "We're traveling for the year and just did some paddling on the Deschutes River."

Jakob: "Cool, how do you like Bend?"

Johnny: "It's awesome!"

Jakob: "Have you been to the Sparrow Bakery?"

Johnny: "Yeah, we love that place."

Jakob: "Well, I am Jakob, a baker at the Sparrow."

Julie: "That's so cool. Do you think we could come visit you at the bakery?"

Jakob: "Sure, I'll be there tomorrow. Just come to the back door at 4:00 a.m. What's your dog's name? He's beautiful."

Johnny: "That's my brother, Max."

Later that night we move our rig and camp in the parking lot of the Sparrow Bakery. The next morning, at 4:00 a.m., Jakob the baker greets us at the back door with a smile. Wearing a white apron, he moves fluidly around the kitchen, mixing flour and spritzing dough. We watch and learn. Jakob pauses to enlighten us about the importance of yeast and mold, as an artisanal, pungent smell seeps into our clothes. A couple hours later, I tear off the heel of a *pain rustique* and dunk it in olive oil. Charlie eats an almond croissant, and Johnny chows down two of the Sparrow's "most enjoyed pastry," an ocean roll—a croissant with cardamom vanilla sugar baked inside. Then we all go back to bed.

The Organic Day-to-Day: A Syllabus of Serendipity We want to point out that life itself can drive the curriculum. If you want to wing it completely, this is your chance. You can string together one adventure to the next—rolling, shaping, mixing, building, and ready for whatever good luck comes your way. Without a heavy backpack of books or the weight of a schedule, you may feel more nimble and spontaneous. You are prepared to say yes to opportunities as they arise. And with nowhere else to be, the timing may be right for any adventure. So, accept an invitation, stay an extra week, wander over the hillside, or return to somewhere you loved.

You might stay up late for a full-moon hike because you can sleep in the next day. Perhaps you spend an entire morning and afternoon building a sandcastle. Or skip your stop because you're having an amazing conversation with someone you've met on the bus. You can truly listen because, today, their stories won't make you late. Let freedom and serendipity illuminate the learning moments of every day.

STEP 5: GATHER YOUR TEACHERS

In a traditional classroom setting, a teacher does the teaching. When we travel, parents, siblings, locals, our senses, time, space, rivers, maps, and coins can be our teachers. For us, the magic occurred when it all came together into one big, yummy stew.

Parents as Teachers

At home, parents often don't have enough time and context for rich discussions with their children about what the kids are learning at school. As a worldschooling family, by virtue of being together in a variety of settings, you can leap right into fluid discussions with real-world learning, leveraging your lifetime of experience and sharing that valuable perspective with your children.

Be creative and share your interests with your kids. Mark, Angela's husband, loves baseball, so he took their family to a game in Tokyo. Stacy, another worldschooling parent, brought her kids to a local tortilla bakery in Hatch, New Mexico, to share her love of cooking. Or consider your profession or hobby as a gateway. Are you a photographer, scientist, writer, geographer, or musician? You might use your professional network to set up a site visit, meet with a colleague or connect with someone in your field, and bring your kids. When you run out of your own ideas, look out the window for other teachers.

Remote Teachers and Tutors

If you will have access to the web, there's a world of online tutors at your fingertips. You might choose to use someone you know from home or connect with someone new. More and more curriculum packages, such as Outschool or Oak Meadow, now offer the enhanced options of 1:1 tutors. Angela's family kept up weekly online Latin tutoring across many time zones for an entire year. Relatives back home can be teachers, too. The Fernandes family had book clubs with their grandma—they decided which chapters to read each week and then had book chats via Zoom. Two of Yasmin Page's three children do weekly math lessons with their granddad. What a great way to keep in touch with family back home!

Learning from Locals

We encourage you to make the most of local resources as potential teachers.

For example, you might hire a kidcentric guide for a day at Pompeii, who teaches your family that the ancient inhabitants ate walnuts to cure a headache. Maybe you join a naturalist-led hike along the Hoh River Trail and learn how the fog and mist make amazing things grow and how an epiphyte plant grows on another plant without harming it. Hiring a teacher is an expense, but sometimes it's a great relief not to be in charge. In Europe and other more traditional travel destinations, there are travel companies that cater specifically to families, such as Europe4Kids Tours and Global Family Travels, which offer kid-centered activities like curated scavenger hunts, gladiator training, pizza-making classes, and other personalized experiences.

Because of her daughter's roots in China, Annika's family wanted to connect deeply to the region, so they prioritized time there. They knew that they needed a guide who was fluent in English and could provide nuanced translations in Chinese if they wanted to get off the beaten path. They splurged on a month with an American PhD student who guided them around China. This was a total leap of faith that worked. Annika put up a request on an alumni board and tapped into her personal network. Her family interviewed their guide online and drafted and redrafted sample itineraries by email. It was a magnificent month.

Internships and Apprenticeships

Internships can simply be an exchange of volunteer work with an organization for access to someone with specialized knowledge. For instance, you can do a beach cleanup in Alabama or help with an olive harvest in California. You can also learn informally throughout your travels by finding a local artist, musician, or tradesperson, maybe even paying a small sum to have them teach their art form to you and/or your kids. A guitarist in Nicaragua? A carpenter in Crete? Play or work alongside them. Learning happens by doing, by observing, by questioning.

Teachers Are Everywhere

- ▶ Jakkarin and his family taught Kai to tap a rubber tree in Krabi, Thailand.
- ▶ The guesthouse owner in rural China showed Lucy how to make steamed vegetable dumplings.
- ▶ Ben, a docent at the Equal Justice Initiative in Montgomery, Alabama, told Lorna about the local communities who work with them, and those who—unfortunately—don't.
- ▶ A New Zealand boat captain instructed Asher on how to navigate and sail on the majestic Milford Sound.
- ▶ The ranger at Dinosaur National Monument, in Dinosaur, Colorado, taught Annika's family about geology, archeology, and desert ecology.

You can search online for ideas in local networks, expat groups, on the Folk Education Association of America's website; or look at WWOOFing, hotel, or Airbnb experiences. On the ground, check out libraries, makerspaces, or community centers, or ask your rental host. Volunteer experiences abound as well; multi- and single-day programs can help the local community while you learn experientially. Check the resources section for more information.

Enrolling in Local Schools

You may not know it, but you can enroll your kids for short-term stints in local public schools in the US. If you're overseas, this may also be an option. Sometimes it's as simple as meeting with the school administrator and showing them a copy of your rental agreement. Private schools and alternative educational models like Waldorf, Montessori, and Forest Schools often allow very short stays, especially if your children have prior experience with these models. This can be a meaningful way to connect with the local community.

Real-Life Worldschooling Plan: Angela

When it came to worldschooling, I overplanned and overpacked.

When our family decided to embark upon a Wonder Year, my number one concern was how we would educate our rising fourth- and seventh-grade kids. They had been cruising along in public school, and we were attentive parents to their progress, but we certainly weren't *in charge* of it. And now we would be, completely. We were also relocating after our travels, so we wouldn't have the opportunity to work with their current schools to create a plan together. We were on our own.

As someone with no teaching experience who had left the education of my children wholly to those public schools, I was starting at ground zero. And as is my way when I don't know much, I dove into researching, planning, and organizing—learning about homeschooling methods and gathering curriculum options, books, websites, and tools. I talked with other homeschooling families and included everything they were using on my list of possibilities for us, wondering how we'd ever choose. All the while feeling quite overwhelmed about how to do it *right*. The fallacy.

My original question of *How will we figure out how to do this*? quickly morphed into *How will we ever choose from all the ways to do it?* I felt an enormous responsibility to keep my kids on track, make sure they could successfully return to "regular" school, and not let them down. Months of research resulted in a game plan—in the form of a spreadsheet—that I now look at and laugh. Truly, best-laid plans.

I made sure we'd cover it all—every subject offered in their brick-and-mortar schools. I identified the times we'd "do school," planned how to balance across two kids and two teachers, allocated days, and designed tracking methods. Then I purchased loads of materials—textbooks, workbooks, teacher's guides, test kits, Kindles, journals, art supplies, and a portable printer. I secured an online Latin tutor for my older son and purchased a piano keyboard for my younger. I gave each kid a school cabinet in our Airstream and a whiteboard to track weekly progress on the RV wall. Game plan: check. We were prepared with a capital *P*.

And then: letting it all go became one of the most gorgeous, revolutionary experiences of our Wonder Year.

Within the first month, the schedule fell apart completely. One day we decided to forgo the two hours of online science lessons we'd planned so we could hike to the bottom of a volcano with friends instead. It was far more fun to hunt through the local woods, competing to find the biggest pine cone. Day excursions took the place of math lessons, and at night we were too tired from kayaking to muscle through reading assignments. But we were *living*. Living in ways we hadn't in a long time and deeply enjoying our extended time together. No one wanted to disrupt a card game to shuffle off for noun/verb exercises. Art lessons? A few, but mostly they felt forced. More engaging were the times we collected shells and researched their tiny inhabitants or cooked a creative meal together in a stranger's kitchen. Schedule: scrapped.

Formal learning ended up feeling like a distraction from experiencing the *now*. We wanted to grab the organic learning opportunities all around us, not look down at books and worksheets. Shifting our gaze created time to explore, absorb, and wonder. The coolest part? Learning as a family. Because we were doing it together, we parents didn't need to "loop in" to what our kids were learning. The teacher/student roles dropped away, replaced by shared experiences. We could ask questions and talk about what we'd seen and heard during our days. If there was something we didn't understand, we researched it when we had Wi-Fi, and occasionally we asked the kids to produce work—a written reflection, presentation, or art piece— to deepen their learning. Our crazy planning was replaced by observing, inquiring, absorbing, debating, and discussing. Once we replaced the *what* to study with *how* and *why* inquiries, our Wonder Year blew wide open.

Practically speaking, our world-schooling ultimately looked like this. We still did a bit of "official" school. We traveled part time in an RV and covered the essential textbook lessons during those times so we didn't have to worry about carrying gear. When we switched to backpacks for international travel, we took photos of key pages to read while traipsing through the desert, but honestly, we left most of the book learning in the dust. We kept some structure for math and language arts since those follow a sequence in traditional school. Math lessons were learning and practice, with no tests. Language arts was lighter still: spelling during car rides, journaling, and story writing during quiet times to practice grammar and punctuation. Everything else—history, science, geography, culture, world language, art, and music—we absorbed through our travels. We were opportunistic with what the world presented to us, and learning became every day, all day—a natural part of living, not separate and distinct from it.

Worldschooling Gatherings

Worldschool gatherings can be an excellent way to tap into the larger world-schooling scene and meet potential new teachers. Some traveling families connect in temporary or permanent communities around the world, and often these offer an educational component. In our next chapter, we'll discuss the community aspects of these gatherings and provide ways to find out more about them—for now, know they are another option for learning. Consider your budget, preferred length of stay, location, and kids' ages as you explore these programs.

Here are some examples:

- Jake and Gillian's family spent six weeks in Andalucía, Spain, and jumped in with a worldschool gathering out of La Herradura. Here they had weekly teen meetups, Spanish-language classes, pottery, and other electives that were organized and met their teen's social needs.

- Stephanie and Scott's family spent six weeks at a gathering in Egypt. For a fee, their girls learned from local teachers and an English-speaking founder, and socialized with other world-schoolers three days per week.

- Viet Nguyen and his family spent three months in a hub in Bansko, Bulgaria. Parents volunteered as teachers and also shared the cost to hire two trained teachers from the Netherlands. And there was plenty of time to ski on the nearby slopes!

If you don't see the educational offering you're looking for at one of the existing gatherings, you might create your own. We spoke with several families who established new programs that they now offer to fellow world-schoolers. It's exciting to watch the evolution of these grassroots, entrepreneurial efforts.

Learning Modalities

Your Wonder Year is an opportunity to get to know your kids through a different lens and to learn how they learn. No matter the approaches you choose, chances are you will get a closer look at their strengths and challenges.

You'll be there to help break down projects into small chunks. You can teach them about setting schedules, reaching goals, and prioritizing. These are the soft skills of executive functioning; and kids will thrive from the step-by-step, individualized instruction. Throughout the year, you can pull back or help them make their own system.

Direct, hands-on experiences result in long-lasting knowledge. Think about that time in middle school when you presented a science project to your classmates. Maybe you asked them to taste chocolate, lemons, salt, and arugula to learn about sweet, sour, salty, and bitter taste buds. Chances are you remember way more from that exercise than from a lecture you passively listened to on the same topic. What does this mean for worldschooling? It means that your children are likely to learn and remember more from their multisensory travel experiences.

Each child learns in a variety of ways, and your teaching toolbox may be bigger than you think. On the road you can employ a full range of learning approaches such as the following:

- Visual and spatial learning happens by seeing the information and thinking in pictures. Kids can explore map reading and photography.

- Verbal or auditory learning works by hearing information and thinking about the meaning of words and sounds. Worldschoolers can interview interesting people they meet or listen to ocean waves, birdcalls, and audiobooks.

- Reading and writing skills are developed through interacting with some form of text. In this mode, we journal, write blogs, or read menus or books.

- Logical or mathematical learning happens through calculating numbers, identifying patterns, and thinking conceptually. Your kids might play logic games like Sudoku or collect coins and calculate and compare their value.

- Hands-on or kinesthetic learning occurs through physical activity, like learning a new dance or the times tables while practicing headers with a soccer ball on a rainy day inside a twenty-four-foot RV . . . for example!

We are not one fixed learning type but rather a constantly changing mixture. Play around with different approaches, and discover together what works for your family. Most importantly, coach your children so they become lifelong, meta learners—those who are aware of their own learning. It all brings you closer; it all brings wonder.

Lisa Keller traveled in an RV with her daughter, Savannah. When it came time to do her schoolwork, Savannah consistently resisted, and Lisa quickly sensed that it was something more than a power dynamic. She found a professional who could do a full educational evaluation. It revealed that Savannah had been struggling with dyslexia her whole life, but in the classroom, she hid it with coping strategies and behavioral distractions. Lisa found the support Savannah needed so her daughter could relax into personalized reading strategies using a less stressful way.

If you have a neurodiverse child, your Wonder Year might have more considerations. One mom, Megan Rudolph, attended an Orton-Gillingham (a type of multisensory teaching approach) training program for dyslexia so that she could more confidently help her two sons in their daily school-work. She also decided to shorten their Wonder Year to six months, to lessen her sons' time away from the seasoned support of their learning center. You could also plan your trip in a way that allows you to return home periodically so that you can tap in and out easily with specially trained teachers. Another mom found that working one-on-one with her daughter, who had ADHD, helped her understand and strategize solutions that carried them both way past their Wonder Year. Sometimes removing the literal and met-aphorical noise is advantageous for diverse learners.

Finding Your Rhythm

With a Wonder Year, you choose the time in which to learn and the space you want to do it in; this flexibility can be one of your most powerful educational tools. You could, for instance, have "school" each morning for one hour. You could have one day on and one day off, or you could have pockets of concentration. You will inevitably adjust these dials to suit your needs and preferences throughout your Wonder Year.

The point is to find a cadence that works for your family. Angela used their RV home base for traditional homeschooling of some subjects. Her family alternated three months of international traveling with three months of domestic road tripping, multiple times over. This gave them a base for desks, storage space for materials, and the time of slow travel to work through their lessons. Annika had "buckle down" time in New Zealand so that she could get through 75 percent of their goals and objectives and then relax into the magical moments of travel, fitting in the remaining goals as opportunities naturally arose.

Be flexible and take advantage of the natural downtimes in travel, such as a long train ride in China, a rainy day in the Everglades, or waiting for food in Greece. Keep flash cards in your purse or backpack. A pair of dice is also good for math exercises: divide, multiply, add, and subtract. Annika kept one big Ziploc with 5" x 7" journals, colored pencils, scissors, and a glue stick for impromptu sketching, scavenger hunts, or journaling. Julie, Charlie, and Johnny always had their "10 essentials" bags handy with things like headlamps, pocketknives, compasses, star charts, and paracords. You never know when there's a knot to be tied, a limerick to be written, a stick to be whittled, or a constellation to be identified.

Worldschooling rhythms can be highly efficient. While classroom teachers fill their seven- or eight-hour day with teaching, classroom management, and breaks in between, most worldschooling families find they can cover material in much shorter times than they ever imagined. We have found that one or two hours per day of focused learning is profoundly effective.

Zeus's front porch.

Naxos, Greece

Past the freshwater spring, the well-maintained trail has been petering steadily out. We find ourselves using arms and legs to scamper up the hillside. A goatherd and his tinkling, shaggy charges are on the opposite valley wall.

"I see it!" says Lucy, pointing to a doorway cemented into the hillside.

"Finally!" says Kai.

Passing the threshold into the cave takes us from arid to humid, from hot to cold, from light to dark, from the profane to the sacred. We have arrived at Zeus's cave, on Naxos in the Greek Cyclades. The cave is more than fifty feet high and at least double that in width. Some stories say that he was born here, others that he hid here during his teenage years from a jealous father, and a man in the village even told us that Zeus received his thunderbolt from an eagle on top of this mountain.

We are silent, walking the smoothed pathways that Zeus walked, breathing the air of his boyish fragility or his teenage angst. He is embodied. Behind the teal and green moss, drip-drops of moisture echo across a dark cavern. The light beam from my phone cannot take in the size of this place; I have to imagine the extent of its reach.

We have been studying the Greek gods, their powers, symbols, and interrelational dramas. We've read classic myths, written our own original myths using Olympian characters, and visited the many temples during our monthlong stay in Greece. Our landlord told us about the cave—turn left at the potato patch and take the right fork at the white square house— giving directions that describe every intersection on the island. Getting here has been an epic quest requiring intuition, clues, research, and asking as many locals as possible.

For a nine- and ten-year-old, the myth and magic are real. "He must have been super tall, even as a kid. Where did he put his head when he slept?" And "Did someone bring him blankets?"

For my thirteen-year-old, the isolation fuels empathy. "Who did he have to talk to?"

We try to orient where he would have cooked and ate. We take in his view when he stepped outside of his cave—to his left, the tallest mountaintop in the Cyclades, currently named Mount Zeus, at 3,300 feet, and to his right, a valley that tumbles into the island-dotted sea below. He could have seen visitors a long way off.

This cave kept our Zeus safe, time-stamped his childhood, and prepared him for his extraordinary life ahead.

When Everything Isn't Awesome

When you are the parent *and* the teacher, what happens when your kid doesn't like your supercool lesson idea? They look at you and say *no*. When you're on the road, your kids will be distracted, tired, and sometimes, it may seem, just plain *over* you. The emotional proximity might make this normal child behavior feel like a personal attack. It's not.

Coping strategies for off days:

- Limit the direct instruction to no more than an hour, maybe even fifteen minutes on a bad day or if you have younger kids. Create some space. Keep stepping back until the dynamic lets you step forward again somehow.

- Find ways for kids to do independent work, maybe an art project or online lesson.

- Remind them that they are not spending all day in a classroom, and that, in your most gentle parenting way, their end of the bargain is to do this schoolwork.

- Kids need you to be their safe space. If long division is causing a divide between you and your child, stop.

- If there are more and more of these off days, find ways to shake it up. Hire an online or local tutor, look for an online class, reach out to loved ones back home for ideas, or offer your kids self-paced books or science kits.

Jake had been teaching his eighth-grade daughter algebra for months, and it had been going great. One day it wasn't anymore. They found an online tutor to step in twice a week for a few months, and then they returned to father-daughter math lessons without stress.

The White family was also seriously butting heads over math, and the friction was rising. In Australia, they found their unicorn—a book that made it possible for their son, Scout, to learn math independently. So, each night before bed, they laid out the book, suggested pages to tackle, and corrected the pages from the day before. Scout loved to wake up early and do his work independently, and Mom and Dad got to sleep in!

Here are some tips for working with differing levels of learners at the same time, especially when the kids outnumber the parents:

- Set one child up to do independent work while you coach the other one.

- Ask one child to help or present information to another child; ask siblings to quiz each other.

- Remind kids to do what they can independently for, say, fifteen minutes, and then go check on them. It's hard to move forward with one child when you are interrupted repeatedly by the other.

- Of course, if it's an option, two parents can coach.

Packable School Supplies

- Journals
- A durable carrier for colored pencils, a glue stick, and TSA-approved scissors
- Hard-shell accordion file folder for drawings, school assignments, or keepsakes that you don't want to get tattered
- Index cards for flash cards, quick diagrams, and other ideas
- Dice for math games
- Binoculars and magnifying glass

- Mini portable photo printer
- Kindles or other e-readers
- Deck of cards and travel board games
- Camera
- Compass
- Laptop/tablet
- USB thumb drive to deliver files to a print shop

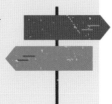

Real-Life Worldschooling Plan: Annika

Our third, fourth, and seventh graders were in a Waldorf School back home, and the teachers were supportive and encouraging of our year away. I brought hard copies of the larger yearly project assignment sheets: animal report, shelter project, and biography. We took advantage of the New Zealand libraries to complete them. The kids wrote monthly postcards to their classes, and their teachers used our wanderings as teachable moments, too. We tried to follow the Waldorf philosophy of little to no screens, but we softened over time.

It was important for me to keep the kids aligned with math back home. As their teacher, I felt the least comfortable with math, so I relied heavily on paperback workbooks from local bookstores. I didn't do much research but found ones that covered roughly the same material as our school did. It was important to me that these books were lightweight. We supplemented with Khan Academy when we could. It was challenging to have enough bandwidth in most rentals to have more than one kid online at one time.

We focused our third and fourth graders on memorizing their times table. We often quizzed them with flash cards when waiting for a train and sang the times table while hiking, and the kids quizzed each other while Will and I were busy doing something else. Mastery of the 7s was cause for celebration with ice cream. We didn't need a formal curriculum to do any of this. The kids often say now that having their times table memorized has served them well.

For writing, we created writing portfolios and read a lot. My three kids read somewhere between fifty and a hundred books each during our Wonder Year! We kept a list, like an informal bibliography. As we hiked, my son would give me plot updates from his books. We would simply discuss them, and I would ask clarifying questions and what his predictions were—but all in a conversational style. It didn't feel like school; it felt like shared curiosity. My kids' fondest memory when they look back upon our worldschooling "curriculum" was the luxury to have the time to read for interest and pleasure. Whenever we had Wi-Fi, we would download ebooks onto their iPad. My husband and I were always reading books aloud in the evenings with the younger ones. I miss those days!

We did "school" about 30 percent of our days. Surprisingly, the three kids enjoyed the structure of "school days." Maybe it gave them confidence that

Lucy
*Finish reading
 notes: Sparta
*Math pages 97+98+99
*One chapter or
 30 pages in Caddy
 Woodlawn
*Journal

Kai
* Two pages cursive
* Twenty Pages in
  Humbug Mountain
* Journal
* Four pages of math

Lorna
*Birth of Renaissance
 Drawing
*Outline
*Reread your Maranui
 post
*List important dates
 for SE Asia
*pg 39-42 mid-test
 (open book)

they wouldn't fall behind? For us, a half-day worldschooling lesson might have looked something like this:

▶ Practice "find the errors" and dictation (see page 223) in their journal, using learning points and spelling words from our geographical location. Review together and help them correct.
▶ Complete two pages in the math book.
▶ Learn about one new thing—for example, paragraph structure, photosynthesis, haiku, or the three Noble Truths of Buddhism.
▶ Do chore(s).
▶ Have forty-five minutes of structured and self-paced writing portfolio time.
▶ Reading time: independent, guided, or with a parent.
▶ Done. Out the door. Go explore.

Culmination Projects

When you have finished your year, how do you make sense of it with your children? How do you document and memorialize what your family has done and learned? How do you present it to your school upon reentry?

There are many ways to capture your children's educational adventure. Take some time to digest, integrate, and share your experiences.

- Create a writing portfolio as a culminating project. Make a cover, create a table of contents, and add some artwork.

- Apply to attend a conference or festival, and once accepted, prepare a presentation or poster for display as an exhibit.

- Keep a running document about some of your kids' favorite unschooling learning moments. Include photos. This is easier to do as you go, rather than cramming it all at the end.

- Create a timeline of your trip, and have your kids list their greatest hits from each place, month, or activity.

- Final exams. *Not what you're thinking.* If your children are nervous about having a whole year out, create a "Celebration of Learning" that circles back to those goals, standards, and objectives you articulated at the beginning of the year. This kind of final is a fun way to show your kids just how much they learned. You might ask questions like:
  - What is the strangest food you ate?
  - What is the capital of Maine?
  - What is the major religion in India?
  - Which countries colonized Vietnam?
  - What are the trees in these photos?
  - Would you recommend a Wonder Year to your friends? Why or why not?

Subject-Area Starter Kits

We want to encourage you to experiment with education, be spontaneous, and trust your instincts. Your confidence will grow. To help you get things started, the following section provides some techniques that worked well for us and other families we interviewed. Many activities and prompts are interdisciplinary, so adapt and blend them with your own. The learning can be woven in through a day of discovery or as themes you return to throughout the year.

We share these ideas not to hand you a script but instead to show how easy it is to encourage learning with just a bit of preplanning. For those who want to go further with actual lessons, we offer example lesson plans on our website (wonderyear.com) on such varied topics as poetry and water use.

LANGUAGE ARTS

Writing

We recommend having your kids each keep a journal in which they can write freely and without suggestions from adults so they can feel safe to wonder, vent, experiment, or puzzle through the world around them. *Writing to learn* through journaling means that we can sort out our thoughts and opinions by writing, finding the why, and seeing cause and effect as our hands scratch the pages. *Learning to write*, on the other hand, provides the structure and style to communicate and persuade effectively. There is a place for both types of writing instruction.

Consider keeping a writing portfolio, to imitate the way that writers actually write—in drafts. You could do early drafts in journals before moving on to revised drafts on fresh lined paper or typed on a laptop. A hard-shell accordion-style folder is handy for drafts and final documents that you can later assemble into a tangible portfolio for each school year.

STARTER IDEAS: WRITING

- Create a scrapbook. Include ticket stubs, flyers, pictures your kids have drawn, or poems they've composed over the course of your trip.
- Write postcards to friends and family back home.
- Ask your kids to write a monthly post to put on your blog. This is a perfect opportunity to take a first-draft journal entry through the editing process and then type it out on your laptop.
- While you're waiting for food at a restaurant, create group haikus or limericks.
- Write a Yelp or Airbnb review.
- Invent worlds and storylines for Dungeons & Dragons or other online gaming realms.
- If your teen or tween has strong opinions (ahem . . .), encourage them to share their thoughts on an online forum or write to a politician or even your federal government (such as whitehouse.gov).

Reading

Oh, the luxury of more time to read! Read with your kids as much as you can. Read out loud together and predict what will happen, connect scenes to your own lives, find clues (foreshadowing), and examine characters, conflict, and theme. The sky's the limit. This one-on-one exchange with time to explore is hands down the *best* way to teach reading. Be sure to give your kids plenty of room to read independently as well, especially if they are older, and keep a running list or informal bibliography of what they've read; it will be a great way to document their work if your kids are returning to traditional school.

STARTER IDEAS: READING

- Find books that take place in your destination, and let your kids teach you about it.
- When your kids are reading on their own, ask for updates on the plot. Ask leading questions: Why do you think they did that or said that? Wait, who is that again?
- Read the placards at national parks or museums. It's a wonderful way to learn how to read nonfiction organically.
- Do a book report. For young ones: Draw your favorite scene or character. Write about the conflict or challenge in the book. For older ones: Compare two books, create an alternative ending, or write a five-paragraph essay on a topic of your choosing. Make a book jacket. Draw a tourist map of the fantasy land.
- Read a local newspaper. Identify any biases, and discuss the sources cited in the articles.
- Leave a book review on Goodreads.
- Listen to an audiobook while traveling on a long stretch of road.

Grammar/Spelling

Try these ideas for grammar in context and to review or learn a few specific skills.

STARTER IDEAS: GRAMMAR/SPELLING

▶ Use Mad Libs to teach parts of speech. After introducing adjectives, pronouns, plural nouns, and adverbs, practice with this high-interest game. It's an entertaining and often funny way to pass time on a long bus, plane, or train ride.

▶ Review your kids' existing written pieces to find error patterns, then create individualized "find the errors" exercises. Adjust for age and ability.

▶ Practice dictation: using the information you have about your current location, read a sentence (or an entire paragraph for the older ones) aloud and ask your child to write it down in their journal. Then review together what they've written and make any corrections with them. Without realizing it, they've also learned some important facts about this new place.

▶ If your kids are really craving structure, create weekly spelling lists using words inspired by the place you're visiting. In Florida, it could be *orange, archipelago, alligator,* or *roller coaster.* Or use the words in your dictation and "find the errors" exercises. Practice writing these words in the sand, if you're at the beach, for bonus fun.

▶ Take advantage of spelling resources. Angela's family had a cool spelling program, but the book was huge. Instead of doing writing exercises, they went through the book and took photos of the upcoming pages for each kid and quizzed them out loud during long journeys.

MATH

This is one subject that builds sequentially, so it may work best with some regularity and order. You can also naturally apply mathematical skills within an unschooling approach. There are so many ways to bring math into everyday life.

STARTER IDEAS: MATH

- Calculate mileage for your RV, flight, or boat ride. You could do this by using a map or odometer, and then create graphs or charts as a visual representation of the data.
- Get your kids involved in keeping track of the budget. You can make a ledger and have them track costs over a day, a week, a month, or the entire trip. They can break down expenses into categories and even help decide where to splurge and where to cut back.
- Play cards, which will reinforce patterns with Go Fish or counting and probability with blackjack.
- Convert metric to imperial measurements or vice versa while baking or cooking, or when measuring distance traveled or volume of water in your RV's clean-water tank.
- Double the recipe while cooking. Voilà, it's a math lesson! Share the extra food with new friends.
- Practice converting fractions to percentages while doing fun things like hiking or kicking a soccer ball.
- Estimate the length of a bridge, the height of a cathedral, the diameter of a tree, or the speed of a motor scooter.

SCIENCE

Science is all around you, in theory and application. Every time you cook can be a chemistry experiment, and every time you move can be an exercise in physics. When you drive, there may be roadside geology exhibits. Simply asking your kids to observe, notice, wonder, draw, or hypothesize about cause and effect can set you up for a science lesson anytime, anywhere.

STARTER IDEAS: SCIENCE

▶ Volunteer for an archeological dig or a river cleanup.

▶ At the airport, check out exhibits or tours open to the public. Maybe you can view an educational display or visit the control tower when your flight's delayed.

▶ Make your own bingo cards and play to identify flora, fauna, and other natural features during a boat trip, land trek, or safari.

▶ Research environmental challenges and how humans are working toward solutions. For example, there are apps for determining air quality in China and tsunami risk in New Zealand.

▶ Use your magnifying glass during a hike.

▶ Study applied physics at one of the many amusement parks that offer special "learning lab" days.

▶ Observe the sunset every day for a week. Sketch the different colors, and explore negative and positive space, shadows, light, and silhouettes.

▶ Spend as long as you want at a streambed. Turn over rocks, wade in the water, and notice what kinds of insects live above and below the surface. Learn the words *riparian*, *habitat*, *limnology*, and *anaerobic*.

▶ Visit a nature and science museum.

▶ Check out ready-to-go science programs, like Citizen Science and Junior Ranger described in the resources section.

▶ Track the night sky. Learn about International Dark Sky Places and light pollution.[37] Take a late-night excursion. Find the North Star. Find the Milky Way. Ask: Can you see Jupiter? Do you want to go to Mars?

SOCIAL STUDIES

Many parents find that social studies is the easiest subject to worldschool. It's literally hard *not* to learn. Just observe, absorb, and discuss.

STARTER IDEAS: SOCIAL STUDIES

- ▶ Talk to strangers. Ask questions. This is the heart of world-schooling. Yes, it really is that simple. Or you can be more intentional and interview people.
- ▶ Hire a local guide: not only will you learn but you will also contribute to the local economy.
- ▶ Read maps: plan the route from your accommodations to the museum, or take the subway to the market.
- ▶ Keep a running timeline that incorporates interesting history facts from every place you visit over the year into a visual representation. This will help your kids see what was happening at different places in different times.
- ▶ Bring historical fiction to life! If you take a tour of Pompeii, ask your kids to write down five, six, or eleven facts that will be incorporated into an imaginary story or scene. This is an adaptable and fun activity that can be done anywhere.
- ▶ Preview a museum's website and use it to create a museum scavenger hunt in your child's journal. Or, better yet, ask your kids to create scavenger hunts for themselves or each other.
- ▶ Take a road atlas or world map and diligently chart your course. Explore cartography through exercises in scale, compass rose, place names, and boundaries. Whose story is being illustrated in the map? Who makes maps, anyway?

SCIENCE, TECHNOLOGY, ENGINEERING, THE ARTS, AND MATH (STEAM)

STEAM encourages students to use creative, out-of-the-box thinking to solve real-world tasks. Kids play with perspective, discovery, and questioning that dovetail effortlessly with worldschooling. Consider banking ideas and family brainstorms for future science or art-fair projects.

STARTER IDEAS: STEAM

▶ Build a sandcastle with moats and tributaries leading back to the ocean.

▶ Make a family trip website and have your kids do the coding.

▶ Help your kids take digital photos and edit them with an image editing program.

▶ Visit science and transportation museums.

▶ When something breaks— a zipper, luggage handle, a bicycle derailleur—pause and let your kids diagnose the problem and brainstorm a solution.

▶ Read inspiring books about real kids who were faced with a STEAM-based challenge and used science to help their communities. A few examples are *The Water Princess* by Susan Verde, *The Boy Who Harnessed the Wind* by William Kamkwamba and Bryan Mealer, and *Iqbal and His Ingenious Idea* by Elizabeth Suneby.

▶ Source websites with coding instruction. For example, Hour of Code has hundreds of free computer science activities for kids of all ages.

▶ Learn CAD and design structures inspired by the places you've visited.

▶ Play chess. It requires multistep thinking, problem-solving, and real manipulatives. Bring a travel version when you're on the road. You can find chess games everywhere in the world, and it can help you find immediate friends who also play.

WORLD LANGUAGES

Languages offer insight into the psyche of a place. In Thai and Mandarin, the "How are you?" greeting literally translates to "Have you eaten your rice yet?" Now that is a window into the culture!

STARTER IDEAS: WORLD LANGUAGES

- Learn a new alphabet. For instance, you could learn how to read the word *train* in Chinese characters. Try to spot it when you can. Or study the Greek alphabet and sound out the names of foods from the grocery store or place names while driving.
- Learn to say "hello," "goodbye," "please," "thank you," and "where is the bathroom?" in the local language of every country you visit.
- Ask for a word a day from a neighbor, a hotel clerk, or new friend. Offer to reciprocate.
- Learn and practice appropriate nonverbal communication, customs, and body language.

For instance, learn how to *hongi* (press your nose together with another person in traditional Maori greeting) in New Zealand; recognize when to make or avoid eye contact, when to remove your shoes in someone's home, or when to say hello with a handshake; or know how to hail a cab in New York versus Istanbul.
- Use online language-learning apps like Duolingo.
- If you're staying in a place for a longer period of time, enroll in a local class.
- Do the obvious: go outside and talk to someone.

MUSIC/ART/CULTURE

This is a great way for kids to interact with their surroundings. You will be so happy to have their Wonder Year art years from now.

STARTER IDEAS: MUSIC/ART/CULTURE

- Find hands-on art activities at your destination that you can join for a day, a week, or more. These are easy to find in online searches. Weaving classes in Cambodia, painting lessons in Guatemala, or pottery classes in Costa Rica are just a few examples.
- Carry colored pencils, charcoals, or watercolor sets and a sketchbook wherever you go. Sketch a temple or cathedral. Copy four artist signatures. Paint a watercolor landscape.
- Begin a museum visit in the gift shop. Let your kids pick a postcard, and then do a scavenger hunt to find that piece. Ask why they were drawn to that particular work of art.
- Find a local music festival and volunteer or do work in exchange for free admission.
- Learn to finger knit, crochet, or hand sew. Travel is a great time to do handicrafts, and you can bring some simple prepackaged kits with you. Insider tip: bamboo knitting needles are TSA-friendly.
- Take a local cooking class or learn a new recipe from the owner of your accommodations.
- Look at billboards and be an anthropologist for a day. What are the values represented? Whose perspective is being shown? What are the cultural norms implied? What is the message?
- Take a one-, five-, or ten-second video that represents each day or week you travel. Create a video compilation and set it to music.

HEALTH AND WELLNESS

Physical activity may be an integral part of your trip. If not, you may need to be more conscientious to get the blood pumping in the course of a day.

STARTER IDEAS: HEALTH AND WELLNESS

- Go to the local park. Carry with you a soccer ball, hacky sack, diabolo, juggling balls, or Frisbee—these are great ways for your children to meet local kids and get a party started.
- With proper research and gear, go hiking on a glacier.
- Get in the water: swim in a local pool, kayak on a lake, or snorkel or surf in the ocean.
- Use the step counter on your phone and chart how much you and your family walk in a day.
- Take a meditation class as a family, and incorporate

mindfulness practices into your lives.
- Try a sport you know nothing about. Netball? Cricket? Kneel jump?
- Learn basic first aid and restock your kit. Learn the signs and treatments for altitude sickness, dehydration, and heat stroke.
- Observe the ways that the locals exercise—is it part of their everyday lives? Consider incorporating new habits while you're there.

LIFE SKILLS

Survival, self-care, independence, and self-esteem all grow as children take on more responsibility and contribute to the team. Whether you are overseas or in your own country, in an Airbnb, in the backcountry, or on 5th Avenue in New York City, you can learn "street smarts" through your travels.

STARTER IDEAS: LIFE SKILLS

- Have a regular family meeting and rotate leadership roles. Share your "roses and thorns," the highs and lows of your day.
- Learn how to read subway routes, bus schedules, or topographical maps. Let your kids lead the way.
- Practice threading a needle and knotting thread. Sew a patch over a hole in damaged clothing.
- Plan for, shop, and cook a meal.
- Practice packing light, keeping track of your gear, and staying organized.

- Climb a tree to put up a clothesline, then hand-wash your clothes and hang the laundry.
- Wash and dry the outside of your van.
- Learn how to build a fire with one match.
- Study and practice the principles of Leave No Trace.[38]
- Learn how to write thank-you notes. Mail them at the local post office.
- Pitch a tent. Anywhere. Everywhere.

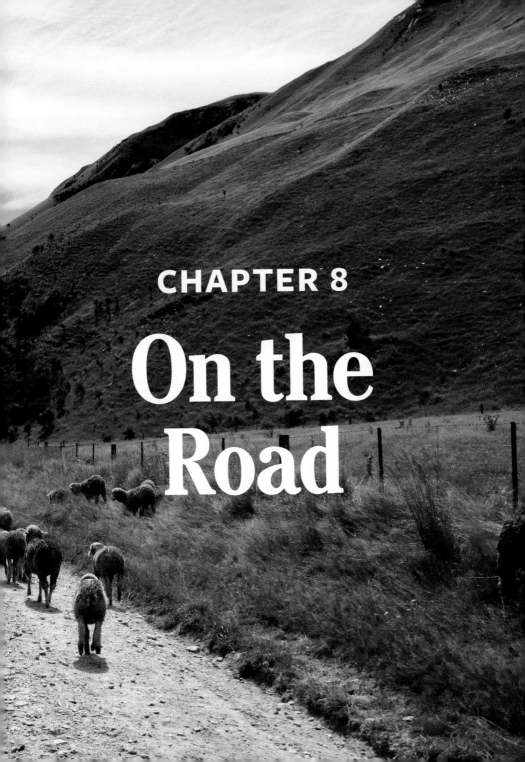

CHAPTER 8

On the Road

The nature of the flower is to bloom.

—Alice Walker

AS YOU HAVE READ THROUGH THE PAGES of this book, we hope you have found some inspiration and nuggets of wisdom that help you make the decision to travel, design your extraordinary adventure, and formulate an approach to education that aligns with your values and your children's needs. Now comes another humdinger: life on the road! Many amazing things come about when you get in motion as a family. This chapter steeps you in it all: the luscious, the ludicrous, and the hanging-on-by-a-thread-but-I-would-do-it-all-over-again.

We've read hundreds of articles, blogs, and books and talked to dozens of traveling families. We've been privy to personal accounts and have heard touching stories as we conducted our research. Without a doubt, the overwhelming majority of current and former travelers paint a similar portrait of their respective family's journey: "Our time on the road was amazing"; "We loved being curious together, solving problems together, trying new things together"; "We are closer, stronger, more alive and attuned to each other and the world."

Gems of the Journey

We coauthors heard some common gifts of a Wonder Year: togetherness, simplicity, freedom, and new perspectives. Of course, there were challenges, too, and some unexpected twists and turns in the journey. In this chapter, we'll share guidance and the inside scoop on extended family travel, from navigating family dynamics and finding community to getting out of your comfort zone and more.

TOGETHERNESS

On the road, togetherness is the default. We see each other's vulnerabilities and bravery, and we cheer and support each other through hardship and growth.

As traveling parents, the joy of togetherness is multiplied. As adults, we interact with new places, people, landscapes, and legends and have wonderful learning experiences. Then, as parents, we pause, look around, see our children, and delight all over again in their joy of discovery. Our common goals and shared experiences strengthen the bonds of the family. Imagine that each person jumps into a pond from different locations on the shore: ripples spread out from each entry point, and when they meet, new patterns and waves of beauty are created. Family travel is collective joy that builds and entwines, tumbles and shines, in a daily repertoire of discovery.

Togetherness for the Brentons had a tropical flare. Their six-month trip in Monteverde, Costa Rica, pulled the family together from the very first night. They arrived at their house near the Cloud Forest Biological Reserve in the dark, during a rainstorm, with no heat or TV; and with creaking frogs, clicking beetles, silent scorpions, tarantulas, and millipedes. The kids shared a bed, which they had never done at home, and the massive change in the environment kick-started their togetherness over their entire journey. Upon reflecting on the impact of their trip, Dad, Mitch, remarked, "You can't bring up any aspect of our trip that doesn't involve all of us. We have a common memory for the rest of our lives. It was awesome."

SIMPLICITY

One of the slow-release outcomes of a Wonder Year is the experience of living simply. On the road, we don't have to juggle a million balls. A lifestyle of noise and busyness can be replaced with focus and clarity. This helps us reprioritize and see anew the essentials—health, sleep, food, learning, experiences, and time together. We can connect in the moment and appreciate the little things. For Julie, a three-minute hot shower made her feel like royalty, and a shot of espresso while sitting in a camp chair made her buzzed for days. We heard from many travelers that they were happy living simply and showing their kids that the "rich" life can be a simple life, independent of material wealth.

Simple Pleasures of the Road

- Really starry nights
- Cotton pillowcases
- Clean socks
- A closet
- Hungarian goulash in Budapest
- Rainier cherries in Washington State
- Turkish coffee in Istanbul
- A new toothbrush
- Stillness
- Dinner with friends
- Raw juice from a coconut sliced open by a machete
- Sunsets
- Real maple syrup
- Noticing
- Being fully in the moment, no multitasking, nowhere else to be, nothing else to do
- Watching a spider spin a web for an hour
- To-do lists that fit on a tiny piece of paper
- Reading a lot
- Reading without a mission
- Every meal together

FREEDOM

When we finally walk out the door to start a Wonder Year, we can exhale and release the tendency to push, produce, and do all the things, all the time. Instead, we can tune in to the rhythm of the world. We can wander, stay longer. The only demands upon us are those we've chosen. Days may be framed by sunrises and sunsets. Kids can sleep 'til they wake up. When you're driving down the road, there's no reason you can't stop in Farson, Wyoming, among the big sagebrush and ricegrass, to watch a pack of wild horses. Maybe three hours later, your kids will edit their photos of horses or write a poem or ask you to turn around and go back to see them again, because you can.

While traveling as a family, we also enjoy the freedom to express ourselves fully. Maybe it's the freedom to try something new or work through things that make you anxious. Kids might feel safe to dabble in new interests without pressure. They might even find new voices, try new styles, or explore identities.

NEW PERSPECTIVES

One common reason why families set out on a Wonder Year is to take their children away from the familiarity of where they've grown up. It's hard to imagine how profound it can be to witness the opening up of our children's minds as they see new places and gain new perspectives. From the moment we leave home, they start processing, considering, trying on new ideas, and testing their beliefs. They begin to appreciate that their ways are not the only ways, whether it's how people eat, sleep, cook, speak, gather, worship, celebrate, dress, live, wash, or play.

New perspectives can emerge when our kids reconcile how they see the world with how the world sees them when they are the *other*—the "foreigner," the "one with the accent," the person who isn't understood. They may catch some of a news broadcast or see in the press a representation of their country that is not the one they know. As they gain cultural literacy, they acquire the critical thinking to challenge their own assumptions and those of others.

Johnny had an extraordinary change in his concept of time. At nine years old, he was walking among the olive trees in Sicily with his seventy-year-old friend, Catarina. Looking across the verdant hillside, Johnny asked about a town off in the distance. Catarina answered, "That's Vita, the new town. It was established in 1609." "New?" Johnny asked, half laughing, and not immediately understanding. The rest of the trip, he told everyone about how awesome it was that Catarina called Vita the "new" town. He got it.

Putting ourselves out in the world is to open our eyes and to keep noticing until we're able to see through someone else's eyes. That's when we've gained a new perspective. It's a beautiful thing to see in our children and a beautiful gift of a Wonder Year. Hopefully, it's also a gift they can keep giving back.

Togetherness, simplicity, freedom, and new perspectives—sounds poetic, right? But perfect? Well, no. Let's also talk through some of the challenges that might come up for your family—dynamics, provocations, and forks in your wandering way. We're here to assure you that with a little preparation and forethought, some luck and good timing, a sprinkle of good karma and a teaspoon of humor, you can navigate almost anything.

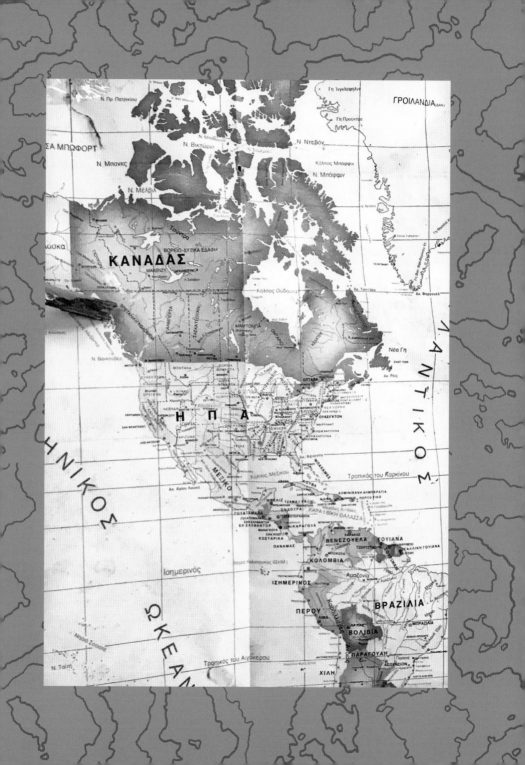

Planning for Launch

Many families experience transitions galore during their Wonder Year, sometimes even before they leave home. As your launch date nears, feeling sorrow or grief is perfectly normal. It's also totally fine to feel none of that and just be excited about your journey.

When it comes time, involve your kids in saying farewell to the things you can't take with you—family, friends, your home, beloved pets. Ceremonies of any kind, whether they are small goodbye dinners or a big bash to send you off, can help kids feel a sense of closure.

Family Dynamics

Once on the road, it's often the things we take for granted, which are routine or otherwise under the radar at home, that pop up and demand our attention. These changes and transitions may unleash a roller coaster of emotions as everyone adjusts their stride and becomes a traveling family.

ROLES AND RESPONSIBILITIES

One of the biggest adjustments is establishing new roles and responsibilities. That process has a bit of an undoing of what was and a bit of creating something new. At home, our days and identities are established and distinct. Kids go off to school. Parents do their work. The bicycle gets parked in the shed; the garbage goes out on Tuesdays. When you begin a road trip, the pieces of the family puzzle may get shuffled. It's likely that your traveling roles are going to diverge from the ones at home you've sorted out over years of practice and living together.

Basic needs remain: food, shelter, hygiene, clothing, medicine, sleep. Toss in education, navigation, recreation, and transportation, and many deliberate choices must be made about who does what. If you are traveling domestically in an RV, someone will have to drive, someone will have to navigate, and someone will have to learn the peanut butter and

How do you decide who does what?
Before we left, Matt was making money
and I was holding down the house.
So, when we got on the road, I did
everything, and he read *The New Yorker*.

—*Nicole*

jelly two-step: open fridge, grab jelly, close fridge before the driver turns or brakes. If you are on a boat, only one person can be the captain. If you are traveling internationally, someone needs to be the keeper of the tickets, the linguist, the wrangler, the reservationist.

For families with more than one adult, there may be friction as you adjust to being a traveling couple or traveling co-parents. Perhaps at home you grew stronger in your relationship by working through sensitive topics like gender stereotypes and parenting styles. Some of these may reappear, as traveling has a way of shaking loose feelings that have settled over the years. There may be a sorting-out period in the early weeks or months of your trip. Treat it like the changing of the seasons: you may need to adjust the thermometer, change your base layer or outerwear, or eat cool food instead of spicy. Adaptation is a learning opportunity, and you'll come together by recognizing the demands on everyone and having each other's backs.

Adults who were accustomed to working outside the home may be less familiar with performing the day-to-day tasks of managing a family. For those who identify as a traditional earner, extended time away from work may challenge ideas of identity and self-worth. Who are you on the road, and how do you matter? The upside is that you might have time to develop or deepen a hobby or skill. Maybe you'll find new uses for your carpentry or navigational prowess or language proficiency. Maybe you'll spend more time with your kids and teach them how to work on engines, fix flashlights, or calculate rates of currency exchange. Perhaps you'll just hang out with them a lot more than you ever did at home, doing both extraordinary and oh-so-ordinary things.

Children can have—and may even need—meaningful roles, too. Age-appropriate work is not only a great way to get stuff done but also builds confidence in our kiddos and can help with their focus and self-esteem. On the road, it may be easier to be patient and give kids time to try tasks and make mistakes. Older kids can read manuals and maps or become experts of any system; they can plan trip segments, make reservations, or even drive the rig. Tweens can check the hours a museum is open or wash pajamas in a hotel sink; they can plan a meal, shop at the market, and cook. Younger kids can help count backpacks, fold bandannas, stir the oatmeal, look under beds for missing socks, or hold someone's hand when walking through an airport to make sure no adult gets lost. Go ahead and delegate! It's good for everyone.

You may have some team building to do as everyone gets tossed into the fishbowl. Be patient. Be kind—including to yourself. Balance the challenges by finding new ways to bond. Maybe it's dinner together every night. Maybe it's setting an intention for 1:1 time with each of your kids. You might have fun coming up with a family nickname, a name for your vehicle, or a theme song for the journey. Roll with your new roles.

PERSONAL SPACE AND BOUNDARIES

In addition to sorting out roles, it's important to make space for yourself and for family members so you all have room to breathe.

For one, your living quarters may be smaller than what you are used to. Maybe you're on a boat, renting small apartments, or living in a string of hotel rooms. You'll have to play Rock Paper Scissors to see who gets the bed, who gets the top drawer, or who gets any drawer. For another, you may find yourselves cramped together in sweaty trains and taxis. The smaller physical spaces may also be tough for family members who aren't comfortable changing into pj's or putting on a swimsuit with everyone around. Might be time to perfect the "deck change"—wrap a towel around yourself, drop whatever you're wearing, replace it with something new—all in the privacy of your terry-cloth "changing room." It's a good skill to have, so there is no better time to learn it.

Physical proximity is one aspect, but adapting to social proximity can be more nuanced. It's all out there in the open. When you're always together, you're always together. Skye White put it like this: "When you're full-time traveling, sometimes you just want to shut the door, but you can't. There's no door." Be prepared to say everything aloud, in front of your kids. Even if you think you are whispering, they can probably hear you! Setting boundaries and claiming alone time can provide great role-modeling opportunities. Maybe you commit to a solo morning walk or time to listen to a podcast or music. Some couples trade off one morning a week or a monthly overnight away to do their own thing. Other families designate "quiet hours," downtime, or headspace time. These physical and mental breaks could coincide with kids' naps or be a new period in your daily or weekly rhythm. If you are traveling with a partner, the time you spend together can nurture a relationship. Traveling reveals different sides of ourselves, and that may be exciting, interesting, and novel. Parenting in broad daylight is full of surprises and full of potential. Simply being together for three meals a day can feed the love.

Finding time for date nights, privacy, and intimacy can be a challenge when you are on the road. You probably need to plan rather than be spontaneous, and think about where your kids will be and who can look after them; then you need to stay awake! Destrie Long and her husband planned date nights. They relied on camping friends to watch the kids while they had dinner in a nearby town, and it worked well for them. Those moments together can be outsized and memorable.

Our advice is to make your time together a priority. Your kids will appreciate seeing their parents hugging or holding hands, talking with each other, working through the ups and downs of travel, and being supportive partners. It's a rare and beautiful thing for children to witness their parents' unfolding as a traveling couple, and they will recognize authenticity in these loving moments.

We can't predict how traveling together will affect your relationship, but we can say from experience that good intentions and openness always help.

ANNIKA'S REFLECTION
Date Nights

We purposely scheduled Airbnbs so that we could have a locked door and not need to worry about the kids' safety. Couple intimacy became an event and created its own sense of intention and wedding-night pomp. One of my favorite nights was at a small guesthouse on a frigid fall night in China near the Great Wall. We had a guide with us at the time, and when we told her that it was our anniversary, she, the innkeepers, and the kids all conspired toward our romantic evening. We were given the best sheets and blankets and the old-fashioned, honorary kang bed. Used in northern Chinese villages, a kang bed is built over steam-vent channels in the floor; the heat from a stove below is directed through flues to warm the bed.[39] Everyone stood in the hallway wishing us a nice evening as Will and I entered the room to a literally hot, steamy bed, candlelight, and some rice wine. My kids were too young to know the details of what this meant, but they did know that this was special alone time for us as a couple. How often can kids understand the sanctity of date night?

SIBLINGS

Sibling dynamics can be wildly tested as your family travels full time. Twenty-four seven in-your-face togetherness may take some getting used to, so be deliberate about creating space for everyone. We've talked about the value of making 1:1 time between a parent and each child. Maybe that can be expanded to create some physical space between siblings. Perhaps there's a suitable event or excursion that would work for a parent and child or for a solo teen. When everyone cannot go off to their own room, you can get creative with how and where you carve out physical space for a quick break. When tensions rise, try calling for quiet time, and redirect kids to get their book, throw a ball against a wall, or head outside for some downtime.

All that together time can also lead to better sibling relationships. We've heard from many parents that they were pleasantly surprised by how much closer their kids became when they had time to sort out their needs and work as a team. When there's a limited number of playmates, siblings start to look pretty good. Or maybe it's because they're not competing for their parents' attention or because they're sharing rooms, beds, and inside jokes. Sometimes the causes of rivalry wash away in shared adventures, and siblings might become best friends.

TEENS

A Wonder Year with teens can have glorious tension. On the one hand, it creates unique opportunities to pull together and deepen connections before they leave the nest. Being on the road can relieve pressure and give teens a break from academic demands and social expectations, which in turn creates openings to connect. Without their peers around, teens also don't have to worry about the "(un)cool factor" of hanging with parents and siblings when the family is on the road.

On the other hand, some teens start to want independence from their parents, make their own money, go on dates, and form a community of peers. These wants might feel antithetical to full-time family travel, and while it can be challenging for all, there are ways for everyone to thrive. Some parents allow their teens the freedom to plan travel segments, take off for a solo jaunt for a couple of weeks or even months, return home for a while, or meet up with friends and then reconnect with their families later in the year. They might connect with other teens at worldschooling gatherings, which we'll talk more about later this chapter. There are also social media communities and online forums that can help fend off feelings of isolation.

Teens wishing to work and earn money during a Wonder Year can find online business opportunities. For instance, they might engage in digital design, writing, podcasting, and other content creation. They can look for tutoring jobs or ways to broker goods in online or physical marketplaces, too. Talk to your teens and help them explore opportunities as global citizens—they may find inspiration and influence from their unique traveling vantage points.

ONLY CHILDREN

Travel can make it easy to celebrate the relative independence and maturity of many an only child. And while they are accustomed to navigating their childhood with mostly adults around, it is still important to think about their personal space and boundaries. Finding 1:1 time is not the challenge. Finding 0:1 time is! You can create comfortable spaces where the parent(s) gets out of the way and the kid rules. Sometimes there are relatives or other trusted adults who are happy to help. Look for ways to connect your kid with peers at drop-in classes, camps, or clinics or at in-person or online worldschooling communities. When traveling kids find each other, it's magic.

Emma Whitman, a single mom from Vermont, taps into expat groups to find local kids for her only child, Caroline, to meet. Caroline gets to hang out with peers while Emma hikes trails she otherwise wouldn't get to enjoy.

ONE-PARENT FAMILIES

Traveling as a one-parent family presents an amazing bonding opportunity between parent and kid(s). As the sole adult decision maker, there's no need for negotiation; single parents may enjoy freedom and ease in matters of planning, education, and spur-of-the-moment decisions. (We recognize that the language around families is evolving; here, we use the term *single parent* with broad and inclusive intent.)

At the same time, there may be unique challenges. There's no other adult to navigate the logistical hurdles at airports, bus stations, and guesthouse check-ins, or to help juggle all the gear. No one is there to respond when you yelp, "Hold this, take that, watch Aidan, I'll be right back." If there's an appointment or meeting you must take care of, there's usually not another adult who can easily stay with your child or children. As a single parent, you may be well synched with your kids, but they can't provide you with adult-sized shoulders for support when you need it.

Other single-parent travelers are out there, and many are savvy, resourceful, and eager to connect and share advice. Check out the increasing number of meetups and local chapters of single-parent travelers as well as social media communities that have helpful information. Some parents tap into expat networks to get recommendations for nannies or babysitters so they can get in some extra work time or enjoy an art-museum visit or dinner out on their own. Others find great utility in a regular Zoom call between kids and family back home.

Visits from family and friends can also provide a welcome interlude. If your budget allows, consider travel companies that cater to one-parent families. Their excursions can offer great adventures as well as opportunities for adult interaction.

COMMUNICATION

Traveling as a family can be a giant exercise in communication. You'll have to talk about logistical, financial, and parenting matters and make decisions about immediate next steps or longer-term arrangements. Travelers may find that their dialogue—even about sticky subjects like finance or work—on the road is better and more immediate than when they are at home. We encourage you to keep the lines open with your family members. You can model what it looks like to listen and agree, or listen and disagree, and come out on the same page. Not always that simple, but do keep trying.

Some families relish the chance to make travel decisions together at a set time or in an impromptu huddle. When kids take part, they have the chance to learn practical skills such as brainstorming, active listening, sharing feedback, negotiating, articulating trade-offs, compromising, and contributing. They can also present some fantastic ideas—you might be amazed by what your kiddos will come up with when given the "speaking baton" and permission to contribute.

Being Out in the World

Your communication and decision-making skills will be put to good use during a Wonder Year. You may find that as a traveling family you adopt principles or rules and identify limits or green lights. We'll talk about a few decisions you'll want to make together, and share some insights about being a family out and about in the world.

RISK TOLERANCE

We all live somewhere on the risk-aversion to risk-seeking continuum, and traveling to new places may change your perception of, and relationship to, risk. Are you okay not knowing where you are going to sleep? Not knowing where you will find food? Not knowing if you have to go left or right when it's getting dark and there are alligators, hyenas, and hill bandits out there? What if you are running out of gas or someone needs to go to the bathroom?

Risk tolerance is simply how much exposure to risk you are willing to handle in terms of where you venture, who you're with, what you do, and who's in charge, as well as physical activities and abilities. While you are traveling, you will need to make decisions, sometimes in the moment, that work for your whole team. You will need to sort out where you stand with your partner and family. If you are with friends or acquaintances, there will be more viewpoints to work through.

We invite you to test your risk tolerance, keeping in mind it's probably not the same profile as that of everyone else you are with. Let's drill down a bit to illustrate the concept. Say you meet a couple of families at a world-schooling summit and you get along well, so you plan to meet up again in the Philippines. One of the moms, a professional rock climber, organizes a canyoneering trip in the Kawasan Falls that will have you navigating water, cliffs, slots, ledges, and waterfalls. On your way from point A to point B, your adventure requires that you launch yourself off a cliff into a pool of water twenty feet below. Does your kid want to jump? Will you let them?

Matters of risk, coupled with cultural differences, can get even trickier. Here are two hypothetical scenarios to test your tolerance:

Scenario 1:

Your kids want to run down the street to a busy city market. There are a lot of people around. It's 8:00 p.m. and dark outside. You want to give them some freedom, and trust they can get there and back safely. Do you:

Say yes and give them some extra cash with a request to bring you a chocolate bar?

Say yes but watch them out the window the entire time?

Say yes but sneakily follow forty feet behind?

Say yes and join them, explaining why you have to go with them?

Say no, but your partner says yes?

Scenario 2:

You've arranged to rent motor scooters to travel around a small island in the Caribbean. You pay for your scooters, and then you walk to the shed to get them. No helmets! Do you:

Hop on and rev the engine?

Politely ask the operator for helmets. They bring you a helmet, but the straps are all cut. Do you then:

Encourage your kid to hop on and tell them to do two thumbs-up so you can snap a photo?

Hop on with a frown?

Politely ask for your money back?

Emphatically ask for your money back?

While you don't want to be the person who offends the locals and keeps the family from doing something fun, you also don't want to expose your family to potential harm. We give you permission to be the adult in the room when you know it's the right thing to do. When locals dismiss, laugh at, or are angered by your ways, here, too, you can hold your line.

Once you feel comfortable identifying and articulating your own feelings about risk, then it's time to communicate within the family. Maybe you'll decide to identify the lowest common threshold, meaning the place where you all feel safe, and that becomes your plan. Or you decide to do more research and education to work through fears and arrive at a compromise. Some families divide and conquer—those who want to do something adventurous can, and those who aren't comfortable choose something different. Be sure to empower your children to speak up, especially if they are feeling scared or uncertain. The practice of honoring, supporting, and working through this exchange with your family can build individual confidence and lifelong family values.

If you are traveling with other families, good communication around risk can avoid awkward moments, discomfort, strained relationships, unsafe situations, or changes of plan. Give yourself the benefit of the doubt: understand what you are exposing you and your family to, and communicate these personal considerations before the point of no return. And when you decide to jump, be sure to make a big splash!

Thermopolis, Wyoming

The first thing that hits us is the eggy smell. We'd been traveling across Wyoming all day, and now we've pulled into the Fountain of Youth RV Park without a reservation. The sun is dropping fast, and we don't like towing the rig along a curvy two-lane highway in the dark.

The campground's signs are all homemade, stencil sprayed on splintered plywood. The skull of a long-horned steer hangs over the door of the office. The man who emerges from underneath it is shirtless, deeply tanned, and seemingly oblivious that his neck and bare chest are covered in mosquitoes. He mumbles something nonsensical but somehow gets us checked in.

The campground is unusually long and narrow, stretched alongside train tracks for high-speed freight. On the way to our site at the far eastern end, we circle around a mustard-colored "volcano" at the park's center, where hot springs—the town's main draw—emerge and sulfur accumulates around its crater. There are a few other RVs, mostly white vinyl boxes with rust stains spreading from fasteners and bolts. Three large spring-fed pools call out to us from the western end of the grid.

Asher and I don our swimsuits and set out for the pools. After dumping our towels on the aluminum picnic tables inside the gate, we slowly submerge into the first pool, but it isn't hot enough—more like tepid bathwater. We decide to go big and try the hottest. No way: scorching. Like Goldilocks, Asher thinks the final one is just right, and we settle in for a good soak.

Next to our pool is a stage with a three-piece band playing bluegrass to one other couple and us. We listen and lounge beneath a violet sky while a chilly desert breeze hisses through yucca and sage. Asher is still young enough to be happily held in my arms. We float and tell silly jokes, reluctant to leave even after the band has stopped playing and we are alone.

The hustle back from the hot springs is cold, with Asher pausing every fifty feet to shake gravel from his flip-flops. Mark and Ronan are playing Uno and listening to the Pixies when we return to our rig. Showering quickly, I dim the lights and make a simple meal of grilled cheese sandwiches and tomato soup while everyone gets into pajamas. As we drift off to sleep in our narrow bunks, a freight train thunders past—the first of many, but the only one we hear. Our sleep that night is deep, filled with dreams and the smell of sulfur in our noses and in our beds.

Fountain of youth.

TRAVEL CADENCE

Travel cadence is the rhythm and speed of your journey. Some families aim to visit as many countries, states, or destinations as quickly as possible. Peripatetic parents, we salute you! Their beat matches their curiosity, and they would dance their way to the moon and back if they could. Others opt for depth over breadth as they settle in for weeks or months at a time.

Your cadence can be intentionally set by your trip itinerary, or it can modulate in response to your family's energy levels, budget considerations, or new opportunities you may hear about en route. For some traveling families, it works great to have off days for moving about freely, and on days to do school. If you have a bucket list of destinations, your cadence may be zippier with shorter stays in each place. If there are countries you want to visit that are more expensive, you may choose to have a shorter stay in those places. Some families get tired and want to slow down; they may need or want to work or enroll their children in a local school. Others simply find themselves in a place they love and want to stay for a while. In doing so, you can minimize your footprint, commit to volunteer work, reduce expenses, or participate in community service or cultural exchange. You can belong to a place.

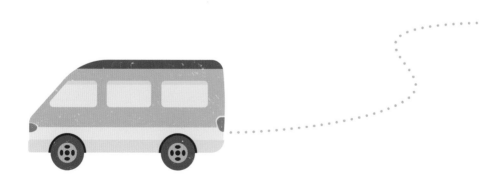

LOCAL CULTURE AND CUSTOMS

Visiting new places may require some study and preparation. Families can learn together about a new country, state, or region—its Indigenous peoples, geography, inventions, art, food, and language. You can practice local greetings, customs, and courtesies. Your research can equip you with practical knowledge about a place while deepening your respect for local customs and beliefs; it can also serve as a great worldschool lesson.

For example, in many cultures elders are treated with reverence—they speak first, and they are served their food first. In some places pointing is rude, or looking someone in the eye is considered offensive. On the other hand, in some cultures, people are more direct in their communication, and you may hear things you might not at home. Annika was told outright she could not be the mother of her daughter Lucy because they are not the same race. People might openly comment on your appearance in ways you're not used to hearing. It's all part of noticing our cultural lens. Our friend Monica's son, Ty, reflected, "The other ways people do things aren't weird; they're just different."

Be prepared to have sensitive conversations with your children as they experience things that are new to them. Some families look for opportunities to examine racial and social dynamics wherever they visit because they want their children to have a deeper perspective of places, not just see the sites. Getting out there, meeting new people, and having conversations can be profoundly enriching for everyone.

PRIVILEGE

Resource disparity and injustice exist everywhere. Many kids have a heightened sense of fairness and tend to notice the inequities around them. Traveling brings these realities to light and provides an opportunity for families to grapple with them in real time. How ready are you to talk about power and privilege? Revisit the ideas in "A Conversation on Inclusivity" in chapter 1 to weave these topics into your family's ongoing dialogue.

Worldschooling, by definition, is going into the world to learn and connect. Some worldschoolers have been criticized for the privilege of being able to move relatively freely while others cannot. They are aware of the tension between using, but not exploiting, that privilege to better understand their place in the world. They also recognize that it might be easier to stay at home and leave the harder questions unexamined. Instead, worldschoolers make the choice to travel, learn about complex issues, engage in meaningful relationships, and build creative solutions.

Toward the end of her year, one worldschooling parent said, "Traveling gave my kids an understanding that the existing power structure treats so many people unfairly, and it has motivated them to make a difference. And for me, interacting directly with other cultures throughout the year exposed my own biases. If these are the things we come to understand over the course of the year, we can consider it our most important lesson learned."

GIVING AND RECEIVING

At its best, travel is an exchange—of ideas, culture, language, and work—and there's a place for both giving and receiving. We hear from some traveling parents that they feel they are taking and consuming more than they are contributing or connecting, and they feel a need to recalibrate their priorities.

Maybe your Wonder Year can be a time to examine your impact, participate locally, or spend time in places that are not just tourist destinations. You could look for opportunities to apply your professional or vocational skills in the service of communities you visit. Perhaps you could support a school by tutoring English or math or donating sporting equipment. While traveling in Thailand, Stephanie Tolk worked hard to find an opportunity suitable for her family to give back. They connected with a local animal shelter that needed volunteers to care for the large number of stray dogs. They walked and fed the dogs, scrubbed the kennels, and cleaned the yard. It wasn't glamorous, but the work was satisfying, and it helped the animals and the community. Traveling helps us expand our thinking about what it means to be fulfilled and happy, moving us beyond personal gratification into a robust and meaningful exchange.

In some cultures, the actual exchange of gifts is a significant gesture and a thoughtful way to show your gratitude in a culturally fitting manner. Many families carry with them small thank-you gifts or handmade cards to share with hosts and new friends. Among our families, we brought inflatable globes and beach balls, deflated soccer balls with a small air pump, handwritten thank-you cards, notebooks, and art supplies to leave as gifts.

It takes composure and grace to receive. Maybe you'll be invited for a meal in a local family's home. Or, on a hot day with a tired kid, passersby might offer a cold beverage and a shaded bench. The more open and attentive we can be, the more we can find contentment in each moment. Savor these encounters. Let yourself give and receive gifts of the road.

CELEBRATIONS AND MILESTONES

Speaking of gift giving and local traditions, you'll likely want to hold on to some customs from home, too. Family traditions and celebrations can provide grounding during a year that may otherwise feel uprooted. These celebrations can take on a new and elevated significance when honored from afar. Do not underestimate how much your kids will love having the tooth fairy visit them in Zambia! No joke.

It can be disappointing to miss celebrations back home, but there are many things you can do to acknowledge special moments and create new rituals. For example, you might pack some birthday candles for the RV or an Elf on the Shelf for your Vrbo rental. If you celebrate Christmas, you might find a fabric store and sew your own stockings with felt. We all learned how to host virtual meetings during the pandemic, so virtual birthday parties with games and laughter can be a fun option. You could Zoom into your cousin's b-mitzvah or create a video or audio recording to be shared with the folks back home. Think small luggage space and big impact, and be spontaneous on the road.

One worldschooling family spent Halloween night at an airport hotel with adjoining rooms in Guangzhou, China. The kids were devastated to miss out on their favorite holiday. So, their parents bought bags of cool Chinese candies, and the kids had to create as many costumes as possible from what was in their combined luggage. After each outfit change, the kids would stand on one side of the connecting hotel-room door, knock, and yell "Trick or treat!" Their parents would open the door and give them their candy.

Academic or extracurricular milestones can also be cleverly celebrated. A visa photo or a US Junior Ranger headshot can stand in for school pictures. Completion of third-grade math or their last day of schoolwork could culminate with a meal of the kid's choosing or a splurge event. With a little forward planning and on-the-go creativity, you'll have a new collection of meaningful and travel-inspired festivities.

Sydney, Australia

I rise quickly from my bed, as I always do, sleep never making me groggy in the morning. The morning sun shoots through the blinds in the room I share with Ronan, making parts of my skin feel hotter. It's my tenth birthday, and I'm celebrating it in Sydney, Australia. I join my dad on the balcony, ten stories above a busy street filled with the sounds of stores opening for the day and the commotion of morning rush hour. Even though it's the middle of the Australian summer, we aren't hot because a brisk wind comes through every few minutes. We sit outside, making guesses about what people are doing and whether they are late to work.

Our tradition is that the birthday kid gets to decide how our family spends the day. I want to go to a local animal-rescue center filled with dozens of beautiful species endemic to Australia. First, we go to a brunch place a few blocks away from our hotel. Inside, it feels like we are back home: loud voices, cool air, the hustle and bustle of coffee makers and people trying to get their food. Everything we could ever want is on the menu: pancakes, waffles, eggs, pastries, fruits, and butter—lots of butter. After our bellies are full, we start the long drive to the rescue center.

When we arrive, the sheer difference of the area truly hits us. The temperature has risen another fifteen degrees, the wind is gone, dust is thick in the air, and we can feel the lack of sunscreen on our bodies. Scattered eucalyptus along the ridge frame our view of the outback. We move over to the shade of a small tent that has been set up for visitors and apply sunscreen, consume large portions of our water bottles, and shed some extra clothes. I can't wait to get going. We are so close to some animals you can't see anywhere else.

We start off with the wallabies, smaller kangaroo-like creatures that are generally nocturnal. We get to feed them from small cups filled with their food. There are two of the cutest owls I've ever seen. They look like furry heads with feet. We enter the koala enclosure to have them climb onto our laps, a total thrill we'd never get back home.

Australia is known for all of the animals that can kill you. Along our path, we see some of the most venomous snakes and spiders in the world. But the scariest thing we see that day isn't the crocodiles, and it isn't the Tasmanian devil (which can run faster than a bike can go). It is the cassowary, an emu-like bird that stands on two long hind legs

Tawny frogmouth owls give us the side-eye.

and is flightless. It looks like a dinosaur and has super-sharp claws. When you look up *cassowary* on the internet, the first thing that pops up is "cassowary attack." That makes sense. Every spot we'd hiked in Australia had signs with stick-bird drawings and red and black text telling us how dangerous cassowaries are and to keep our distance.

Our final stop is the kangaroos. It is so weird to be seeing an animal for the first time that you've always seen in picture books. A tiny joey pokes his head out of his mother's pouch and looks us straight in the eyes.

Tired from the heat, Ronan and I take naps on the drive back to our rented condo in Sydney so we can feel rejuvenated for my birthday night. Back at our room, I request cheeseburgers for my birthday dinner. Mom treks a few blocks to a local grocery store for the ingredients while I make my birthday calls home to family. I talk to my mom's side of the family in Ohio and my dad's side in Missouri. My mom returns and cooks the burgers and serves them up on plates with tater tots she's baked in the oven. We top off the meal with a giant container of Neapolitan ice cream, and I am allowed to eat some directly from the carton. But first, we put candles on top and sing "Happy Birthday," just like at home.

261

Roadblocks and Detours

No matter how much planning, communicating, and going with the flow you muster, extended travel may not go well for everyone all the time. The mental, emotional, and physical transitions take time, and you may need to get past early jitters and a rocky start. People may adjust at different rates, too. We'll briefly share some remedies and strategies for coping, and we encourage you to hang in there. It can be challenging as you confront homesickness, burnout, or just not finding your groove.

HOMESICKNESS

We are all likely to miss people dear to us, favorite places, beloved activities, and the familiarity of the lives we left. Kids are sensitive, and homesickness can show up as sadness or in unexpected ways such as disrupted moods and sleep, unusual behavior, or even physical ailments. It will typically pass, but know that a tummy ache might not be caused by something they ate. Redirecting attention to a favorite book or card game, taking part in physical activity, and providing tenderness can ordinarily remedy a bout of homesickness. Accentuating the positives of your time away can also help bring a new perspective. Perhaps the most effective remedies to homesickness are time, connecting with loved ones back home virtually or in person, and making new friends as you travel.

BURNOUT

Another bump in the road might be burnout. Yup, sometimes you need a vacation from your Wonder Year. Many traveling families hit a wall of exhaustion, loss of inventiveness, or just get sick of all the togetherness. Like any endurance event, there are peaks and valleys both physically and mentally. Practice self-care especially through these times. Take a week or two off of planning and moving about, and make some time to chill. Or hunker down in a place you love and rent an Airbnb for a month or more. Establish simple routines. Spend some time with your hobbies or look for short-term employment or volunteer opportunities. Most likely you'll get a second wind if you can hang in there.

WHEN YOU JUST CAN'T FIND YOUR GROOVE

But what if that second wind never comes? Sometimes family dynamics are too rough to navigate, stress goes up, or parents know their kids aren't thriving. Sometimes there are real budget shortfalls or medical problems. The visit from Grandma did not help; your week at the beach did not help. If the stress on the family is too intense, it's okay to explore other options, including cutting your trip short and returning home. It happens, and we know families who wrapped up early. And who's to say that a six-month Wonder Year is any less valuable than a sixteen-month one?

The contingency plan you put in place before you left exists for these reasons. Destrie Long's goes like this: "My husband and I decided that if things ever get too far off track between us while we're traveling, we'll buy a home and settle into a routine we know works well for our family. No argument or difficulty is bigger than this beautiful life we've built together."

There, we said it and you read it. So, tuck this conversation away in the bottom of a duffel bag, but know it's there if you need it. If the flip-flop were on the other sandy foot, we would have wanted you to give us a heads-up, too.

Staying Connected on the Road

People have different reasons for seeking connection. It could be for support, to gain information, or to stay in touch with your community back home. It could be to get a break from your immediate family or to give them a break from you. Many worldschoolers want to connect with others to cultivate their shared vision of community, and help the kids and adults find new friends.

SOCIAL MEDIA AND OTHER ONLINE PLATFORMS

Your friends and family back home are going to want to know what you are up to during your Wonder Year. A website or blog with trip reports is a great way to keep lots of people apprised of your whereabouts. Get creative with your kids and include photos, journal entries, or poems, as well as other records of your travel activity, such as itineraries, names of towns, restaurants you loved, and more. Years out, you'll be happy to have a colorful, detail-rich archive of what may well be the best time of your life.

With so much communication happening on social media these days, we all know it can be a powerful tool for connecting with others—and that it can quickly become consuming. Decide how you want social media to fit into your family's time. It can be a small part of your day or an intensive quest for the perfect capture. Some families are super creative, and they get into digital storytelling and produce professional-grade content, but please know you don't have to become an expert videographer with a drone and professional editing skills. We encourage you to relax and keep it fun. Or maybe, just send a postcard to Grandma and call it a day.

Social media also makes it easy to connect with other travelers and get timely information about the locations of current worldschoolers. There are many active social media communities of worldschoolers or full-time traveling families. (See the resources section for a list of some of the larger, more established groups.)

There is also a slew of inspirational accounts on Facebook, Instagram, TikTok, and YouTube where families post about destinations and worldschooling experiences. Note that the most popular platforms and active accounts are always changing. If you're looking for families who are currently traveling, you can join and inquire on the Facebook Worldschoolers page. You can also explore popular hashtags such as #familytravel, #takeyourkidseverywhere, or #brownfamiliestraveling to discover more opportunities for connection. Sometimes good old-fashioned Google searches can lead you to a cool family. We've found that an account is most active during the first year of a family's adventure and seems to wind down over time or when they return to a stationary lifestyle. A few entrepreneurial families find longevity and are able to fund their ongoing travels with an online presence.

Some of the most effective ways to use social media during your Wonder Year might be the following:

- Solicit input on where to travel based on your criteria: "Our family is looking for a place that offers this, this, and this . . . Any ideas of where we should go?"

- Ask for specific information about a region you plan to visit or are currently located, such as educational opportunities or places to check out or things to do or learn about while you're there.

- Connect with others ahead of time, or even in the moment: "We're going to be in Lyon, France, in late April—anyone else?" or "We're currently in Bozeman, Montana—anyone else here?"

- Inquire about current hubs, pop-ups, and other organized communities (see more on that in a few pages).

- Seek ways for you or your children to connect with others virtually. Ask a parent-to-parent question, find Minecraft or D&D groups for kids, request pen pals, or just have a chat.

- Ask questions and share resources about travel or worldschooling. While we hope this book is answering most of those questions, we believe social media can still be a great supplement.

VISITING YOUR HOME CREW

Virtual is all fine and good, but let's face it, sometimes you need to connect in person. If you want to move out of the digital world, a great option is to swing back home for a visit with family and friends. This can be part of your itinerary, a surprise, or in response to medical or family necessity. Whatever your reason, that first hug is amazing.

Set up some playdates, let your teens loose, eat at your favorite restaurants, have grown-up conversations with someone other than your partner, or host a family gathering. These things can fill up your bucket. It's okay to enjoy some of your old routine and get a taste of what you might return to after your Wonder Year.

If you do come home midtrip, it might feel a little awkward. You'll be in travel mode while your neighbors, friends, and acquaintances are on ordinary time. It's okay. We'll talk more about the carnival of reentry in the next chapter.

THE CREW COMES TO YOU

Having your friends and family visit you on the road can be equally fulfilling and may be an even simpler solution. The anticipation of an in-person visit is a great antidote to homesickness and travel fatigue. Kids have a chance to be the travel guide by showing their friends or grandparents around a new place. Friendships and relationships may deepen during these times around the campfire, at the dinner table, or walking along the beach.

There are benefits for your visitors, too. They get to go somewhere that might be on their bucket lists while spending time with people they've missed. Perhaps friends and relatives who travel with you will understand your Wonder Year a bit better upon your return, easing your reentry.

Finding Community on the Road

WORLDSCHOOLER GATHERINGS

For all of the together time during a Wonder Year, the road can get lonely. For some, family is enough, but others might need connections with adults and kids outside of their traveling unit. Some traveling families tweak their plans to connect with others for a couple days or weeks. These touchpoints might allow them to restock their ideas pantry, refresh their lists of books to read or places to see, or just present a chance to kick back, laugh with other parents, and let their kids play together. Some families build their plans around connecting with other worldschoolers at both temporary and permanent locations around the world.

Summits

Project World School Family Summits are temporary gatherings for traveling families to come together for community, learning, and support. Cofounded and run by Lainie Liberti, a long-standing and important influencer in the worldschooling community, summits are offered once or twice per year in different locations. Lainie writes and speaks on teens, parenting, mental health, worldschooling, and alternative education, and her organization also offers retreats, immersive learning events, and classes for both adults and teens.

Brandon Pearce and his family hosted the popular Family Adventure Summit, which met both in the US and internationally for several years. Though this particular gathering ended in 2020, given the burgeoning interest in worldschooling and the increasing number of traveling families, it is likely there will be new events going forward.

Hubs and Pop-ups

Worldschooling hubs are more established communities in a specific location where attendees tend to stay longer. They may be run as a co-op or by an owner/sponsor, and they may be for profit or not for profit. Hubs might offer classes, workshops, meetups, trips, activities, and other events. Costs vary dramatically.

Pop-ups (sometimes called meetups) are temporary, time-limited gatherings to bring worldschoolers together and allow them to explore surroundings and participate in organized events or educational offerings. Some pop-ups are organic, one-time occasions organized at a grassroots level. Others are planned and managed by centralized organizations, which may offer several pop-ups each year across various locations.

Most often, gatherings are started by former or current worldschooling families, then shared and publicized through Facebook groups, social media posts, and word of mouth.

What's key across all of these events is this: the offerings and locations are always changing, and even most of the published lists of hubs and pop-ups become outdated quickly; it's often easiest to ask a question on the Facebook groups to find out what is currently available.

Given the investment of your time and resources required to attend, it's good to have a "know before you go" approach for all these gatherings. Here are some things to keep in mind:

- Consider what you are looking for. Some criteria might include location, length of stay, cost, educational offerings by age group, workshop topics, daily/weekly schedule, living situation (coliving as a group or individually booked accommodations with social gatherings), social activities for kids and adults, interaction with local communities and culture, volunteer opportunities, and the amount of coordination required by the family rather than handled by the hub/pop-up sponsor.

- Each gathering will have its own vibe—from laid back and homegrown to more scheduled and organized, and all the shades in between. Use websites and social media to find out what is offered, and make sure it's a good match for your family.

- In addition to the community built during the event, attendees note that it's great to connect with other traveling families ahead of time (via WhatsApp or other messaging or social media apps) and afterward. Many cite lasting friendships, some even sharing that they now plan portions of their travel around reconnecting with families they met at worldschooler gatherings.

As of this writing, there are also a few newer organizations on the scene that are establishing worldschooling membership communities, with a wide range of service offerings and prices.

CONNECTING WITH EXPATS

Expat communities can be a wonderful resource during your Wonder Year. Expats are typically tied to a geographic location through work, family needs, visa requirements, or simply by choice. This used to mean a family was in place for an extended period, but the line between "expats" and "slow travel" is increasingly blurred as more families are becoming nomadic and home base options grow more flexible. Many expats are already worldschooling by design, either because they are oriented to living outside their home country and learning from the broader world and/or because they use their expat location as a home base and then travel around it with a worldschooling focus.

It's encouraging to connect with people who share a common background and are in the know about your chosen destinations. Because expats typically stay in one location longer than other travelers, they tend to build expertise about the area—and thus, become an excellent resource for things like local schools and alternative education options, accommodations, safety and emergency information, governmental processes, employment opportunities, things to see and do, and ways to plug in to the local culture and community.

Expat groups tend to be cooperative about sharing information and resources, and they often have a "We're in it together" vibe. They can also offer a helpful way to find quick connections within an established community; we know worldschoolers who have used expat groups to find local nannies, dentists, and hairstylists and to connect socially via barbecues and book clubs. Many expat communities have Facebook and WhatsApp groups, so poke around to find out what you can join.

CONNECTING WITH LOCALS

Homestays and house-sitting arrangements make it easier to feel part of local communities, but while longer-term stays can help you plug in, they aren't necessary. Some families find ways to connect through kids' programs such as summer camps, sports, and hobbies or lessons like surfing or fishing. Place yourself in residential neighborhoods, go to parks, eat at locally owned restaurants, strike up conversations at markets, and attend community events. You'll often find parents who are thrilled to have new playmates for their kids, which can give the adults a chance to connect, too.

Also, ask for help. People the world over love to help visitors. Angela's family was lost on a side street in Japan, searching for a raved-about restaurant at the address posted online. An older woman watering her flowers nearby noticed their confusion and gestured that the restaurant had recently moved its location. Rather than try to provide directions across the language barrier, she instead locked her door and led the family on foot to the new location six blocks away, turning around and waving farewell once they could see the restaurant's sign.

CONNECTING THROUGH COMMONALITIES

You can build connections around your personal interests. There are existing affinity groups you might tap into for community and resources related to your specific type of travel, such as the PanAmerican Travelers Association Facebook group, Vanlife Facebook group, or multiple RV member organizations and affinity groups online.

The Or family, who are Chinese American, visited Chinatowns everywhere they went. It was great to speak their native language with other people, and often they would connect socially with store owners' friends and family after their initial visit.

Annika's family found immediate connections at vegan restaurants, talking philosophy, recipes, and poetry. Dog owners meeting during evening walks at campgrounds can swap stories of breeds and best off-leash hikes nearby. Joining local sports clubs/teams, religious services, or holiday camps can also build connections.

IF YOU BUILD IT . . . WILL THEY COME?

If you really have gumption, you can build your own community. Abigail and Jeremiah Kovacs attended and enjoyed a school in the Dominican Republic but then decided they wanted to be more on the move. They hired a traveling teacher and recruited other families to join the Traveling Circus, a community and educational program that moves between locations every few months. Other travelers we talked with are working on creating their own communities, too.

Of course, your family may not be "joiners" or feel the need to seek connection. Or you may want to leave it all to chance and serendipity. Johnny met his buddies, Gabe and Remi, while biking in the Coconino National Forest. Annika's family clicked with a solo Chilean female traveler named Paz while trekking in Nepal; they stuck together for weeks and keep in touch to this day.

Bangkok, Thailand

Once we settle in the taxi and get the address up on the map, I start asking the driver about his night, whether he's eaten his rice yet (see page 228), how long the rains might last this season, and if he thinks the military junta will allow elections soon. Bangkok city lights cast reflections on the wet streets. My hair begins to swell in the humidity. We talk easily as our taxi floats on the raised highway, built since I was last here. I turn to check in on the kids behind me. Wide-eyed silence. They're stunned.

"Mom, you speak Thai!"

"I told you I did."

"But, like ... you *speak it*, speak it."

My husband laughs.

I had lived and worked in Thailand for almost two and a half years with the US Peace Corps right out of college. Work and life brought me back and forth until I was almost thirty. This was a home to me, a home that I had been away from for seventeen years.

My kids look me up and down. They turn their heads and squint from the side, as if I'm a spy, or at least someone very different from their mother. I *feel* very different from their mother. I feel like the girl I was when I first came to Thailand, started my career, and first tasted mangoes and sticky rice. This whole Wonder Year is about learning from the world, but it's also a time to remember and share parts of myself with my kids. They could hear me say that I lived in Thailand in my twenties, but to introduce them to my Peace Corps site, share fried noodles wrapped in banana leaves, show them how to offer early-morning alms to the monks, or talk to a taxi driver is about sharing a piece of my heart.

Out of the context of home, I am recalling previous chapters of my life that brought me joy and a sense of accomplishment. Perhaps this remembering shows me an unabridged, more integrated version of myself. I'm more than the laundress, more than the lunch packer, more than the carpooler. I can't help but wonder what this time will mean for me as a mom.

"This was a home to me, a home that I had been away from for seventeen years."

273

Self-Discovery and Personal Growth

You probably dreamed up and decided to pursue a Wonder Year for your *family*, but while you are out there, you might discover a lot about yourself beyond being a parent. Perhaps the clarity of your Wonder Year will reveal that *you*, too, are a main character in this adventure. *You* are alive, receptive, and likely to change. As the safety and predictability of prior habits fade away, foregone conclusions, choices we've made, beliefs, and perspectives may all break open. Travel brings to light nuances of family dynamics and illuminates aspects of your essential identity. How will the experience of traveling in the world affect you?

Many traveling parents tell us that during their respective Wonder Year, they felt grounded because they were living in line with their values. Perhaps that comes from turning off the autopilot of home life and reflecting on the purposeful decisions made during travel. One mom told us that she spent her year living with all her senses wide open, which helped her reclaim who she really was and peel back the masks she had put on to fit into her cultural and societal roles. Sometimes pulling ourselves out of the comfort zone of home helps each of us see our essence.

For some, you'll have the opportunity to explore new interests or learn what makes you tick. Gillian, who had a regular meditation practice back home, attended a spiritual retreat nearby while her husband covered the home front. For others, journal or blog post writing and photography became new skills for life. Josie had always kept a pollinator garden. During her Wonder Year, she read one book, then another book, then another, and then did some online research about the environmental issues facing bees and butterflies. When she settled back home, she replanted her garden fivefold and became a local advocate for Bee Safe. Her kids love honey.

Allie Rockwell told us that motherhood had consumed her in ways she didn't see coming. It demanded all of her, and she felt that parts of her prior identity were lost. Once her family got on the road, she felt her groove coming back. Allie said, "I was a traveler way before I was a mom." Speaking to us from her van in Belize, she shared that reclaiming herself and that place of wholeness makes her a better mom.

Destrie Long called herself "super social" before she, her husband, and their two kids decided to try full-time RVing. When they were boondocked in the backcountry for three months, she was struck by the quiet, the stillness, and the alone time. She struggled to figure out who she was when she's not entertaining others. She had to ask herself, *What do I enjoy? How do I want to spend my days?* It was hard at first to live in more isolation, but after some trial and error—and time spent in busier campgrounds with more families—she learned how to hear herself and find balance.

Amanda Dishman, who had a successful career in the military, now lives on a boat full time with her family. Her husband grew up around boats, but she knew nothing about them before starting their journey. Now she's weathered literal storms, become fluent in knots and navigation, and is a resilient #boatlife badass.

Our best advice can be summed up in a word: *Be.* Or in two words: *Be Ready.* Or in four words: *Be Ready for Anything.* We'll circle back around to personal identity and how to bring home your new self in the next chapter.

CHAPTER 9

Reentry

Why do you go away?
So that you can come
back. So that you can see
the place you came from
with new eyes and extra
colors. And the people
there see you differently,
too. Coming back to
where you started is not
the same as never leaving.

—Terry Pratchett,
A Hat Full of Sky

AT SOME POINT YOU WILL EITHER return to the nest or land in a new hometown. You will park the car, enter your home, unpack your belongings, and put your luggage into storage. You will put your passports in a drawer and pay bills. This return may look different for other people. You may be a person who skips home with alacrity and kisses the front stoop while platters of "welcome home" food arrive from your beloved community waiting on the lawn. If you're this person, welcome home and you can skim this chapter. Or maybe, you will decide to set down roots in a place you discovered while traveling. It felt like home, you made connections, and your kids are excited to be there again.

If coming home is more complex, then you're with the majority of worldschoolers, and you will benefit from thinking about reentry even before you leave for the trip. For some, coming home can be the hardest part of a Wonder Year. Peace Corps Volunteers have an entire three-day training process for "coming home," and they are prepared and equipped by career counselors, psychologists, and even nurses for unexpected possibilities that swirl around this giant step of reentry. No matter where you've wandered, you have changed. Perhaps your home has, too.

This chapter will give you tips for an easier homecoming, permission to grieve the end of your trip, and avenues to weave meaning back into your life at home. We'll cover the logistics of reentry and suggest ways to create a softer landing.

JULIE'S REFLECTION
On Reentry

Coming home was harder than I thought it would be. While I was focused on the motion of reentry, I failed to consider the emotion of reentry. Something I loved so much had ended. I grieved. Johnny and Charlie defaulted back to normal as their flow state became soccer, fifth grade, trumpet lessons, friends, work, and staff meetings. My job went away while I was gone, which I knew was a possibility. Before I resigned, I had asked my employer for a leave of absence, to "save my job" for the year. They declined, so thirteen months later, I was unemployed. Adding injury to inertia, I came home with a broken elbow and was in a fixed brace for three months. I couldn't lift boxes, brush my teeth with my dominant hand, or sleep. I don't need to spoon-feed the metaphor. I was immobilized.

It took me three weeks to muster the mustard to write a final blog post on juliafreedom: Travels with Charlie (and Johnny and Max) because I didn't want our trip to end. I felt like I should have been able to wrap it all up with a pretty bow, share a few lessons learned, and embrace home sweet home. But I couldn't wrap up the most amazing year of my life. Not with a bow, duct tape, a bungee cord, or words.

We looked and felt like travelers when we came home. I wore the same ratty jeans with holes in the knees and frays on the seams. I clipped key chains onto my belt loop, noticed each moon phase and sunrise, and called every vehicle a "rig." We were all shocked by the number of forks in our fork drawer and the volume of shelves in the pantry.

And yet, while difficult, returning was not bitter. It was sweet. We eased back in, spending two nights as guests in a cottage at Chautauqua, a regional park nestled at the base of the Flatirons, on the western edge of Boulder. Charlie's mother joined us for a summer wind-down in our beautiful hometown. We sat, talked, and came back to ourselves. The actual drive into our neighborhood wasn't planned; we just pulled over at a friend's house and turned off the engine. Johnny bounced on the trampoline and mowed their lawn. These friends and family were our cushion that made for a soft landing. Slowly we reconnected with others over a meal or a walk or at our old stomping grounds—Ideal Market, Vic's coffee shop, Moe's Broadway Bagel. After a couple of months, close friends hosted a gathering where we had the honor of sharing our slideshow with our community.

There had been a series of uncanny, undeniable signs that it was time to come home. My wallet, lost the week before we left for the trip, turned up at a local Boulder bank thirteen months later. Charlie's phone, lost midtrip, was mailed back to his office. We tearfully and effortlessly sold the RV on Craigslist, leased a hybrid electric vehicle, and rejoiced in the juiciness of local Palisade peaches.

We were often asked, "So, where was your favorite place?" My answer: anywhere in Alaska; Fern Canyon in Redwood State Park; Canaan Valley, West Virginia; hundreds of magnificent places over thousands of miles; and not one day the same as any other. My favorite places, though, were not the destinations; they were the long stretches in between destinations, the unplanned space where we were simply travelers. And every day still, even after being home for a few years, we are enriched by the year of wonder, the memories and lessons, the colorful perspectives, complex relationships to home, and a familial closeness that will never, ever unravel. I would do it all over again and again. And again. It was the best year of my life.

The Winding-Down Mindset

When the final months and weeks are upon you, your family might behave like those proverbial horses steering back toward the barn. Your minds may start to gallop home even as your heart wants to linger in the pasture. You may start marking the days with both sadness and anticipation.

You can start openly talking about things that you may all be thinking individually. Discussions about things you'll miss or won't miss may be equal parts joking and venting. You might be eager to see friends, curious about being home, anxious about all that responsibility that was packed away into cardboard boxes and stored in the garage for the year, excited for a hot soak in a tub, and yet uneasy about getting back into your routine. Perhaps remind your kids that you'll be right there with them when the family's gears shift. And then start focusing on all the good things waiting for you: friends, pets, favorite foods, clean laundry, *that* pillow.

Where will your last night be? You might, for example, camp on top of Independence Pass in Colorado, rig facing east, heading home. Or you might be in an airport hotel in London with your passport and burning through the last of your shillings. Eager but unready. It's a common feeling among returned travelers that you are straddling two parts of yourself, that your peace of mind is now ringing between two clanging cymbals. Some family members may be more than ready, whereas others may not.

Creating a Soft Landing

Coming home can be an emotional process. We've found some tricks to make it easier, and we offer these suggestions to soften the landing.

- Spend some time, say, months or weeks before you return home, to get ahead of important tasks. If you start scheduling the appointments—trips to the orthodontist or dermatologist, for example—that may have piled up, you won't be inundated with them at one time. Some need to be scheduled months ahead, so yes, you will need to use that calendar again.

- If you are not already working from the road, don't be afraid to think about work before you get home. Explore employment ideas before you land.

- Make your reentry gradual. Try not to go from treehouse living in Laos to suburban sprawl in forty-eight hours, or from RV living in Utah to an apartment in Manhattan with sand still in your shoes. Instead of a direct flight home, consider driving or taking a train from the coast or a major city to help your kids visualize their unique place on this planet. You are still world-schooling, always seeing a teachable moment.

- Think about staying with a sympathetic family member or friend for a brief interlude before moving back into your house. Perhaps give yourselves two or three days of anonymity: don't tell your friends when you are arriving. The big group chatter can be more overwhelming than helpful. Perhaps try recon-necting with those special people first; this can be especially comforting for your kids.

- If you're returning to your old house, try to reenter your physical home without an audience of friends or family to welcome you back—you may have to manage their questions and small talk, and your family might be simply worn out.

- If it feels too easy to slip back into the old, busy way of life, perhaps you want to stay loose, flexible, and keep the options open. It's okay to say no to an invitation and yes to more family downtime.

- A soft landing can simply mean building in two to three weeks before anything important is expected of you once you are home.

Parenting through Culture Shock

While you're managing the details of reentry, you will no doubt need to be extra present with your kids and find ways to support their reentry experience. We might know what culture shock is—the feelings of uneasiness caused by experiencing a new culture—but reverse culture shock, when your old world feels unfamiliar, can be more surprising.

The effects may be different for kids at various ages, so expect a mix of emotions. Your children might jump on their bikes and peel out of the driveway on flat tires before you've been home thirty seconds. Or they may cry for most of the first week home. Kids are probably digesting much more, both positive and negative, than they can verbalize, so use those strategies that have always helped them process—it could be physical activity, an art project, or extra time to connect with you before bed. For right now, just be present.

When your family has been in close quarters in a camper, a boat, hotel rooms, or small rentals, the standard home can feel too big and isolating. You may find that you all still congregate in the same 100 square feet, even if your house is 3,000 square feet. For each of our families, this was a good thing: we wanted to be close (except for some teenagers, but that's for the best). You will naturally start to drift apart physically again.

Like so many parenting conundrums, perhaps the best approach is to follow your kids' lead. If they're mourning the end of the trip, reminisce about it—tell stories and look at journal entries and photos—so they know it's still living in your family memories. You can help spark their excitement at being back home by hosting friends, unpacking special things from storage, and spending time with pets.

Kids' willingness to share their experience varies. Some kids want to talk about their Wonder Year with everyone they see. Others, perhaps the older ones, desire to blend in and be like everyone else. Still other kids overshare, and you may need to coach them on what's appropriate.

Depending on who you are and where you've traveled, your children may grapple with the disparities of the world. We found that our older kids especially began to recognize all that they had. They tended to see education as a privilege rather than a chore. But what if a deeper confusion comes? What if the awareness becomes painful? If this happens in your family, keep that hands-on learning alive. Link up with organizations that do work that has meaning to your children. Annika's daughter, Lorna, began volunteering with a local nonprofit that raises and distributes college scholarship funds. The Hunter family found purpose in making it their mission to reject all single-use plastic, a cause that united them during their Wonder Year. There are so many ways to use this type of questioning for forward motion.

On Reentry

The overgrown lilac and salvia bush made our usual side entrance to the house feel more like a return to Sleeping Beauty's castle than the home we left a year before. We opened the door, into the collective space of our past, ready to kiss it back to life. We dispersed in different directions. I was in a stupor and struck by the space, the sheer square footage. Recently vacated by renters, the house had been rearranged and was absent of the jetsam and flotsam of our previous lives. It felt as generic as a furniture catalog. There were no dogs or rabbits; no half-finished art projects or dishes drying. Was this really home?

Then I walked around the yard and saw the cherry tree full of perfectly ripe cherries—for the first time since it was planted three years before—and realized that the pie must be made today. Time sows its constraints, and cherries will not wait long. The mental to-do list had started. I turned to Will, and he said, "Let's go. Let's just not unpack the car and just keep going." We looked at each other and laughed. And cried. Holding hands outside of our house, next to the electricity and gas meters, we realized that we were choosing to land, choosing to find meaning in one fixed place on the planet and plant our roots like the cherry tree. At least for a year, we could give it a year.

The happiest part of coming home for me was *putting things in drawers*. It's astounding how much pleasure that gave me: to open a drawer, arrange my things inside, run my hand along the folded clothes, and then *close the drawer*. No longer was I digging through duffels, fumbling with zippers, or finding that something had leaked. A close second-best thing was my friends: although Will and I grew as a couple and deeply enjoyed each other's company, there were some topics better discussed with friends. When I would talk with him about the complex set of emotions in letting my hair grow gray, he tried in earnest to find the discussion meaningful for the twenty-seventh time. And would often ask, "Did I do okay?" And yes, he did, but there's something so much better about that conversation with other women in their forties. There is just so much to talk about with gray hair. And it is so yummy to have female conversations in real time with my beloved friends.

Back to the hum of the utility boxes and the urgency of the cherries, we grieved the loss of our family as a distinct unit. Our thirteen-year-old couldn't wait to put the air in her tires before biking over to visit a friend. She literally rode off on a flat back tire as I stood in the driveway to watch her go, feeling enormous gratitude for our year and watching it end just like that. *Poof.* It's healthy for kids to go their own way, and yet I would miss our shared time, our yearlong team build.

I feared that the best year of my life was waving at me from the rearview window. How could anything top the year of wonder, laughter, the expanse of time without hurry, and a year when family was the priority? Not like a kitchen-plaque motto or life-coaching exercise, but an in-your-face, 24-7 reality? This was my thought as I stood by the cherry tree: I will miss them.

In my first month, I started filling up my calendar in the way I used to. I quickly had three places to be in different parts of town at the same moment: a class picnic at one school, a class picnic at the other, and a Suzuki Strings group class three miles away from either one. My throat felt tight, my guilt at having to tell someone that I couldn't do it all made me sweaty. But how was this possible? How could I be in three places at the same time? And the answer was: I couldn't. The old me couldn't see this impossibility. The new me said, *Well, that's unhealthy.*

The new me also messed up my scheduling. A lot. I was like a pink Cadillac with loose shocks and a broken fuel injection trying to merge onto the Autobahn. To complicate matters, my phone somehow thought I was still in the time zone of the Aegean Islands (and mentally I probably was), but somehow I knew that we were probably not meeting with the tax adviser at 3:00 a.m., which left me always second-guessing the veracity of my schedule. I was simply out of practice in looking at my phone. As the muscle memory began to kick in, I tried to be mindful of when I truly needed to be accessible and when time and its dictates could be more mysterious and muffled. I vowed to not simply acclimatize to the way I used to be, to remember that my phone was not an appendage. I vowed to edit the family's activities and not feel the guilt. I vowed to remember that time could be expansive and did not hold me captive.

Returning to Community

Be gentle with yourself while reconnecting with social circles. In the early days of reentry, you're processing differently, and you're not in sync yet. You have changed, and your friendships may rejigger themselves—some relationships may strengthen and others might wane. If you're moving to a new place and folks know your story, you might have the awkward celebrity introduction of a Wonder Year family.

Stepping out of the box to take a Wonder Year can seem like a provocative move to other members of your community, and their reactions to your choice might be surprising. After asking about your favorite place, some people will want a concise summary of your Wonder Year. Help your kids work out an easy go-to reply. There's a lot to unpack mentally; our kids felt overwhelmed by the questions and the expectation that there was a simple answer. Other friends and acquaintances may ask how they, too, can do it. (We wrote this book because so many people asked, and we had so much to share.) Perhaps your return can be a passing of the torch to another family.

You might also need to manage others' feelings about your trip. Comments like "You're so lucky; *we* could never afford that," or "No one got sick or hurt?" They may comment on the way you look. Maybe it's great, gray, more groovy. Or maybe the best one is, "Well, back to reality. You can't do that forever!" And to that, we thought some version of, *Sometimes I wonder if that was reality—living each moment out loud—and this is a dream.* Hopefully, your friends are waiting with open arms and want to hear how you've grown, how kind people are out there, and they'll gamely eat all those new dishes you want to share.

Kyla Hunter had loads of relatives and friends come visit her family for various portions of their Wonder Year, so the line between their traveling selves and their community was more blurred. Shared experiences, inside jokes, and stories helped them feel understood and eased the transition home.

Capturing Your Year

It may be hard to fathom now, but one day your trip will be five or ten years behind you. Your recall may not be what it once was, and you'll crave the details. Keep a record of funny stuff your kids said, observations they made, the magic you created. For nostalgia and a hundred other reasons, please make time to document your travels. For keeps. Write it. Frame it. Sculpt it. Keep it in whatever medium speaks to you. But please do it! Here are some lessons we learned.

For one, don't wait to put together your final slideshow or photo album. It gets harder every day as new demands compete for your headspace. For another, get an early start on assembling your kids' art portfolios and their flag or sticker collections. As you assemble these things, let your travel experiences wash over you, like a high tide on a remote sandy beach. After you document your year, you can also share it with your community. Here are some ideas:

SHOWCASE YOUR ADVENTURE WITH A MULTIMEDIA SLIDESHOW

This won't be your grandparents' slideshow of their trip to Mount Rushmore. Involve the kids and strive to make meaning, tell stories, and explore conclusions. With all our easy-to-use photo-editing technology, you could simply choose your favorite shots, click *slideshow*, set it to music, and let 'er rip. You could also pick themes and let each child present one with accompanying slides.

THROW A COMMEMORATIVE PARTY

For true extroverts, you may want to throw a party for said slideshow. You could host trivia games like "Pin the Capital on the Country" or organize an "Our Trip by the Numbers" quiz (how many miles traveled? beds slept in? number of toes on Ernest Hemingway's polydactyl cats?). Share foods you tried on the road or dance moves you learned. This is a quick, courageous way to share your year.

GET CREATIVE WITH OTHER KEEPSAKE PROJECTS

One Wonder Year parent was an Instagram holdout until month ten of the yearlong trip, and he didn't want any kind of following other than his closest friends. The minute he landed in the US, he began posting one photo each day to remind him of the trip, of what his family had experienced exactly one year ago. This was a way to communicate nonverbally what his year had meant to him. Rather than trying to do it in real time, you could work on your keepsake project once you're home.

There are so many creative ways to memorialize your trip. We encourage you to find your medium and hold on to your journey.

Preparing Your Kids for School

Maybe you've fallen in love with worldschooling and you plan to bring the mindset home. Some families are so transformed by their Wonder Year that they change their education approach from what they did before they left home. They might become full-time homeschooling families, change schools, or even choose to keep traveling. *Wonder* is their middle name.

For everyone else, we hope that you'll still hold a worldschooling mindset for whichever approach you take with school. Here are a few considerations for kids going back into classroom learning:

- If you are returning to your same school district, we recommend meeting with your contacts there soon after you arrive home. Let them know what you did. They may ask to see some type of record that details what your kids learned. If you were more DIY with your educational approach, this is when all the explicit goals, standards, and objectives might come into play. Maybe they will ask your kids to take a placement test or to see samples of student work. This is where that journal, reading bibliography, writing portfolio, math workbook, or printout from online programs will really come in handy.

- The more you've leaned into unschooling, the more challenging a traditional scope and sequence might feel for your kids. For most of us, a Wonder Year is not something that we can do indefinitely. That might be hard to grapple with if this year made you all the happiest learners of your lives. (Two families we interviewed each completed a one-year trip, came home for a few years, and then went back out for Wonder Year, part two.) By contrast, you may be totally relieved that you can pass the baton back to a cadre of professionals. Either way, prepare your kids to see that school is just one more tool for learning. The world isn't going anywhere.

- For those kids reentering a traditional school, help them transition in the weeks before. If you feel like there were some holes in their learning, take time to evaluate that now and/or consider hiring a tutor. Reach out to old friends or, if your kids are entering a new school, ask if there's any new student-buddy program. Having a connection can alleviate a lot of stress.

- Know that the immediate effects for Wonder Year kids might also be a renewed appreciation of home and a new perspective of their education. They might find certain subjects become more alive (and less abstract) for them, like geography, geology, or history.

- Six, twelve, twenty-four months without sitting in a traditional classroom reprograms a kid. They will probably be asked to sit still for longer than they have for a long time. Many kids spend most of a Wonder Year in flip-flops, and dress codes can feel stifling. Buy some school clothes that fit, and do what you can to get them prepared. Yes, there may be apprehension, but your kids have already proved they are adaptable.

Keeping Worldschooling Alive

Just because you're settling down again and unpacking those suitcases doesn't mean your mindset needs to be stationary, too. There are still ways to learn from the world around you and keep your eyesight trained to that larger perspective, the farthest horizons.

Translate your traveler's experience into being a superstar host. Make it a priority to meet the family of the new kid at school or on the block. Invite exchange students into your home for a semester. Extend invitations to all those people you met on the road or friends and family you want to see. Sometimes the invitation is all that's needed.

Your family may have developed passions for cross-cultural connections. Perhaps you've discovered a cause or issue that motivates you to learn more. Continue to feed those interests by watching documentaries, finding a pen pal, or exploring museum exhibits. Look for volunteer work or fundraising opportunities. Many communities have intentional cultural exchanges or organizations that link individuals and families with ESL learners.

You can even approach your shorter vacations like a Wonder Year. You might feel more inspired to visit regions close to home that you never have before. Maybe you have a specific area of interest, say, American blues music, and you've never been to Mississippi, or perhaps you've longed to visit Washington, DC, as a family, to learn more about the American political system. You could have more of a Wonder Year–styled spring break than a pure mission of relaxation. The beauty is that there's room for both.

On Reentry

I was standing on the musty, shadowed wraparound porch of an old farmhouse, looking for the first time at a view that would soon become familiar. Mark and I were on a late-December house-hunting trip to Colorado while the boys were with family in Ohio.

A week before, we'd taken our final safari drive in the lush rains of Botswana, parked the jeep at an airstrip, then flight-hopped across thirty-seven hours and nearly ten thousand miles to land in the frigid, leafless suburbs of Cincinnati. Jarring, but worth it to reach my parents' welcoming home and spend the holidays together. Especially since we had no home to go to—not even a hometown. That also meant there was no pressure to return to a house and unpack or to be anywhere else. No one knew we were back, so we could fly under the radar and get our bearings.

We'd been watching this house as we traveled across two continents. It needed loads of work, but there were job opportunities nearby, and it was on a sweet bit of land at the intersection of mountains and prairie. Having spent so much time in nature during our time on the road, we needed space to breathe as we put down new roots. We negotiated the purchase, but the house wouldn't be ready for a while, so first we settled into a bland corporate apartment furnished with hard mattresses and hotel soap. It was bigger than most of the places we'd stayed in during the past two years; I preferred the coziness of our RV and single-room rentals. We sold the RV, and I was sadder to see it go than anything we'd ever owned.

We tried to calibrate into a semblance of "normal," although I wasn't quite sure what that meant anymore. Ronan, fourteen, enrolled in an entrepreneurship program so he could meet some kids his age. He wouldn't start school for many months and was navigating a rocky social road in the meantime. We visited California so he could spend some time with his old crew. For Asher, now eleven, we found a temporary spot in a quirky experimental school with self-paced learning, a chicken coop, and daily chores. He was psyched to be with peers again but missed unstructured days and the ocean.

Setting up shop in a new place was like a tailwind of our Wonder Year, and we threw ourselves into becoming Coloradans. The boys learned to ski, and Mark and Ronan ran the BOLDERBoulder 10K with fifty thousand new friends. We went to concerts at Red Rocks. I worked for a state ballot campaign and joined a hiking group to stay connected to my boots and the earth. Our home served as a rest stop for friends and family headed into the Rockies, giving us a chance to be the hosts rather than the hosted.

That fall Ronan and Asher both started at new public schools. District administrators didn't blink an eye at their odd academic histories, slotting them into grade years based on their birthdays with no questions asked. Asher was elected to student council, and Ronan attended his first homecoming. Mark found a good job, the two-year gap on his résumé inconsequential. He was away a lot, and I missed him.

Months in, I couldn't shake my attachment to the old cross-body purse that held my essentials while traveling. It was absurdly dirty with remnants of both jungle and desert on its worn leather. I missed the weight of the camera pack that was usually slung over my shoulder with it. Mostly I missed being outside a ten-mile radius and spending time together as an unhurried, unscheduled family.

It became a running joke that we kept finding ourselves all together in the same room of the house—four humans and a canine. Timber, our dog, was enthralled by the elk that passed through our woods but terrified of Colorado thunderstorms. One evening we returned home to an enormous black bear in our front yard. For a fleeting moment, life felt wild again.

But. A creeping realization set in. The structure of our lives was looking a lot like before. Unconsciously we had recreated the way things were prior to our Wonder Year—and what a folly that was, since we had intentionally stepped away from *the before* to find ourselves. But there was no shedding the impact of a Wonder Year; things couldn't just go back to the way they were. Why had we rebuilt our lives to look almost the same, just in a new place?

And with that awareness, we spent the next several years undoing it all again. Finally untethered once more, we took a Wonder Summer, and some Wonder Weeks and Wonder Weekends, to recover the real *us*. We had a better sense of what *us* looked like now. We recognized those people when we saw them, and we liked inhabiting their skin.

Personal Identity

As you insert your new self into your old world, try to resist becoming exactly who you were before. Instead, weave meaning and perspective into this new, more purposeful existence.

Reentry might be bumpy, but try to approach it with the same sense of novelty with which you visited new places in your Wonder Year. Start with the noticing. Be part anthropologist and part poet. Notice your first reactions, the smells, the light, and the shape of your past life. Notice where your child goes first. Notice your yard, the sounds, and the smells of your neighborhood. It's like the first peach of the season or the first drop of water after you forgot your water bottle for the hike. Notice. This is one of the best reasons to leave—the sweet sensations of the return.

As the days roll by, notice who your children have become and the choices they make—it may surprise you. Annika noticed that her kids stopped asking for prepackaged snacks, like single-serving chip bags or lemonade in a plastic bottle. (Walking on a "beach" with foot-high plastic debris will do that.) Her abstract protestations against all that packaging now made sense. Your children may reach out to "the new kids" more. They may think globally and read the tags on their clothes to see where things come from. After living with so little stuff for a year, Angela's kids had nothing on their holiday wish list.

Ongoing Reentry: One, Three, or Ten Years Out

For many returned Wonder Year families, nostalgia is ever present. The trip lives in the idealized world of life with fewer constraints. Its essence is aspirational. These families play the "remember when" game and always have stories on hand to rebond.

As time rolls on, you might find that your kids, now young adults, continue to identify as world citizens and carry with them a love for adventure and curiosity. Living on the road shows them that it's okay to want a life of togetherness, simplicity, freedom, and perspective. Annika's sixteen-year-old daughter, Lorna, who had been back for almost three years, remarked, "I don't like living in one spot for too long." Meredith Davis, back in Austin, Texas, for fourteen years now, said, "My son has taken a nontraditional path to education. After starting off at a four-year university, he grabbed the opportunity to join a touring band and finish his education while also holding down a part-time job. He lived a different way at nine and ten. He isn't afraid to do it still."

Another common theme for returned families is an added sense of confidence. Many feel they did something hard and out of the ordinary. They managed logistics; they helped make decisions; they connected with people whose cultures and backgrounds were different from theirs. They've been out there and know that, despite what the news might show them, the world is not scary, people are kind, and difference is beautiful.

Endings Are Also Beginnings

Dear reader, when you return from your Wonder Year, you'll see that you've accomplished something profound. You've climbed mountains—metaphorical mountains and maybe literal ones, too. Stop for a second to realize what you have created. And then step back for a landscape view.

As we wrap up this book, we want to offer you the metaphor of a Tibetan sand mandala. Picture a team of monks, working together, sometimes with a low, rumbly chant, for countless hours to create a complex design with painstaking detail out of brightly colored sand. The minute the design is complete, they hold a ceremony and sweep the sand into jars. *Oh, how sad!* you might think. *What a waste of time!*

Those monks then wrap the mixed-sand-filled jars in silk and float them down rivers to release the sand back into the world. This is what you are doing. You are releasing beauty, perspective, and wonder back into the world. Like the sand mandalas, moments and years of beauty are impermanent, and their passing is also a gift. The grand design that you helped lay on the ground with so much effort and intention will always be with you. So, put some metaphorical sand in your pocket, keep some in a bottle on your shelf, and sprinkle the rest around your world as you reconnect. Celebrate and watch how the brightly colored memories take shape in new, unexpected, and wonder-full ways.

Resources

Below is a curated list of resources to help you start planning for a Wonder Year. We've aimed to provide credible sources, but inclusion in this collection does not indicate our endorsement or affiliation.

ACCOMMODATIONS

Airbnb An online site for hosts to list available places, and travelers to book accommodations and experiences. The site has expanding functionality and offers search features to locate special-interest accommodations such as islands, national parks, tiny homes, monasteries, etc. **airbnb.com**

Booking.com An online platform to reserve transportation and accommodations for both hosts and travelers. Available in forty languages with 24-7 customer support. **booking.com**

Couchsurfing A website, Facebook group, and app-based membership service to connect travelers interested in community. Offers a free exchange of hospitality. It has 12 million active members in over 200,000 cities. **couchsurfing.com**

Furnished Finder A website for travelers interested in longer-term stays. Created to serve roaming professionals and medical providers, some slow-traveling families may also find furnished-housing options here. **furnishedfinder.com**

Home Exchange An online membership-based home-exchange platform available in over 150 countries. **homeexchange.com**

Home Swap An online membership program for home swaps, active in over a hundred countries. Free trial period and tiered membership options with varying features. **lovehomeswap.com**

Hostelling International An over 100-year-old nonprofit that works with youth hostel associations around the world to promote affordable, sustainable, and good-quality accommodations. Many hostels are family friendly; check to see if there are age limits or restrictions. **hihostels.com**

House Sitting Magazine A magazine and website that provides useful information and resources for house sitters and pet sitters around the globe, including house-sitting sources (for a fee) and location-specific information. **housesittingmagazine.com**

Vrbo An online resource that helps families looking for accommodations find and reserve entire homes around the world. Expanding functionality serves the needs and budgets of various travelers **vrbo.com**

Workaway An online resource to connect travelers who wish to work and immerse themselves culturally with hosts who need some form of help such as gardening, baby-sitting, or other tasks. **workaway.info**

Worldschool House Swap/Sit/Rent Facebook group A private Facebook group for worldschoolers to post available accommodations and to search for places to stay. **facebook.com/groups/worlschoolhouseswap**

CULTURAL EXCHANGE

AFS Intercultural Programs USA American Field Service (AFS) emerged out of WWI and WWII with the goal of advancing cultural exchange. Today, AFS hosts exchange students from eighty countries. **afsusa.org/host-family**

The Pen Pal Project A partnership between WeAre Teachers and the United States Postal Service that connects classrooms around the world to foster friendships and build tolerance and understanding. **about.usps.com/newsroom/national -releases/2021/1108-usps-introduces-pen-pal-project.htm**

HEALTH AND SAFETY

Association for Safe International Road Travel (ASIRT) A nonprofit organization that provides helpful information to travelers worldwide about road conditions, local laws, and other road-safety topics. In the interest of safety, ASIRT partners with many organizations including the United Nations and the World Health Organization. **asirt.org**

Centers for Disease Control and Prevention (CDC) The CDC's Traveler's Health website is a comprehensive travel health resource that includes a disease directory, information on finding a clinic, travel notices, country-specific information, and a helpful FAQ page. Additionally, the CDC website provides information for immuno-compromised travelers. The CDC also publishes the Yellow Book, a resource for health care professionals who treat international travelers.
wwwnc.cdc.gov/travel/destinations/list
wwwnc.cdc.gov/travel/page/yellowbook-home-2020

Environmental Working Group (EWG) A nonprofit organization that publishes consumer guides on the efficacy and safety of various consumer products, including sunscreen and insect repellent. **ewg.org**

Food Allergy Research and Education (FARE) A US-based nonprofit that supports individuals living with food allergies. The FARE website has comprehensive information on traveling with food allergies, including a travel checklist.
foodallergy.org/resources/traveling

Transportation Security Administration (TSA) The TSA website provides useful information for persons with disabilities and medical conditions, including passing through security checkpoints with medications, liquids, and other accessories. **tsa.gov/travel/special-procedures**

United States Department of State A credible and up-to-date source of information on critical topics including health and safety and country-specific travel advisories, as well as lists of embassies, consulates, diplomatic missions, doctors, and hospitals. It also provides information pertinent to high-risk-area travelers, special-needs travelers, LGBTQ+ travelers, and US travelers in Europe to help them prepare before departure and handle life events while abroad.
travel.state.gov/content/travel/en/international-travel.html
travel.state.gov/content/travel/en/international-travel/before-you-go/your-health-abroad.html

UNWTO/IATA Destination Tracker A user-friendly platform providing travelers with information on health-related travel restrictions and requirements. unwto.org/tourism-data/unwto-iata-destination-tracker-easy-travel

INCLUSIVE TRAVEL

ABC Travel Green Book A resource available in both paperback and ebook formats with information to celebrate and inform Black travelers across the globe. abctravelnetwork.com

Autism Travel A website that helps families choose travel options that are safe and supportive of all family members. It lists certified travel resources and tools that are recognized by the International Board of Credentialing and Continuing Education Standards. autismtravel.com

Green Book Global A travel review website that seeks to empower and inspire Black travelers to explore the world through a destination rating feature and crowd-sourced travel tips. greenbookglobal.com

IGLTA, the International LGBTQ+ Travel Association A website that provides information and resources for LGBTQ+ travelers. IGLTA works to "promote equality and safety within LGBTQ+ tourism worldwide." iglta.org

Lonely Planet's Accessible Travel Online Resources A free, easy-to-read guide that provides country-specific information to aid with planning and finding destinations and suitable activities for travelers with disabilities or access challenges. shop.lonelyplanet.com/products/accessible-travel-online-resources

Tourism Diversity Matters (TDM) An industry resource that seeks to improve the effectiveness of the tourism industry's diversity, equity, and inclusion initiatives through research, data, and expertise. In 2021, TDM announced a partnership with the US Travel Association to broaden its impact. tourismdiversitymatters.org

UNESCO World Heritage and Sustainable Tourism Programme A multistakeholder program intended to spawn tourism development that respects natural and cultural assets. The website provides information about UNESCO sites, partnerships, publications, and activities. whc.unesco.org/en/tourism

United States Department of State LGBTQI+ Travelers Site This governmental site provides useful information for LGBTQI+ travelers to help with planning, security screening technologies, and staying safe while traveling overseas, as well as many other resources. **travel.state.gov/content/travel/en/international-travel/before -you-go/travelers-with-special-considerations/lgbtqi.html**

United States Department of Transportation - Passengers with Disabilities A US governmental website that provides information about laws, regulations, rights, and support for travelers with disabilities. **transportation.gov/airconsumer/passengers-disabilities**

Wheel the World An online repository of information to help travelers with disabilities find places to stay, things to do, and accessible trips. **wheeltheworld.com**

PETS

BringFido A website and mobile app that shares information and booking options for pet-friendly accommodations and sites around the world, including hotels, restaurants, hiking trails, and parks. **bringfido.com**

Rover An app and website that connects dog (and cat) guardians with pet lovers for boarding, house sitting, drop-in visits, doggy day care, and dog walking by location. **rover.com**

SUSTAINABLE TRAVEL

B Corp A nonprofit network that seeks to build a global economy that delivers environmental, social, and community benefits. B Corp certification for travel companies may indicate alignment with sustainable practices. **bcorporation.net**

Center for Responsible Travel A nonprofit organization that serves as a research center and promotes and informs responsible travel. **responsibletravel.org**

Environmental Defense Fund (EDF) The Environmental Defense Fund's Travel Carbon Footprint website is an interactive tool that lets travelers calculate and look for ways to reduce their carbon footprint based on flights, car travel, rail travel, and hotel stays. **edf.org/travel-footprint-calculator**

Future of Tourism Coalition A coalition of six nongovernmental organizations, including the Center for Responsible Travel, Tourism Cares, and others that have come together to drive positive global change. **futureoftourism.org**

Global Sustainable Tourism Council A global organization that develops sustainability criteria and manages its use in a variety of sectors. **gstcouncil.org**

Impact Travel Alliance A global nonprofit that educates travelers, promotes sustainability, and hosts meetups and chapters around the world. **impacttravelalliance.org**

United Nations World Tourism Organization (UNWTO) A leading intergovernmental organization that seeks to inform and promote sustainable tourism. **unwto.org/sustainable-development**

US RV TRIP PLANNING

Boondockers Welcome For an annual membership fee, travelers can find places for overnight camping without utility hookups (boondocking) on private property. **boondockerswelcome.com**

Boondocking.org An online site to find dispersed free camping sites in the US, outside of developed campgrounds. Travelers can leave reviews and add new sites to the database. **boondocking.org**

Harvest Hosts A membership program that invites travelers in RVs to camp at wineries, breweries, farms, and attractions within an expanding network. **harvesthosts.com**

Recreation.gov A partnership of several US federal agencies including the National Park Service, Forest Service, Bureau of Land Management, and Smithsonian. Recreation.gov lists over 100,000 reservable outdoor sites in the US for recreation and cultural travel. **recreation.gov**

RV Communities Many communities of RV and van travelers can be found online. Here's a sampling:

- ▸ PanAmerican Travelers Association **facebook.com/groups/panamtravelers/**
- ▸ Vanlife **facebook.com/groups/1218937564804262**
- ▸ RV Life with Kids **facebook.com/groups/403708457666927**

RV Trip Planner Apps There are many RV trip planner apps and websites, typically with a fee, that include features such as navigation, campground search, road conditions, and points of interest. Some apps and sites to check out:

- ▶ The Dyrt PRO **thedyrt.com/pro**
- ▶ RV Life Trip Wizard **tripwizard.rvlife.com**
- ▶ Roadtrippers **roadtrippers.com**

US TRAVEL DOCUMENTATION

AAA | American Automobile Association A membership organization that supports travelers by providing roadside assistance, information resources, and 24-7 mobile and online support. The AAA website provides additional resources including an online application form for an International Driving Permit (IDP). **aaa.com/vacation/idpf.html**

REAL ID - United States Department of Homeland Security A US governmental website with information for domestic travelers eighteen years and older, who, as of May 2025, will need to have a REAL ID card to board domestic flights and to get into certain federal facilities. **dhs.gov/real-id**

Smart Traveler Enrollment Program - United States Department of State The Smart Traveler Enrollment Program gives travelers the opportunity to find the nearest US embassy. Enrollment lets travelers receive important information from the embassy about safety concerns in each country of interest and lets the embassy know how to contact travelers if there are emergencies such as a natural disaster or civil unrest. It also makes it possible for family or friends to reach families in an emergency. **step.state.gov**

Trusted Traveler Programs - United States Department of Homeland Security A US governmental website with information about TSA PreCheck, Global Entry, and other programs, all of which can help speed up entry in US airports and when crossing international borders. **ttp.dhs.gov/**

United States Postal Service (USPS) The USPS website provides useful information and services for obtaining and renewing passports, including scheduling appointments, downloading applications, and expediting passport requests. You can also get information about mail holds, address changes, and PO boxes. **usps.com/international/passports.htm**

USING TRAVEL POINTS AND MILES

Miles Momma A one-stop shop for traveler information about miles, points, hotel rewards, banking, and more to help family travelers stretch their dollars. Miles Momma also offers family travel tips, location-specific information, and suggestions for cash-back shopping. **milesmomma.com**

The Points Guy A website that provides news, tips, deals, and reviews of credit cards to help travelers maximize reward travel. **thepointsguy.com**

VOLUNTEER TRAVEL

A Beginner's Guide to Voluntourism A beginner's guide to volunteering that can help potential volunteers ensure the work they are engaging in is helpful, respectful, and beneficial to the local community. **nationalgeographic.com/travel/article/a-beginners-guide-to-voluntourism**

GoAbroad An online search engine with information about international travel programs to review and compare options. **goabroad.com**

Go Overseas An online community site that provides reviews, photos, and information about thousands of overseas programs, trips, and jobs including volunteering. **gooverseas.com**

Grassroots Volunteering An online resource that helps travelers connect to communities in the places they're visiting. The site maintains a database of organizations around the world. **grassrootsvolunteering.org**

Worldwide Opportunities on Organic Farms (WWOOF) An organization and website that links visitors with organic farms around the world. Hosts get help on the farm while visitors gain education, cultural immersion, and typically room and board. **wwoof.net**

WORLDSCHOOLING

Citizen Science A US governmental website that uses crowdsourcing and publicizes opportunities for people to participate in scientific research across the US. **citizenscience.gov**

Common Sense Media An online resource that provides reviews and advice about apps and websites for learning. It also offers free lessons and resources on topics such as digital citizenship. **commonsense.org/education/selections-for-learning**

Junior Ranger - United States National Park Service A free, activity-based program run by the US National Park Service that encourages children to learn about parks and share their "ranger story" with others. The Junior Ranger program is available at almost all national parks and many state parks in the US. **nps.gov/kids/become-a-junior-ranger.htm**

PBS Learning Media An online collection of educational resources designed to support learning with digital media. It offers free resources for students from pre-kindergarten through grade 12. **rmpbs.pbslearningmedia.org**

In addition to the sources above, you might consider joining any of the following online communities to learn more about worldschooling and get answers to questions:

- ▶ Worldschoolers **facebook.com/groups/worldschoolers**

- ▶ We are Worldschoolers **facebook.com/groups/weareworldschoolers**

- ▶ Worldschoolers Explore the USA **facebook.com/groups/1842724762611474**

- ▶ Worldschoolers - Single Parents **facebook.com/groups/WorldschoolersSoloParents**

- ▶ Worldschoolers - People of Color (POC) **facebook.com/groups/WorldschoolersPOC**

- ▶ Worldschooling Central – A Family Travel Community - Education with Travel **facebook.com/groups/worldschoolingcentral**

- ▶ Roadschooling - Families Homeschooling on the Road Group **facebook.com/groups/roadschooling**

- ▶ Roadschooling Europe **facebook.com/groups/1305020486300270**

- ▶ RoadschoolingUSA **facebook.com/groups/RoadschoolingUSA**

Appendix A
CHECKLISTS

Here's a checklist, distilled from the book, of things to do and think about before you go. While it's not comprehensive—and not all items will apply to your family—we hope this provides a helpful starting point for your Wonder Year.

MONEY

- ▶ Review any savings as a possible funding source.
- ▶ Downsize belongings for possible sale.
- ▶ Sell or donate downsized items.
- ▶ Check any financial investments as a funding source and consult a financial adviser.
- ▶ Decide whether your current residence will be sold or rented, or if your lease will end.
- ▶ If renting your home, find renters and/or engage a property manager.
- ▶ Decide if you're interested in house swapping; if so, create an online profile and list your property.
- ▶ Decide if you're interested in house sitting; if so, create an online profile and research properties.
- ▶ Identify any couchsurfing options.

- ▶ Decide whether any family members will work while traveling.
- ▶ Check with your current employer about a remote work arrangement.
- ▶ If you own a business, arrange for management while away.
- ▶ If you plan to work while traveling, identify your marketable skills.
- ▶ Look for employment opportunities via remote or planned destinations.
- ▶ Research income-tax implications.
- ▶ Decide whether you're borrowing funds for travel.
- ▶ Identify volunteer opportunities to pursue while traveling.
- ▶ Create a travel cost-management plan.
- ▶ Create a draft income-and-expense budget.
- ▶ Draft financial contingency plans.

CLOSING UP LIFE AT HOME

- ▶ If renting your current home, notify your landlord of your termination date, or arrange to sublease.
- ▶ If selling your current home, contact a real estate agent or prepare for self-listing.
- ▶ Modify or discontinue homeowners or renters insurance policies.
- ▶ Modify or discontinue utility accounts—gas/electric, water, sewer, trash, internet.
- ▶ Talk with your current employer about end date, or transition to remote work.
- ▶ Determine logistical and technical needs for any remote work plan.
- ▶ Notify kids' schools; complete necessary paperwork to unenroll or change status.
- ▶ Review kids' sports, extracurriculars, and lessons—identify end/pause date, and work with coaches and instructors on plans during travel.
- ▶ Pause or discontinue memberships and other recurring payments.
- ▶ Arrange for federal and state income-tax filing.
- ▶ Arrange to receive mail while traveling.
- ▶ Establish a plan for voting while away.
- ▶ Sell, lease, lend, or store vehicles; adjust auto insurance accordingly.
- ▶ After any downsizing, determine where remaining belongings will stay or be stored.
- ▶ Decide who will care for your pets while traveling.
- ▶ If pets are coming along, ensure all travel regulations have been researched and addressed.

TRAVEL LOGISTICS

- Ensure each family member has a passport with current name and expiration date that extends six months beyond currently booked travel.
- Research and secure any required visas for planned destinations.
- Get an International Driving Permit.
- Establish Power of Attorney for any legal needs at home.
- Find a debit card that minimizes or eliminates foreign transaction fees.
- Load debit and credit cards into a digital wallet.
- Practice the security-line process with your kids.
- Research security-checkpoint rules for planned destinations.
- Complete applications for any security process programs you deem helpful for your family: TSA PreCheck, CLEAR, or Global Entry, for example.
- Confirm onward travel documentation requirements for planned destinations.
- Research requirements for border crossings by road.
- Pack a daypack for each family member that includes time fillers for any travel delays.
- Identify technology connectivity needs for travel, including Wi-Fi, cell phone plans/SIM cards, and/or a GPS phone.
- Determine whether streaming services are useful for travel; cancel any that are not.
- Talk as a family about plans for technology use while traveling.
- Research and select insurance as need dictates:
  - Travel insurance
  - Belongings coverage
  - Medical insurance
  - Evacuation and repatriation coverage
- Sort your remaining belongings to leave most valuables and sentimental items at home.
- Label and photograph items you are taking on your journey.
- Organize and create a checklist for packed items.
- Inform credit card companies of travel plans.
- Set up transaction alerts to monitor debit/credit card activity while traveling.
- Bring along a list of phone numbers for your insurance, bank, and credit card companies.
- Record everyone's laptop models and serial numbers; keep the list at home.
- Update antivirus and firewall programs on your laptops.
- Secure a VPN if you plan to use one while traveling.
- Purchase any desired RFID-blocking wallets or bags (for identify-theft protection).
- Pack! See separate appendix for details.

HEALTH AND SAFETY

- Set up a medical appointment for each family member for updated exam and lab work and to talk through physical/mental health needs for travel.
- Secure any needed medication prescriptions, and make a plan for filling ahead of time or while away.
- Carry paper prescriptions for medications and glasses/contacts while traveling.
- Complete updated specialist exams—dermatologist, gynecologist, allergist, etc.—prior to departure.
- Make a final dentist (and orthodontist, as needed) appointment for each family member, or arrange to complete these visits while traveling.
- Research and take vaccinations required/desired for travel.
- Obtain preventive medications for planned destinations.
- Arrange for any disability-related travel needs.
- Plan and complete any physical fitness preparation, including carrying weight and acclimatizing to altitude when possible.

- Plan for:
  - Reproductive health items: menstrual, contraceptives, UTI prevention
  - Insect prevention/treatment
  - Motion sickness prevention/ treatment
  - Ear pain prevention/treatment
- Prepare for any high-elevation travel.
- Get EpiPens and/or food allergy cards.
- Ensure all kids are water safe; have them take swimming lessons prior to travel.
- Reserve or bring along strollers, car seats, high chairs, and babyproofing supplies.
- Carry medical information for each family member in daypacks.
- Create a plan with kids for what to do when lost or injured, including carrying important contact info and securing help when needed.

REENTRY

- ▶ Preplanning: consider your itinerary and think about end-of-trip transitions.
- ▶ Check with your school district to find out about important deadlines (signing up for sports, submitting physicals, shadowing new programs, etc.).
- ▶ Connect with friends; set up get-togethers and playdates.
- ▶ Consider a gathering to share your trip with relatives and friends.
- ▶ Set up a date to pick up pets.
- ▶ Visit your library for some real books!
- ▶ Check in with movers.
- ▶ Get a car, bicycle, or bus pass.
- ▶ Schedule medical appointments:

  - Wellness exams/physicals
  - Dental/orthodontic checkups
  - Vision screenings
  - Mammograms and other routine screenings
  - Specialty providers

- ▶ Line up employment as needed, and make sure you include your Wonder Year on your LinkedIn account or résumé!

Appendix B
PACKING LISTS

This is an extensive list of things you might need for your Wonder Year. Of course, you cannot bring everything here and still pack light! Create your own personal packing list from this reference inventory.

LUGGAGE

- Checked suitcases
- Carry-on suitcases
- Kids' backpack(s)
- Luggage tags
- Hip packs
- Luggage, backpack, and/or cable locks
- Packing cubes
- Dry bag and/or pack covers if you're caught in rainy weather
- Camera backpack
- Hand-held digital travel scale (for shifting contents between bags to prevent excess weight fees)

DAYPACK ITEMS

- Toilet paper
- Hand sanitizer
- Plastic bag to carry trash
- Sporks
- Reusable straws
- A few $20 bills
- Sunscreen
- First aid kit
- Whistle
- Reusable bag(s)
- N95 masks
- Book
- Journal
- Snacks
- Packed meal just in case!
- For transit days:
  - Compact stroller
  - Ear plugs and nasal spray
  - Eye mask (for napping)
  - Hard candies or ginger chews to settle upset stomachs

CLOTHES/ACCESSORIES

- Clothes in similar tones and colors to mix and match
- Lightweight, midweight, and outerwear layers
- Pajamas
- Multipurpose everyday walking sandals/shoes
- Gym clothes and exercise shoes
- Scarf to "dress up"
- Underwear
- Hats
- Sunglasses
- Waterproof jacket

BABY GEAR

- Sling or backpack for wearing
- Stroller
- Car seat

WATER SPORTS/GEAR

- Swimsuits
- Rash guards
- Goggles
- Snorkel and mask with cover
- Swim aids: water wings or life jacket
- Sarong or microfiber towels
- Water shoes

PERSONAL CARE

- Ear plugs
- Eye mask
- Glasses
- Contacts and contact lens solution
- Hairbrush, ties, and barrettes
- Shampoo
- Conditioner
- Lotion
- Favorite skincare products
- Toothbrushes
- Toothpaste
- Dental floss
- Razor
- Deodorant
- All-purpose hand, face, and body soap
- Washable, reusable wipes and face pads
- Reproductive care: reusable menstrual cup or cotton supplies, contraceptives, UTI prevention
- Nail care: scissors, file, or clippers

TECH EQUIPMENT

- ▶ Cameras and camera gear, tripod
- ▶ Phones
- ▶ Backup battery
- ▶ E-readers
- ▶ Headphones
- ▶ Headphone splitter to enable tech sharing
- ▶ Charging plugs
- ▶ Charging cords
- ▶ Bluetooth speaker
- ▶ Solar charger for tech
- ▶ Selfie stick and a chest strap
- ▶ Laptop(s)
- ▶ Tablet and protective cases
- ▶ Universal plug adapter

WORLDSCHOOLING RESOURCES

- ▶ Journals/notebooks/scrapbooking supplies
- ▶ Paper
- ▶ Small watercolor paint palette and brushes
- ▶ Drawing and coloring pencils in a roll-up bag
- ▶ Basic stationery including erasers, sharpeners, mini stapler, scissors, and writing pencils
- ▶ Black pens for outlining drawings and writing
- ▶ Hard-shell case to keep kids' work organized and unwrinkled
- ▶ Books
- ▶ Craft supplies

TOYS AND GAMES

- ▶ Stuffed animals
- ▶ Travel games; dice, backgammon, chess, Scrabble
- ▶ Playing cards
- ▶ Travel puzzle and activity books

PHYSICAL DOCUMENTS

- ▶ Passports
- ▶ Visas and supporting documentation
- ▶ Medical/vaccination records
- ▶ Prebooked hard-copy travel tickets
- ▶ Debit cards
- ▶ Extra passport photos
- ▶ Destination guidebooks and translation books
- ▶ Cash

HOUSEHOLD

- Duct tape: great for everything from babyproofing electrical sockets and table edges to repairing luggage
- Refillable water bottles
- Water-purification pen or other system
- Soft-sided cooler bags
- Ziploc bags
- Laundry pins: for curtains and laundry
- Carabiners: universally useful
- Headlamps and spare batteries
- Sleep sacks
- Laundry soap, laundry brush, and bungee clothesline/detergent strips
- Universal sink stopper
- Reusable shopping bags
- Sunscreen
- Carbon monoxide monitor
- Sewing kit

HEALTH AND PERSONAL SAFETY

- Prescription info for medicine/eyeglasses
- Insect repellent; mosquito net
- Thermometer
- Moleskin or similar for blisters
- Band-Aids
- Bandages/gauze
- Antibacterial ointment
- Diaper cream: good for any chafing or skin irritations
- Prescription medications
- Vitamins and supplements
- Pain relievers
- Allergy medicine
- Diarrhea medicine
- Pedialyte or similar rehydration powder
- Cold and flu medicine
- Broad-spectrum antibiotics, if your medical provider will prescribe
- Sting reliever: for bug bites and insect stings
- Ear infection drops
- Swimmers' ear drops
- Steri-strips or "butterfly stitches" for wound care
- Pediatric pain relief
- Antihistamines
- Tea tree and lavender oils
- Throat lozenges
- Doorstop
- Whistle
- *Where There Is No Doctor*, the classic health care manual in print or ebook

ADVENTURE TRAVEL

(key items to get you started; you may also want to research other destination-specific items)

- ▶ Trekking poles
- ▶ Insulating layers
- ▶ Waterproof layers
- ▶ Hiking shoes or boots
- ▶ Fishing pole
- ▶ Tent/camping gear
- ▶ Satellite communicator
- ▶ Topographical maps
- ▶ Bivouac or tarp
- ▶ Fire-starter kit
- ▶ Trowel
- ▶ Bear bag/canister
- ▶ Pocket knife or multitool
- ▶ Bear spray

Traveling by RV/Camper/Car

KITCHEN

- ▶ Tableware
- ▶ Flatware
- ▶ Nonbreakable beverage containers
- ▶ Tablecloth and clips (worth it, a lovely touch to have a tablecloth, and it doubles as a ground cloth for picnics)
- ▶ Cloth napkins (bandannas work)
- ▶ Cookware

  - – Small pot
  - – Bigger pot
  - – Good knife
  - – Fry pan
  - – Cast iron skillet (did you know you can use it on an open fire?)

- ▶ Cooking utensils
- ▶ Measuring cups
- ▶ Measuring spoons
- ▶ Cutting board (lightweight, doubles as portable desk)

- ▶ Serving dishes and bowls
- ▶ Hanging fruit basket
- ▶ Coffee setup (seriously, think about it because it will matter)
- ▶ Teapot
- ▶ Small appliances

  - – Immersion or small blender for smoothies and soups
  - – Slow cooker
  - – Mini food processor
  - – Toaster

- ▶ Salad spinner (or if limited space, a terry-cloth drawstring bag works well)
- ▶ Containers for leftovers
- ▶ Basic spices and oils
- ▶ Dish soap
- ▶ Mesh bag for hang-drying dishes after washing
- ▶ Hand soap

HOUSEHOLD

- Clothesline for drying clothes and cloth napkins
- Cleaning supplies
- Microfiber cloths for cleaning
- Waste management system
- Mini recycle bin, trash bin, drawstring bag for laundry
- Mini broom or mini vacuum
- Wooden or plastic crate for worldschooling supplies
- Bedding: sheets, blankets, pillows
- Showering items
- Shower caddy
- Toiletries
- RV-friendly toilet paper
- Quick-drying towels and washcloths
- Books
- Board games
- Portable speaker
- Storage baskets/bins
- Decorative items (favorite photos, houseplants, flags, art, or outdoor lights)
- Portable grill or fireplace
- Small cooler
- Picnic bag/basket
- Grill and fire supplies: lighter, starter briquettes, etc.
- Outdoor mat
- Outdoor chairs
- Lanterns
- Insect repellent
- Sunscreen
- Pet supplies
- Worldschooling supplies

TOOLS AND RESOURCES

- Tool set
- Water hoses
- Sewer tubes
- Leveling blocks
- Solar tech device charger
- Vehicle registration
- Proof of vehicle insurance
- Road map

Notes

Introduction

1 "River Heroes," River Network, accessed November 5, 2022, rivernetwork.org/our-impact/awards/river-heroes.

Chapter 1

2 Mark Ellwood and Laura Dannen Redman, "The Science of Wanderlust," *Condé Nast Traveler,* June 12, 2017, cntraveler.com/story/the-science-of-wanderlust.

3 "Santiago de Compostela (Old Town)," UNESCO World Heritage Convention, accessed November 5, 2022, whc.unesco.org/en/list/347.

4 *The Economist*, Twitter post, January 24, 2019, 4:00 a.m., twitter.com/theeconomist/status/1088406294179008513.

5 Barbara Jacquelyn Sahakian, Christelle Langley, and Victoria Leong, "Why is Cognitive Flexibility Important and How Can You Improve It?," World Economic Forum, June 25, 2021, weforum.org/agenda/2021/06/cognitive-flexibility-thinking-iq-intelligence.

6 "Our Mission," International Baccalaureate, last updated August 23, 2022, ibo.org/about-the-ib/mission.

7 Debra Kamin, "Tour Companies Pledged to Address Racial Inequality. Those Promises Are Taking Shape.," *New York Times*, February 23, 2022, nytimes.com/2022/02/23/travel/group-tours-diversity.html.

Chapter 2

8 John Higham, *360 Degrees Longitude: One Family's Journey Around the World* (n.p.: Prospecta Press, 2012), 4.

9 *Minimalism: A Documentary About the Important Things*, directed by Matt D'Avella (Catalyst, 2015), film.

10 "United℠ Explorer Card," Chase, accessed November 5, 2022, chase.com/personal/credit-cards/united/united-explorer-card/earn-rewards.

11 "U.S. Citizens and Resident Aliens Abroad," IRS, last updated June 2, 2022, irs.gov/individuals/international-taxpayers/us-citizens-and-resident-aliens-abroad.

12 "Figuring the Foreign Earned Income Exclusion," IRS, last updated November 16, 2022, irs.gov/individuals/international-taxpayers/figuring-the-foreign-earned-income-exclusion.

Chapter 3

13 "Homeschool Laws by State," HSLDA, accessed May 12, 2022, hslda.org/legal.

14 "Topic No. 304 Extensions of Time to File Your Tax Return," IRS, last updated November 3, 2022, irs.gov/taxtopics/tc304.

15 "USPS Hold Mail® - The Basics," USPS.com, December 2, 2021, faq.usps.com/s/article/USPS-Hold-Mail-The-Basics.

16 "PO Box™ - The Basics," USPS.com, November 12, 2021, faq.usps.com/s/article/PO-Box-The-Basics.

17 "Absentee Voting Information for US Citizens Abroad," Travel.State.Gov, accessed November 5, 2022, travel.state.gov/content/travel/en/international-travel/while-abroad/voting.html.

Chapter 4

18 "Great Pacific Garbage Patch," *National Geographic*, accessed November 5, 2022, education.nationalgeographic.org/resource/great-pacific-garbage-patch.

19 "Travel," Travel.State.Gov, accessed November 9, 2022, travel.state.gov/content/travel.html.

20 "Sustainable Development," World Tourism Organization (UNWTO), accessed November 5, 2022, unwto.org/sustainable-development.

21 World Economic Forum, *Powering Sustainable Aviation Through Consumer Demand: The Clean Skies for Tomorrow Sustainable Aviation Fuel Certificate (SAFc) Framework*, June 2021, www3.weforum.org/docs/WEF_CST_SAFc_Demand_Signal_Report_2021.pdf.

22 "Road Traffic Injuries and Deaths—A Global Problem," Centers for Disease Control and Prevention, last reviewed December 14, 2020, cdc.gov/injury/features/global-road-safety/index.html.

23 Heather Long, "1 Million Americans Live in RVs. Meet the 'Modern Nomads.'," *Washington Post*, November 12, 2018, washingtonpost.com/business/2018/11/12/million-americans-live-rvs-meet-modern-nomads.

Chapter 5

24 "LGBTQI+ Travelers," Travel.State.Gov, last updated March 31, 2022, travel.state.gov/content/travel/en/international-travel/before-you-go/travelers-with-special-considerations/lgbtqi.html

25 "Schengen Area," European Commission, accessed November 5, 2022, home-affairs.ec.europa.eu/policies/schengen-borders-and-visa/schengen-area_en.

Chapter 6

26 "Get Vaccinated Before You Travel," Centers for Disease Control and Prevention, last reviewed August 1, 2019, cdc.gov/vaccines/parents/travel-vaccines.html.

27 "Respiratory Disease in Adults and Children," *European Lung White Book*, accessed November 5, 2022, erswhitebook.org/chapters/outdoor-environment/respiratory-disease-in-adults-and-children.

28 "Altitude Sickness," Cleveland Clinic, accessed November 5, 2022, my.clevelandclinic.org/health/diseases/15111-altitude-sickness.

29 "Altitude Sickness," NHS, last reviewed March 13, 2020, nhs.uk/conditions/altitude-sickness.

30 "Traveler's Diarrhea," Cleveland Clinic, last reviewed April 24, 2022, my.clevelandclinic.org/health/diseases/7315-travelers-diarrhea.

31 Allergy and Anaphylaxis Australia, *Airline Comparison for Passengers with Food Allergy*, January 2018, allergyfacts.org.au/images/pdf/Airline_comparison_for_food_allergic_passengers.pdf.

32 "Swimming and Diving Safety," Centers for Disease Control and Prevention, last reviewed October 6, 2022, wwwnc.cdc.gov/travel/page/safe-swimming-diving.

33 "Civil Unrest: Travel Advice and Planning," Harvard Global Support Services, accessed November 5, 2022, globalsupport.harvard.edu/travel/advice/civil-unrest-planning.

34 Randy Pausch and Jeff Zaslow, *The Last Lecture* (New York: Hyperion, 2008), 160.

Chapter 7

35 Milton Gaither, "John Holt," *Encyclopedia Britannica*, accessed November 6, 2022, britannica.com/biography/John-Holt.

36 "Earn College Credit with CLEP," CLEP, clep.collegeboard.org.

37 International Dark-Sky Association, darksky.org/our-work/conservation/idsp.

38 Leave No Trace, lnt.org.

Chapter 8

39 "Improving Energy Efficiency of Traditional Chinese Kang Beds in Rural Areas," Beijing Forestry Society, accessed November 5, 2022, www.bjfs.org.cn/en/product/61.mhtml.

Index

Acknowledgments

T O THE WONDERWELL TEAM: Maggie Langrick, Allison Serrell, Eva Avery, Jenn Jensen, Jesmine Cham, Morgan Krehbiel, and J Cisneros. Thank you for believing in *Wonder Year* and our author team. We're so appreciative of your guidance, expertise, and enthusiasm. We've enjoyed sharing Wonder in name and vision.

For the trusted sources who helped bring dimension to this project: Mark Steele, Normandie Rainwater, Jen Louden, David Petrush, Amanda Elend, Hana Rivers, Catherine Greener, and Fran Reuland. Thank you for going the extra distance to help us sharpen our thinking, expand our impact, and connect with the vast community of traveling families.

Thank you to the friends and colleagues who shared your counsel, impressions, and camaraderie with us: Shari Caudron, Andy Clark, Lee Strongwater, Jeff and Kim Greenberg, Jason Gruhl, Kita Murdock, Brad Pivar, and Florence Williams.

Thanks to the amazing traveling families who shared your stories with us: Nadia Adnan Abdulrehman, Holly and Bob Bendz, Nathan and Juliann Blew, Laura Brenton, Zoe and Ray Carr, Meredith Davis, Sarah De Santi, Kristin Dennett, Justin and Nancee Gold, Gillian and Jake, Kyla Hunter, Mitch Jacob, Guðrún Jóhannsdóttir, Lisa Kieffer, Jen Krigsman, Abigail and Jeremiah Kovacs, Elissa Langenegger, Terry Butler Lebobe, Destrie Long, Kelly Masters, Viet Nguyen, Hin and Holly Or, Yasmin Page, John Leigh, Brook Leigh, Eydie Pines, Allie Rockwell, Megan Rudolph, Mary Solio, Stephanie Tolk, Lindsay Vandermyde, Astrid Vinje, Cynthia Matthews von Berg, and Tiffany Wilding-White. Your words bring texture and truth to our book and will inspire other families for years to come.

And to the many others who shared experiences and insights that enhanced our understanding and shaped this book, thank you.

FROM ANGELA

To Mark, my brilliant partner, devoted best friend, and ideal travel companion. I'm so grateful for all of our adventures and the innumerable ways you have supported me and the creation of this book. To Ronan, who moves through the world with sensitivity and strength—life is so much richer because of all I learn from you. Thank you to Asher, my curious adventurer who loves to say yes. I am in awe of your enduring optimism and appreciate the joy and care you bring to my days. To my parents, Russ and Joan, who gave me the foundation to step confidently into the world. I appreciate you always embracing our crew with so much openness and love. To my sister, Kate—thank you so much for lifting us up, and for being my childhood playmate and grown-up friend. To Iris and Alyssa, thank you for celebrating and encouraging us and providing soft places to land. To Cynthia, Debbie, and Stacey, many thanks for supporting my family's journey and for continuing to love us from afar. And to my grandparents, Ed, Esther, Wally, and Edna, who enveloped me with warmth and acceptance, and who taught me the card games that keep my family happily occupied as we travel the globe. I love you all so much.

FROM ANNIKA

To my first traveling family, Poppa, Grandma Lorna, sister-Daisy, Val, and Davenport. Thank you for modeling curiosity, adaptability, a sense of humor, and offering a safety net in case my adventures didn't work out. To my travel muses, Kathy Dragon, Chris Yager, and Uncle Ed (who visited the Great Wall in a wheelchair and never tired of crisscrossing the beauty of this country by train). To my quilling partners Bets McNie and Lew Gibb for Zooming through the dark pandemic days, and my dear Alliterati for your kindness and keeping the bar high. To everyone who made our trip possible: Dana Runge, Lilo Michel, the Hunter-Buckley family, the McNeil family, Steve and Veo Schipani, Anthony Harnett, and the entire Lama family. To friend-Daisy for always reminding me to think big, live large, and laugh. To my Lorna, who feels with wisdom and moves through the world with bravery. To Lucy, for your enthusiasm, caring, and wonder for . . . everything. To Kai, for always being kind, calm, and ready for a game. And to Will, my partner, for always having a soundtrack at the ready, never letting me take anything too seriously, and living with intention. Thanks for being you and making space for this project.

FROM JULIE

To Char, thank you for sharing the extraordinary journey. To paraphrase John Muir, going out into the world with you felt like coming home. To Johnny boy, thank you for your support and for enriching my life with your love of adventure, ingenuity, and teamwork. To Char's family and to mine—Debbie, Margot, Andrea, and especially Mom and Sol—thank you for the grounding, strength, love, and chutzpah in encouraging me to go after big dreams, whether it's traveling the world or writing a book about traveling the world. I appreciate and love you all, my dear family.

I am thankful for my traveling friends—John and Eydie, Kaitilin and David, Agnes and Serge—your love of nature, creativity, and can-do attitude is sweet nectar. To the amazing crew that helped our Wonder Year flow, it's been a while, but we are forever grateful for your part in what was the best year of our lives—Katherine Luscher, Gever Tulley, Phil and Mary Deriemer, Gershon Cohen, Kate and Colm Sweeney, Esther Schneider, Michael Stroh, and Eugene and Kamenna Lee. To our beautiful friends in Boulder, thank you for the rocking send-off and open-armed return. After seeing the world, there is no other village we would rather have come home to. Thank you, Caroline, Dana, Katri, Kita, Tina M., and Tina F.

TO OUR COLLABORATION

This book is born of curiosity, optimism, and friendship. We are grateful for each other and for the inspiration and creativity we found through this process. Our shared conviction that *Wonder Year* had to be written kept us at work for years, and the alchemy of our collaboration made it a memorable and beautiful journey.